ACKNOWLEDGEMENTS

This book was made possible by the Social Trends Institute (STI), an international nonprofit research institute that offers institutional and financial support to academics in all fields who seek to make sense of emerging social trends and their effects on human communities. STI focuses its research on four subject areas: family, bioethics, culture and lifestyles and corporate governance.

STI organizes experts meetings that bring scholars together to present and discuss their original research in an academic forum. These meetings are intended to foster open, intellectual dialogue between scholars from all over the world and from different academic backgrounds, disciplines and beliefs. STI aims to publish a single volume of the meeting papers, which are reviewed and edited in light of the discussion that took place during the sessions. This volume is the result of one such meeting, held in 2006 under the leadership of Professor Ana Marta González. To learn more about STI, see the website www.socialtrendsinstitute.org.

· STI ·

Social Trends Institute

IDENTITIES
THROUGH
FASHION

A Multidisciplinary Approach

Edited by
Ana Marta González
and Laura Bovone

B L O O M S B U R Y
LONDON · NEW DELHI · NEW YORK · SYDNEY

Bloomsbury Academic
An imprint of Bloomsbury Publishing Plc

50 Bedford Square
London
WC1B 3DP
UK

1385 Broadway
New York
NY 10018
USA

www.bloomsbury.com

Bloomsbury is a registered trade mark of Bloomsbury Publishing Plc

First published 2012 by Berg
Reprinted 2014

British Library Cataloguing-in-Publication Data
A catalogue record for this book is available from the British Library.

ISBN: HB: 978-0-8578-5057-7
PB: 978-0-8578-5058-4
ePUB: 978-0-8578-5118-5
ePDF: 978-0-8578-5119-2

Library of Congress Cataloging-in-Publication Data
Gonzalez, Ana Marta, 1969–
Identities through fashion: a multidisciplinary approach/edited by Ana Marta
Gonzalez and Laura Bovone.
p. cm.
Includes bibliographical references and index.
ISBN 978-0-85785-058-4 (pbk.)
1. Fashion—Psychological aspects. 2. Fashion design. 3. Identity
(Psychology) I. Bovone, Laura. II. Title.
TT507.G587 2012
746.9'2—dc23 2011048951

Typeset by Apex CoVantage, LLC, Madison, WI.
Printed and bound in Great Britain

IDENTITIES THROUGH FASHION

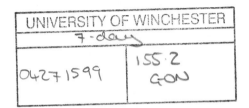

CONTENTS

ABOUT THE CONTRIBUTORS

RAPHAEL M. BONELLI, MD, DMedSC, is associate professor at the University Clinic of Psychiatry in Graz, Austria. He received his medical doctorate degree from the University of Vienna Medical School, Austria, a doctor of medical science degree in psychiatry from the University of Graz Medical School, and did his postdoctoral studies at Harvard Medical School and the University of California Los Angeles. His medical doctoral thesis, for which he was awarded a prize by the Austrian Medical Association for outstanding scientific research, deals with the compliance of bipolar patients. Since 2003 he has been the director of the neuropsychiatric outpatient clinic at the University Clinic of Graz and group leader of its biological psychiatry research group. His basic scientific research interests include Huntington's disease, psychopharmacology, psychiatric MRI research and geriatric neuropsychiatry. He has published more than 150 scientific articles and serves as a scientific peer reviewer for various medical journals.

LAURA BOVONE graduated in philosophy and is a professor of Sociology of Communication, director of the "Centro per lo studio della moda e della produzione culturale" and the master's program "Comunicazione per le industrie culturali" at the Università Cattolica del Sacro Cuore in Milan, where she is also in charge of the doctorate in sociology. She was chair of the section Cultural Processes and Institutions of the Italian Sociological Association in 2002–2005. Her main research interests are micro theories and methodologies, postmodernism and communication processes, city cultures, cultural production and consumption and fashion. She has published a number of books on these topics as well as articles in various journals, such as *Theory, Culture and Society* 10 (1993), *International Journal of Contemporary Sociology* 40 (2003), *City and Community* 4 (2005) and *Poetics* 34 (2006).

ANN MARGARET BRACH is deputy director of the second Strategic Highway Research Program (SHRP 2) at the Transportation Research Board of the National Academy of Sciences in the United States. She is responsible for overseeing research on the role of driver behaviour in highway safety and on renewal of aging infrastructure. She also carries out legislative analysis related to federal highway and transportation research. Prior to holding this position, Dr. Brach served as the study director for the development of SHRP 2. In addition, she has completed studies of funding trends, congressional earmarking and stakeholder involvement in federal transportation research programs. Before working at the National Academy of Sciences, Dr. Brach was research and technology program manager at the Federal Highway Administration and chief of the Research and Technology Division of the Maryland State Highway Administration. Dr. Brach obtained her BSc in civil engineering from Northeastern University in Boston. She received her MSc and PhD from the Massachusetts Institute of Technology, where she focused on management of research and innovation in the construction industry. She is a registered professional engineer in the Commonwealth of Virginia. In addition to her work in research management and policy, Dr. Brach recently completed a MA in philosophy at the Catholic University of America, where she studied the phenomenology of Edmund Husserl and wrote a thesis dealing with his treatment of cultural objects.

COLIN CAMPBELL is emeritus professor of sociology at the University of York. He is the author of half a dozen books and some one hundred articles dealing with issues in the sociology of religion, consumerism, cultural change and sociological theory. Prof. Campbell is probably best-known as the author of *The Romantic Ethic and the Spirit of Modern Consumerism* (Macmillan 1987, Alcuin Academic edition 2005), while his other publications on consumerism include *The Shopping Experience* (co-edited with Pasi Falk, Sage, 1997) and 'The Craft Consumer: Culture, Craft and Consumption in a Postmodern Society', *Journal of Consumer Culture*. In the sociology of religion, he is known for his contributions to work on the cult and the cultic milieu, as well as irreligion (see *Toward a Sociology of Irreligion*, Macmillan, 1971), while his contribution to sociological theory is evident in *The Myth of Social Action* (Cambridge University Press, 1996). Prof. Campbell's latest book, *The Easternization of the West*, was published by Paradigm Publishers in 2007.

FRANCESCO CECERE is a psychiatrist and a psychotherapist. He is the director of the Eating Disorders Center, a public outpatient clinic for people suffering from anorexia nervosa, bulimia nervosa, binge eating disorder and obesity. He is also the director of a Daily Service for Eating Disorders, a facility for long-term, severely anorexic and bulimic patients. These two services are related and are located in the centre of Rome. He is also a consultant for Vatican tribunals. He is a member of important scientific societies, such as the Society for Psychotherapy Research and the Academy for Eating Disorders.

DIANA CRANE is professor emerita of sociology at the University of Pennsylvania, Philadelphia. She has also taught at Yale University, Johns Hopkins University, University of Poitiers (France), Erasmus University (the Netherlands) and Columbia University in Paris. She received her PhD from Columbia University. She has been awarded a Guggenheim Fellowship, been a member of the Institute for Advanced Study (Princeton, New Jersey) and been a visitor at the Bellagio Study and Conference Center (Rockefeller Foundation, Bellagio, Italy). She has held Fulbright Awards in France and the Netherlands. She was chair of the Sociology of Culture Section of the American Sociological Association in 1991–1992. She has been a member of the advisory board of *Poetics* since 1992. A specialist in the sociology of culture, arts and media, she is the author of numerous articles and several books, including *The Transformation of the Avant-Garde: The New York Art World, 1940–1985* (University of Chicago Press, 1987), *The Production of Culture: Media and the Urban Arts* (Sage Publications, 1992) and *Fashion and Its Social Agendas: Class, Gender and Identity in Clothing* (University of Chicago Press, 2000). She is co-editor of *The Sociology of Culture: Emerging Theoretical Perspectives* (Blackwell Publishing, 1994) and *Global Culture: Media, Arts, Policy and Globalization* (Routledge, 2002). Her books have been translated into Chinese, Italian, Japanese, Korean, Turkish and, most recently, Spanish.

JOANNE FINKELSTEIN is the dean of the School of Humanities and Social Sciences at the University of Greenwich. She has a particular interest in the visual imagery of consumer culture, including labels, advertisements and packaging, and has published widely in Australia, the United States and Europe. She has recently been a director of the board of Food Science Australia, part of Australia's premier science research organisation CSIRO (Commonwealth Science and Industry Research Organisation). Her books include *After a Fashion* (Melbourne University Press, 1996) and *Slaves of Chic: An A–Z of Consumer Pleasures* (Minerva, 1996).

ALEJANDRO NESTOR GARCÍA MARTÍNEZ is a lecturer at the University of Navarra in the subjects of sociology, social theory, and history of social theory. He has also been a research member in the same university of the following research programs: *Perspectiva Sociológica de la Civilización* (Sociological Perspective on Civilization), *El proceso civilizatorio y la dinámica de la Cultura* (Civilizing Process and Culture), *Estrategias de distinción social* (Strategies of Social Distinction) and *Cultura emocional e identidad* (Emotional Culture and Identity). He is the author of numerous articles and several books, including *La sociología de Norbert Elias: una introducción* (*Introduction to Norbert Elias's Sociology*, Servicio de Publicaciones de la Universidad de Navarra, CAF serie de clásicos de la sociología, 2003), *El proceso de la* *civilización en la sociología de Norbert Elias* (*The Civilizing Process in Elias's Sociology*, Eunsa, 2006), and *Distinción social y moda* (*Fashion and Social Distinction*, Eunsa, 2007). He earned his PhD from the University of Navarra.

ANA MARTA GONZÁLEZ is associate professor of moral philosophy at the University of Navarra in Pamplona, Spain. She has led several research projects, exploring intersections between moral philosophy and social sciences. She is currently leader of the Emotional Culture and Identity research project at Navarra. Prof. González serves as academic leader of STI's Culture and Lifestyles branch. Among her recent publications are *Kant's Contribution to Social Theory* (Kant Studien, 2009), *Practical Rationality and Human Agency* (with Alejandro Vigo, Olms, 2010), *La ética explorada* (Eunsa, 2009), *Razón práctica y ciencias sociales en la ilustración escocesa* (with Raquel Lázaro, Anuario filosófico, 2009), *Ficción e identidad: ensayos de cultura postmoderna* (Rialp, 2009), *Contemporary Perspectives on Natural Law: Natural Law as a Limiting Concept* (Ashgate, 2008) and *Distinción social y moda* (Eunsa, 2007). She was a Fulbright Scholar at Harvard in 2002–2003, where she worked with Christine Korsgaard on the relationship between nature, culture and morality in Kant's practical philosophy. She earned her PhD from the University of Navarra.

MARÍA ELENA LARRAÍN received her first degree in psychology from the Pontificia Universidad Católica de Chile. She has worked in psychoanalytically oriented psychotherapy and drug and alcohol prevention programs with adolescents in Santiago. In 1998 she began studying philosophy in a postgraduate program at the Universidad de Los Andes. She was recognized as a psychotherapist (1999) and clinical supervisor (2004) by Colegio de Psicólogos de Chile, Sociedad Chilena de Psicología Clínica and Comisión Nacional de Acreditación de Psicólogos Clínicos. Since 1999, she has been director of the School of Psychology of the Universidad de Los Andes. She has taught developmental psychology and psychoanalytically oriented psychotherapy for children and adolescents. Since 2002, she has taught professional ethics to students of psychology. Her research interests have centred on the influence of different means of communication, particularly Internet use in adolescents (2002), and psychoanalytic theory, treatment modalities and diagnostic studies.

MARIA TERESA RUSSO graduated in literature and philosophy and obtained a PhD in philosophy and human sciences theory from Roma Tre University. She is a professor of anthropology at Campus Bio-Medico University in Rome and teaches social ethics at Roma Tre University. She is a member of the European Society for Philosophy of Medicine and Healthcare; she coordinates the scientific secretariat of the scientific journal *MEDIC: Methodology & Education for Clinical Innovation*. Her research is focused on the anthropological issues of health care and on the transformations of the female body. Among her publications on these topics are *Corpo, salute, cura. Linee di antropologia biomedica* (Rubbettino, 2002) and *La ferita di Chirone. Itinerari di antropologia ed etica in medicina* (Vita e Pensiero, 2006).

EFRAT TSEËLON is a Professor of Cultural Theory who joined Leeds University School of Design as Chair of Fashion Theory in 2007. She has a BA in social psychology and an MA in media and communication (specializing in translation and discourse), industry experience in organizational and marketing consultancy, and a social psychology PhD from Oxford on "Communicating via Clothing" (1989). In the field of fashion studies she has pioneered the study of "wardrobe research," masquerade, critique of methodology, and critical examination of visual language and ideology.

She is the author of *The Masque of Femininity* and of *Masquerade and Identities: Gender, Sexuality & Marginality*, and is the editor of the journal *Critical Studies in Fashion and Beauty*.

PREFACE

JOANNE FINKELSTEIN

This book takes the reader deep into the beguiling mysteries of modern fashion and cleverly unravels its multiple expressions and functions. We learn that fashion is a technique for ordering the world, for providing a sense of control over the social environment; at the same time, it is a massive machine for capital growth and an aesthetic expression of human ingenuity. It is a sign, an effect, a system, an appetite and a subtle form of social bondage.

Fashion is no longer a preoccupation of the elite. Its critical origins in art history, costume design and textile manufacture have been expanded into new areas of research and scholarship. It now addresses itself to psychology, sociology, philosophy, economic history, film studies, marketing and trade. In the past three decades, the study of fashion has developed a sophisticated theoretical and empirical base using, as hard-working pivots, the earlier classic texts of Georg Simmel, Guy DeBord, Fernand Braudel, Norbert Elias, Roland Barthes and Lisa Jardine. The following chapters engage a wide range of questions, from understanding adolescent rebellion expressed through clothing styles to the obsessive overvaluation of celebrity artefacts such as the auctioning of Yves St Laurent's collectibles after his death. These ideas and more are explored with probing detail, and the result is a highly satisfying overview of the phenomenon of fashion.

Popular writing on fashion was quickly absorbed by the mass media during the boom years of the service economy in the 1970s and 1980s. An expanded workforce was engaged in identifying itself as the new mobile professionals. A self-help literature was produced for them about how to dress for success and how to garner power through the effective assemblage of colours. Not for the first time, clothing became a sign of status and identity. Sumptuary laws were no longer in effect, but high street fashions began to dictate how to dress, and a new language of dubious authority gained currency. The sensible, almost invisible woman in the pink-frilled shirt and grey skirt was supposedly telling her co-workers she had a feminine, frivolous soul, and the man in the double-breasted pinstripe suit was claiming moral rectitude and managerial authority (see John Molloy, *Dress for Success*, 1975; Alison Lurie, *The Language of Clothes*, 1981). The reductive simplicity of these pop psychology texts was soon countered by a more intellectual and insightful literature on the functions of dress and appearances, the exercise of status, power, celebrity and social mobility.

In an era of abundance, where fashionable consumption has a multiplicity of expressions, there is a generalized acceptance that dress and styles of self-presentation have significance, that they do somehow reflect the individual's substantive identity grounded in gender, ethnicity, religion and so on. On closer examination, this taken-for-granted assumption does not hold. Indeed, it is continuously challenged from both the mainstream and the margins. Vivienne Westwood has presented her latest designs during fashion week using the usual gawky female models but with the additional facial markings of a crossover beard. The current style for men to shave their facial hair into intricate geometric designs has been copied by Westwood's models, who paint their faces with a thin black line of a moustache and goatee. Drag kings and queens have long made use of this confusion in gender insignia. Questions about such ambiguous styles of appearance resonate through the fashion world, but what are we to make of it when Westwood brings this into the mainstream? Are we to interpret it as a trickle up or down effect, as the new androgyny, as the collapse of reliable signs in an era of loquacious appearances?

The field of fashion now examines such complex questions about aesthetics and cultural identity, the variety of public spaces in which fashion stakes a claim and the display and spectacle of image as forms of mobile art. Such fluidity in a scholarly field has made it an exciting intellectual enterprise, and the following chapters provide a well-formed, almost perfect overview of a field that now pursues questions beyond the expected, beyond the ethics of the manufacturing industries and global economics, the consequences of conspicuous consumption and aesthetic collapse. These collected chapters push deeply into the mysteries of self-presentation and stylized identity by overturning the conventional assumptions about fashion and its functions. The text will remain a classic reference for some time.

1 INTRODUCTION

DIANA CRANE

Fashion is a complex, multifaceted subject that has been studied in many academic fields. Scholars from disciplines in the humanities and in the medical and social sciences are interested in similar issues related to the phenomenon of fashion, but they approach them in different ways and rarely communicate their conclusions to their counterparts in other fields. The goal of this volume is to show that our understanding of fashion can be enhanced by juxtaposing perspectives from several disciplines, including communication, cultural studies, medicine, philosophy, psychiatry, psychology and sociology. These chapters suggest that a few scholars, both classical and contemporary—such as Georg Simmel, Gilles Lipovetsky and Jean Baudrillard—have provided theoretical frameworks that constitute a basis for research by scholars working in very different fields.

Propelled by increasingly intrusive media, fashion is very visible in contemporary society and has both positive and negative effects. Definitions of fashion focus on four concepts that refer to various aspects of its manifestation. The simplest type of definition is that fashion is a form of material culture related to bodily decoration. Laura Bovone, a sociologist, links fashion to a major aspect of contemporary societies, the use of consumer objects and choices to communicate one's perceptions of one's place in society. In her chapter 'Fashion, Identity and Social Actors', she says that 'the concept of fashion needs to be inextricably linked to the concept of consumption.'

A second type of definition focuses on fashion as a signifier. Here the emphasis is on fashion as a kind of language in which clothing styles function as signifiers. Clusters of norms and codes constitute recognizable styles at any specific time. These norms and codes are continually being revised and modified, usually in relatively minor ways, but from time to time substantial changes occur. The meanings of some items of clothing are stable and singular, like the man's suit, while the meanings of other items are constantly changing and may at times be ambiguous, as in the cases of the blue jean and the T-shirt. Fashions are often confused with fads. The term *fad* refers to specific items which become very popular for a few weeks or months and then disappear.

A third type of definition views fashion as a system of business organizations in which fashion is created, communicated and distributed to consumers. The public performs an important role in the dissemination of fashion. Dissemination formerly occurred largely through imitation from elites to non-elites. Now, role models include celebrities from popular culture and members of minority subcultures.

A fourth type of definition identifies the hypothetical effects of fashion, such as the reinforcement of social differentiation, the expression of aspirations for social mobility and the resolution of anxieties regarding social identity. One indication that fashion is not a trivial and ephemeral phenomenon is the way in which fashionable clothing and accessories are and have been used to express and shape personal and social identities.

The study of fashion is complicated by the fact that fashion is continually changing, not just in its substantive content but also in its relationship to social institutions and the public. Ann Margaret Brach, an engineer, concludes that the essential characteristic of the content of fashion is continual change. In her chapter 'Identity and Intersubjectivity', she says: 'The matter or content of fashion must change for fashion to exist at all.' Alejandro Nestor García Martínez, a sociologist and a philosopher, argues that the instability inherent in fashion differentiates fashion from style. Style refers to behaviour that is relatively stable. Several of the authors in this volume take the position that in order to understand the nature of fashion today, it is necessary to examine how its role in Western societies has evolved in the past two hundred years. The characteristics and impact of fashion have changed as the nature of society has evolved from premodern to modern and from modern to postmodern. Major changes in clothing styles are generally indicators of important shifts in social relations and levels of social tension. The processes of diffusion and the effects of fashion differ in different types of societies.

In premodern and modern societies, members of the upper class and later the bourgeoisie used fashion to indicate their social position or the position to which they aspired. Identification with social class influenced the way individuals perceived their identities and their relationships with their social environments. According to Simmel (1957 [1904]), fashion was a major tool in the quest for social distinction. In postmodern societies, fashionable styles reflect the complexity of the ways people perceive their connections with one another. Different styles have different publics; there is no agreement about a fashion ideal that represents contemporary culture. Lipovetsky (1987) perceives this so-called 'empire of fashion' as liberating for the individual who obtains the capacity for self-expression. By contrast, Baudrillard (1970) views the individual as being trapped in a consumer society where fashion, along with other cultural goods, is useless and ultimately meaningless.

The authors in this volume explore different aspects of the connections between fashion, identity and self-image. Laura Bovone provides a useful definition of identity. She distinguishes between personal identity (what makes an individual unique) and social identity (what makes an individual similar to others in her social group). How has fashion been used to express these two types of identity? How have these connections evolved over time and in various circumstances?

Ana Marta González, a philosopher, examines the views of classical thinkers of the Enlightenment and romanticism—including Kant, Rousseau and Schiller—who, in her opinion, still define the intellectual background of our world and hence of fashion. González's question is: How did classical thinkers shape the ways we perceive ourselves and others and hence our proclivity towards fashion? She notes the affinity between Simmel's conception of fashion as 'a principle of social distinction and assimilation' and Kant's recognition that the individual relies on fashion to facilitate assimilation with others in her social environment or, alternatively, to distinguish herself from others. She explains how philosophers, prior to Simmel, conceptualized the relationship between the individual and public space in which fashion unfolded. She agrees with Bauman (1996) that the problem of identity takes different forms in modern and postmodern societies. In modern societies, individuals used fashion to construct unique selves, but, in postmodern societies, they prefer to avoid commitment to a specific identity, so as to remain free to experiment with alternative identities.

González argues that the conclusions of Lipovetsky and Baudrillard concerning the reasons for the importance of fashion in postmodern societies are exaggerated. Lipovetsky overemphasizes the level of hyperindividualism that supposedly elevates the role of fashion while Baudrillard overstates the extent to which the individual lacks a coherent sense of self that could provide a basis for selecting among fashions and consumer goods. González challenges the theory of the 'minimal postmodern self', which supposedly shifts from one identity to another, on the grounds that traditional identities, as defined by classical philosophers, are not entirely irrelevant in contemporary society.

García Martínez provides an alternative explanation for the importance of fashion in contemporary societies. Drawing on the work of Norbert Elias (1994), he argues that the prominence of fashion has resulted from a general civilizing process in Western societies which has gradually spread from elites to other social classes. This process has produced structural transformations, which have led to greater social differentiation, and changes in individual personality, such as an increase in individualism and in the desire for social distinction. As a result of increased social differentiation, there is greater diversity in people's tastes and, in turn, enormous variation in choices offered by the fashion system. An abundance of new and ephemeral fads and fashions are created and adopted by members of youth and minority subcultures. These changes have led to an increase in the visibility of fashion as a phenomenon but have also resulted in a decline in shared codes of sartorial meaning across different social groups.

Laura Bovone and Colin Campbell (the latter is also a sociologist) attempt to clarify the relationship between fashion and identity in contemporary societies. For Bovone, fashionable clothes are consumer objects. The consumer, not the worker, is the most important actor in modern society. Clothing and personal appearance in general are important indicators of other people's behaviour. More than any other type of consumer object, fashion expresses our social identity because it provides, according to Bovone's chapter, 'Fashion, Identity and Social Actors', 'opportunities to place ourselves socially via situated practice, to communicate to the outer world our belonging or exclusion, or even our ambivalence and instability'. Rather than seeing fashion as a meaningless but oppressive phenomenon, as does Baudrillard, Bovone emphasizes the role of fashion in providing aesthetic choices that enable the consumer either to conform or to rebel, to assimilate or to subvert the dominant culture.

Campbell, like García Martínez, attempts to explain the significance of fashion in contemporary society. He attributes the appeal of fashion partly to what he calls self-illusory hedonism or daydreaming that leads to an 'insatiable desire for novelty'. In his chapter, 'The Modern Western Fashion Pattern, its Functions and Relationship to Identity', he states that 'the essential activity of modern consumption is not the actual selection, purchase, or use of products so much as the imaginative pleasure-seeking to which the product image lends itself.' He also attributes the importance of fashion to its role in providing an aesthetic standard of judgment for consumer goods. Fashion expresses personal identity in the sense that the style of the products that individuals purchase, use and display 'says something about who they are' and serves as an indication of their social identity along with other aspects of their lives. However, Campbell does not agree that individuals select or create new personal identities through their choice of consumer goods, including fashion, with the possible exception of members of minority subcultures. Instead, he concludes that, for most people, the connection between fashion and personal identity in the modern world takes the form of 'discovering their true identity by a process of monitoring their responses to the various styles that are brought to their attention . . . as a part of a process of coming to realize "who they really are" '.

Brach is critical of the role of fashion in contemporary society. For her, the freedom for self-expression that some observers have associated with postmodern societies is illusory. The increasing domination of fashion as an economic system imposes a specific type of identity on consumers through the mass media. Images transmitted through the media encourage continual experimentation with fashion but do not lead to self-discovery or to a stable personal identity. Maria Teresa Russo, a medical anthropologist, is also critical of contemporary fashion, specifically the way in which fashions generated by business organizations in search of profit undermine the individual's capacity to develop a personal style. She points to the role of the fashion brand, which expresses an impersonal lifestyle and turns the individual into a 'walking advertisement'. Although fashion is used in different ways by different social groups, the fashion system is particularly oriented toward the tastes and interests of youthful consumers, some of whom become obsessed with certain aspects of fashion. Russo argues that young people in contemporary society are susceptible to the dictates of fashion because their identities are based on 'appearing rather than being'. Fashions are not chosen in order to express their personal outlook. Instead, young people use fashion to conform to ideas about personal appearance that emanate from the media.

Efrat Tseëlon examines the issue of fashion and identity in a different way by showing that clothing research and sartorial reality produce quite different indications of the meanings of clothing. She argues that fashion researchers have concentrated on 'pockets of homogeneity' with regards to clothing rules and their meanings while academic researchers have emphasized that sartorial meaning is 'contextual, complex, contingent and negotiated within a context'. Both types of researchers suggest that the meanings of clothing and of fashionable clothing can be compared to a language. Through empirical research, Tseëlon tested the idea that 'clothes and personal appearance are means of non-verbal communication used to exchange personal and social information.' By studying whether and how well peers were able to interpret the meanings that individuals intended to communicate through their clothing, she found that the messages conveyed by ordinary people's wardrobes were much more ambiguous and less stereotypical than previous research on fashion has indicated. She concludes that the reality of wearing clothes is 'fragmented, random, fluid and idiosyncratic . . . no clear code is followed by all'.

The three authors in the volume who are specialists in the medical and behavioural sciences are particularly concerned with the negative effects of fashion on adolescents. María Elena Larraín, a psychologist, examines the connections between fashion and the process of identity formation in adolescence. Some adolescents become excessively concerned about their bodies and about their appearance generally. Their anxieties about themselves are reflected in exaggerated levels of attention to their clothing.

Francesco Cecere, a physician, and Raphael M. Bonelli, a psychiatrist, discuss the role of fashion and the media in the generation of pathological behaviour in the form of eating disorders, including anorexia nervosa, bulimia nervosa and binge eating disorders. Although thinness as an ideal is widely disseminated by the fashion media, Cecere finds that the medical literature on eating disorders pays little attention to fashion. He suggests that this neglect is unfortunate since studies of the media have found that the media play an important role in generating and perpetuating eating disorders. For example, even brief exposure to music videos showing images of very thin women increases the level of dissatisfaction with their bodies among adolescents. Bonelli is disturbed by the alarming impact of fashion magazines on the level of satisfaction of women with their bodies. Although psychological problems are the determining factors in eating disorders, the fashion media play a major role in the internalization of the ideal of thinness among adolescent women. Cecere argues that public health services that are attempting to develop strategies for preventing eating disorders need to involve media and fashion professionals and make use of the kinds of language and images that occur in the media in order to attract the attention of their target population.

Bonelli argues that fashion has both positive and negative aspects. In spite of having negative effects on some social groups, an interest in fashion and personal appearance is a sign of mental health. Psychiatrists are able to infer changes in mood from changes in their patients' clothing. He says that observation of the outfit is part of the diagnostic method. Psychiatrists consider that both an exaggerated interest in fashion and a complete disinterest in fashion are unhealthy. Bonelli also observes that fashion is an important influence on a person's lifestyle, a set of behaviours that influence mental and physical health. The study of lifestyle is an important topic in public health medicine.

As the authors in this volume show, fashion is not simply a matter of seasonal changes in clothing styles. Closely allied with the mass media, the fashion system influences the ways in which we perceive and use our bodies; it also affects our conceptions of our personal and social identities, although members of some social groups are more likely to be affected by fashion than others. Larraín, in her chapter 'Adolescence: Identity, Fashion and Narcissism', stresses that 'fashion is a complex phenomenon that cannot be explained by a single theory.' Therefore, a multidisciplinary approach, such as has been used in this volume, provides a variety of perspectives that contribute to our understanding of the phenomenon and suggests new directions that future studies should take.

References

Baudrillard, J. (1970), *La société de consommation*, Paris: Denoël.

Bauman, Z. (1996), 'From Pilgrim to Tourist—or a Short History of Identity', in S. Hall and P. du Gay (eds), *Questions of Cultural Identity*, London: Sage.

Elias, N. (1994), *The Civilizing Process*, Oxford: Blackwell.

Lipovetsky, G. (1987), *L'empire de l'éphémère*, Paris: Gallimard.

Simmel, G. (1957 [1904]), 'Fashion', *American Journal of Sociology*, 62 (May): 541–58.

PART I FASHION AND IDENTITY

2 THE MODERN WESTERN FASHION PATTERN, ITS FUNCTIONS AND RELATIONSHIP TO IDENTITY

COLIN CAMPBELL

I begin this chapter by tackling the question of why fashion has become such a significant feature of modern industrial societies, or, to put it another way, what crucial function or functions could fashion be said to be fulfilling in the contemporary developed world? There are, I believe, two related answers to this question. But first, before outlining these, it is wise to define the terms used. In contemporary discourse we tend to refer to *a fashion* to mean the prevailing style, while to talk of *the fashion* is usually to mean that which is the latest or most approved; unfortunately, however, the term *fashion* is also sometimes used as if it were simply a synonym for *custom*, or indeed for any practice that is currently popular and widespread. Now, not only do I wish to reject these latter meanings, but I would also like to use the term to refer to a distinctive institution—that is to say, to a widespread, established, persistent and valued pattern of conduct, one that—following McKendrick, Brewer and Plumb (1982)—I shall refer to (with a slight modification) as the 'modern Western fashion pattern'.[1] The significance of using this term is to emphasize how the modern phenomenon of fashion is very different from that which preceded it (see also Polhemus and Proctor 1978; Wilson 1985). Indeed, what we have come to know as 'fashion'—what I am calling the 'modern Western fashion pattern'—only really came into existence in the eighteenth century, and what distinguishes it from that which preceded it is the exceptionally rapid pace of change that occurs in the prevailing or dominant style or styles. Of course, even in traditional societies fashions changed over time. However, this change was never rapid and often occurred at such a slow pace that it was not actually discernible to its members, who as a consequence frequently believed styles to be unchanging. What happened in the eighteenth century in Western Europe marked a dramatic break with this pattern of slow and gradual change. The critical events appear to have occurred in England in the reign of George II and were followed by what has been termed a 'fashion frenzy' early in the reign of George III. At this time, instead of changes occurring gradually, they were occurring frequently—effectively annually in the case of ladies' clothes, as each year the new fashion doll came across the channel from France. Thus, in 1753 for example purple was the 'in' colour for ladies' dresses, while in 1757 the fashion was for white linen with a pink pattern; in 1776 the fashionable colour was *'color de Noisette'*, and in 1777 it was dove grey (McKendrick et al. 1982: 54–60). These rapid changes were most apparent in dress, but it is also important to note that this was a time when fashion became important in relation to a whole range of consumer goods, such as crockery, furniture and furnishings, which had in many cases remained relatively unchanged in nature and design for decades.

FASHION AND MODERN CONSUMPTION

It is no accident that the modern Western fashion pattern emerged at this time, just as the industrial revolution was getting under way. Obviously, rapid change in the style of commodities required a flexible and efficient as well as a large-scale mode of production. Of more significance, however, and this is the first of my two answers to the question of why fashion is of such importance in the modern world, is the fact that this pattern emerged just as the first modern consumer society was coming into being. For, as I have argued elsewhere (Campbell 1987), modern fashion lies at the very heart of modern modes of consuming, with the link between the two taking the form of autonomous or self-illusory hedonism, a phenomenon—commonly understood as daydreaming—that results in an apparently insatiable desire for novelty.

To understand the nature of this link, it is necessary to recognize that individuals do not so much desire satisfaction from products as they seek pleasure from the self-illusory experiences that they construct from their associated meanings. The essential activity of modern consumption is thus not the actual selection, purchase or use of products so much as the imaginative pleasure-seeking to which the product image lends itself, 'real' consumption being largely a resultant of this 'mentalistic hedonism'. Viewed in this way, the basic motivation of consumers can be regarded as the desire to experience in reality those pleasurable dramas that they have already enjoyed in their imagination, with the consequence that 'new' products are preferred to familiar ones because they are seen as offering the possibility of realizing that ambition. However, since reality can never provide that especially perfected form of pleasure experienced in daydreams, each purchase leads to literal disillusionment, something that necessarily contributes to the extinction of the want for that particular good. However, what is not extinguished is the fundamental longing that daydreaming itself generates, and hence individuals remain as determined as ever to seek out new products that can serve as replacement objects of desire.

Viewed in this way, the emphasis upon novelty becomes comprehensible, as modern consumers reproduce the cycle of desire–acquisition–use–disillusionment–renewed desire in their continuing attempts to close the gap between an imperfect present and a perfectly imagined future; the practical effect of such activity being the creation of a permanent disposition to seek out the strange, novel or unfamiliar. The fact that any so-called new product may not in reality offer anything resembling either additional utility or a truly novel experience is largely irrelevant, since all that is required in order to satisfy this desire for novelty is the presence of objects in the environment that can be 'taken as new' to some degree. That is, commodities that can be differentiated in style from those currently being consumed to a sufficient extent to be identified with illusory images. Hence, it is this basic taste for novelty that helps explain both the ability of modern consumers to generate endless wants, as well as the existence of the modern phenomenon of fashion. Indeed, it follows that the modern Western fashion pattern involves little more that the consumption of novelty, while it is the fact that modern consumers possess this basic 'taste for novelty' that explains not only why they embrace new fashions so enthusiastically, but also how they are able to change their actual tastes so easily. This is not primarily because they are being manipulated into doing so, or because, à la Veblen (1925) or Simmel (1957 [1904]), they have an overwhelming concern with status, but simply because they are addicted to novelty (for a critique of the Veblen-Simmel model of fashion behaviour, see Campbell 2002). The importance of fashion to modern consumerism can be seen in the fact that fashion accounts for more of the demand for new goods than technological innovation (even accounting for planned obsolescence) and replacement purchasing combined.

Now, we can see evidence for this addiction in the extent to which fads and crazes are widespread features of modern societies. However, what generally distinguishes novelty fads such as using a hula hoop, streaking or collecting Pokemon cards, for example, is that these lack the critical aesthetic ingredient. Thus, such activities are not normally considered to be 'attractive' when in fashion or 'ugly' when their time has gone. On the contrary, they are simply judged to be outdated, old hat or passé, which is also how one generally regards formerly fashionable places that have since lost their appeal, such as holiday resorts or restaurants. But fashion in the true sense involves a second ingredient in addition to novelty, and this is aesthetic significance. An activity, place or person, or even an idea or belief, may be fashionable for a while before becoming old hat or passé, but a style of dress or decoration that has gone out of fashion is more than simply passé. It is also no longer considered attractive or beautiful. That fashion plays this crucial role of acting as an aesthetic standard of judgement is of immense importance and helps provide my second answer to the question of why this institution has become of such critical importance to modern societies. But in order to understand its crucial role in this respect, it is first necessary to appreciate what happened to ideas about beauty and aesthetics at the dawn of the modern era—that is, in the eighteenth century.

FASHION AND AESTHETIC STANDARDS

Throughout the history of the West, from Greco-Roman times until the eighteenth century, it had been taken for granted that there was a universal and unchanging standard by which beauty, both in nature and art, could be judged. This was the classical ideal, as originally set out by Aristotle, and although commentators were well aware that aesthetic standards did in fact differ (between individuals, societies and over time), this variation was generally put down to the influence of custom and ignorance—hence, in effect, to the lack of an appropriate education in the arts. In other words, the assumption that there existed universal and unchanging rules or laws by which objects in both nature and art could be judged as pleasing and there-fore beautiful remained unquestioned for many centuries. However, with the onset of the Enlightenment, it was no longer possible for this proposition to be accepted as true simply because it was supported by the authority of tradition. The new spirit of rational enquiry required that such truths should be supported by reason, if not also by evidence produced through empirical investigation. Thus, while continuing to assert that the aesthetic rules enunciated by the ancients were indeed correct, eighteenth-century thinkers began to look for ways of demonstrating or confirming their truth. This they hoped to achieve either through thoughtful introspection or through careful observation of that common denominator in aesthetic judgements that, it was assumed, all people possessed. So it was that a generation of thinkers, generally known as the 'aesthetic' or 'British' empiricists, sought through psychological investigation to discover those objects and qualities that were deemed universally pleasing by all men and women.[2]

Now, although these writers were convinced that an ideal and universal standard of taste (and hence beauty) did exist, their efforts were not only unsuccessful in demonstrating what this might be, but their arguments actually tended to under-mine each other, with the result that a general doubt and uncertainty concerning the nature of aesthetic standards became widespread. At the same time, a strong current of popular opinion emerged—stimulated by the developing consumer society—that was dismissive of the confused and conflicting opinions of these thinkers and aestheticians and which favoured a simple, democratic solution to the problem. This was to claim that, as with matters of purely gustatory taste, individuals should be free to decide for themselves what was (and was not) beautiful (Hooker 1934). In other words, all issues of taste were to be considered as purely individual and subjective matters, not open to general debate or dispute. Hence, an individual's likes and dislikes, in art and aesthetics as much as in food and drink, were to be considered purely personal, subjective and therefore unchallengeable.

That a populist movement of this kind should occur at this time is entirely understandable. For, of course, 'taste' is the crucial concept that links imaginative hedonism, and hence modern consumerism, with the institution of modern fashion, given that, as linguistic usage suggests, this term embraces both the patterning of pleasures and the process of aesthetic discernment. However, although this populist reaction against aesthetic paternalism was a significant factor in rendering the efforts of the aesthetic empiricists irrelevant, it was not really a tenable position. In one respect this was bound to be the case, given that, once matters of taste are extended beyond the simply gustatory, they are no longer purely subjective in character but necessarily reflect the wider culture into which individuals are socialized.[3] However, of more crucial significance is the fact that attempts to 'de-aestheticize' taste in this way and render it an entirely personal and subjective matter are bound to fail if only because of the inescapable link between the aesthetic and the ethical (something that is again very apparent in linguistic usage, given that the term 'good taste' can refer to conduct as well as aesthetic appreciation). Thus, whereas the nature of an individual's gustatory taste is rarely likely to be a matter of much social comment and judgement (unless it is exceptionally unusual), a person's aesthetic taste most certainly will be, for it is deemed a personal quality that is indicative of both character and social standing. Consequently, an individual's likes and dislikes in such matters are never likely to be a matter of indifference either to society at large or, indeed, the individual concerned. Moreover, aesthetic judgements are not made simply by individuals acting alone in the marketplace. They are also made by couples and families, as well as by associations, organizations and the wider community in general, while it is obvious that in all these cases there will, as a matter of necessity, have to be some measure of agreement.

This means that some standardization in aesthetic matters must exist, just as it must in relation to moral and ethical issues, if societies are to function successfully. And it is here that the modern fashion pattern has come to be of critical importance because it emerged, towards the end of the eighteenth century, as the de facto answer to the problem none of the aesthetic empiricists could solve, which was to find an aesthetic standard acceptable to all. These writers, while perceiving the need for such a standard, had understandably assumed it would be universal and unchanging in nature; however, the sociological necessity was merely that there should be a widely accepted standard in operation at any one time (so that ordered and meaningful interaction could occur), while, as we have seen, the psychological necessity arising out of the form of modern hedonism that underpins modern consumerism demanded change. The consequence was the development of that institution for the continuous but orderly change in aesthetic taste that was previously referred to as the modern Western fashion pattern. For it is this that serves to provide society with an aesthetic standard by which, at any given time, objects, events and, indeed, the appearance of people can be judged to be pleasing, beautiful or ugly, while also ensuring that styles (and hence such judgements) are subject to rapid change. Indeed, it could be said that, in one sense, the institution of modern fashion does meet the aesthetic empiricists' demand for a universal and unchanging aesthetic standard. It is merely that this standard is not embodied in any one set of aesthetic principles, but rather in a preference for whatever it is that occupies that point in time where familiar styles are in the process of being displaced by the soon-to-be-familiar.

FASHION AND IDENTITY

I should now like to turn to the issue of fashion and identity and consider whether fashion has any connection with social identity; and the answer I should like to give to this question is a rather equivocal yes and no. That is, yes if what is meant by this statement is that the style of the products that individuals purchase, use and display 'says something' about who they are. But no if what is meant is that individuals, by choosing to buy and display certain commodities, while rejecting others, are thereby involved in the process of selecting or even creating an identity, one that had, up until that point, not been a significant part of 'who they were'. For in one respect it is self-evident that the goods we purchase and use (and hence their fashionability) must say something about who we are. But then, so too does our occupation, where we live, the people we associate with and even the way we speak (to name just a few from a long list of possibilities). In short, our overall style of life necessarily says something about who we are, while dress and appearance, like the other criteria mentioned, are necessarily aspects of that overall way of life. In that respect, our consumption pattern is an index or indicator of our social identity in much the same way as is our income, occupation or education.[4] The key question therefore is not whether one can make a connection of some kind between fashion and identity, but rather whether there are any good grounds for believing that the consumption of goods, and especially the following of fashion, has any special significance in this respect. That is to say, are there any grounds for believing that the identities of members of contemporary Western-style societies are somehow more closely linked to their manner of consumption than to any other aspect of their lives, and especially, are there any grounds for believing that their identities are *principally derived* from their mode of consumption? Or, to put it in the simple slogan in which this idea is sometimes expressed, is there any truth in the claim that 'we are what we buy' or, perhaps more especially in the context of this discussion, that 'we are what we wear'?

Now, it is important to stress that there is nothing at all new about the idea that an individual's mode of consumption, and especially his manner of dress, is an indication of his social identity; for this has been the case for most of human history. Indeed, the very prevalence and persistence of sumptuary law, much of which was aimed specifically at ensuring that individuals dressed (and behaved) in a manner consonant with their social position, attests to the ubiquitous assumption of an intimate and necessary connection (see Hunt 1996). Of course, the whole point of sumptuary law was to patrol and enforce this link and thereby prevent individuals from trying to claim an identity they did not possess by 'dressing above their station'.

It is generally assumed that 'the sumptuary project' is long dead and that, in the modern (or perhaps especially the postmodern) world, no such restrictions apply. Hence, the assumption that today people can dress as they like (subject, of course, to the constraints of their pocket) and therefore by implication that individuals can 'pass themselves off' as anyone they please.[5] But clearly this is an important distinction from a situation in which, because few if any restrictions exist, individuals may choose to adopt any style of dress that they fancy, especially one in which they can adopt any identity they wish. Obviously, for this to be the case, identity would have to be largely, if not exclusively, determined by dress and appearance, a very different proposition from the claim that these attributes are merely indicators of one's social identity. So, are there any grounds for assuming that individuals can change their identity simply by changing their dress?

The first thing to note about this thesis is its suspect logic. For if, indeed, we live in a society in which anyone can dress in any way she likes, then it follows that dress cannot be a significant indicator of social standing. Sumptuary law was important because it operated in societies in which dress was a direct and unambiguous indicator of a social identity connected directly with social standing. The absence of similar laws and regulations in contemporary societies indicates that dress has no such significance today, which strongly suggests that changing one's style of dress is unlikely to have much impact on one's position in society. In any case, would not those people who have attained the pinnacle of success in a society be quick to ensure that the marks of their success were ones that 'lesser people' could not easily imitate or adopt? Surely the fact that one can change one's style of dress with ease rather argues *against* the suggestion that social identity—especially in the sense of social standing—is closely linked to dress.

But then there is another strong objection to the suggestion that social identity is directly linked not simply with dress and appearance but also with its fashionable aspect. This is that such a claim would imply that very rapid and continuous changes in identity occur as a matter of course. In other words, if different styles are indicative of different identities, then the sheer rapidity of change characteristic of modern fashion suggests that modern individuals change their identities at least annually, if not seasonally, which, on the face of it, seems exceptionally unlikely. For surely it is implausible to suggest that each change of style involves a corresponding change in an individual's sense of who she might be, let alone that whole societies change their collective sense of identity each time a new fashion becomes widespread.[6] What is rather more plausible is that an individual's sense of identity might be related to her perception of her position in the fashion cycle, something that would not thereby necessarily change as styles themselves change. Thus, she might see herself as an especially fashionable person, in which case she would be among the first to adopt each new fashion, or alternatively, she might see herself as, if not actually unfashionable, at least indifferent to fashion and, hence, among the last to adopt the latest fashion (if indeed she ever does get around to it). Thus, identity (or at least an aspect of identity) would seem to be linked, not to particular styles as such, but rather to an individual's position in the ever-changing fashion cycle. But then, of course, this is simply to recognize that the valuation of and sensitivity to fashion is necessarily an element in a person's overall complex of cultural values and beliefs, and hence to cast it as a product of an individual's social identity, and not as its cause.

Indeed, the topic that really needs to be discussed is why the claim that identity is mediated through appearance, or even that identity is dependent upon appearance—and hence necessarily linked with fashion—is so popular with sociologists; there are, I believe, three main reasons why this might be the case. The first is because appearance, and especially dress, is often employed as a mark or badge of subcultural membership (see Hebdige 1979; Brake 1985; and Thornton 1995). Thus, a young person may announce the fact that she has joined a group such as the hippies, the punks or the goths through a marked change in her dress, and evidence such as this often is cited to support the contention that there is a close connection between appearance and identity. But there are two points of importance to note about this example. First, experimentation with identity is a defining feature of that stage of life called adolescence or youth. In other words, young people do not so much change their appearance because fashions change as because they themselves are changing, and consequently they seek out a style that signifies their particular chosen mode of youthful rebellion. Mature adults, by contrast, having passed through this stage of identity experimentation and consequently relatively confident in their sense of who they are, are unlikely to feel the need to make such dramatic changes in their appearance.[7] The second point to note is that the differentiations in styles of dress that are relevant here—that is, those that tend to distinguish subcultures—are only loosely connected with the fashion cycle. They do, of course, change over time, usually on a generational basis, such that the styles of adolescent rebellion that marked the 1950s differed from those of the 1960s, the 1960s from the 1970s and so on. But such changes do not correspond with the far more rapid and differentiated shifts that mark the fashion cycle at large. Indeed, youth subcultural styles tend to be rather resistant to rapid change, with some, such as those which characterize the bikers or rockers, for example, persisting relatively unchanged for decades. Thus, although it is clear that evidence from subcultures demonstrates that significant changes in identity may indeed be manifest or 'signalled' through dramatic changes in dress, this process tends to be disconnected from the fashion cycle.

The second reason why the 'identity depends on appearance' thesis is so popular with sociologists has to do with the theory, and in particular with the widespread tendency to assume, that how people see themselves is dependent upon how others regard them—a perspective that is largely considered to derive its theoretical support from the work of George Herbert Mead (in addition, in a rather different manner, from writers such as Erving Goffman). However, it is important to note that Mead's observations on the self and its relationship with others are commonly misinterpreted by sociologists. For Mead's emphasis on how the nature of the self is related to an individual's ability to 'take the role of the other', and hence to see herself as others see her, applied merely to the initial development of the self. That is to say, in order to become an object to ourselves we must first place ourselves in the position of others. However, Mead makes it very clear that, 'after a self has arisen, it … provides for itself its social experiences, and so we can conceive of an absolutely solitary self' (1934: 140). In other words, Mead's work does not lend any support to the view that the conduct of adults is guided or controlled by the way others see them. There is thus little theoretical support for the claim that personal identity, or 'the self', must be linked to a person's appearance since it is necessarily dependent upon the attitudes of others. Of course, this does not mean that it might not be so connected. But neither Mead's work nor that of any other theorist provides any unquestionable grounds for assuming that, in the case of mature adults, how individuals are viewed by others has to be a major determinant of how they regard themselves; in this case, appearance cannot have the crucial role that such a theoretical assumption would necessarily accord it.

The third and final reason why the 'identity depends on appearance' thesis is popular has to do with aspects of postmodern philosophy and, in particular, claims about the decline of tradition. To summarize a complex argument rather briefly, it is claimed that statuses that had traditionally served as the principal sources of personal identity, such as those derived from nationality, religious affiliation, community, occupation and family membership, have lost their significance, with the result that individuals have been left with no firm basis or anchorage for their sense of self. It is then claimed that individuals, unable any longer to rely on these traditional sources, have no choice but to embark on the task of 'creating a self' for themselves using whatever symbolic resources are to hand. And it is in this context that commentators have been inclined to claim that individuals have turned more and more to their 'public image' as manifested in their dress and appearance (and consequently to fashion) in order to resolve this dilemma. However, in order to be certain that they have succeeded in their efforts to acquire their chosen image, individuals need the confirmation that can only be acquired through the affirmative responses of others. That is to say, increasingly uncertain about who precisely they might be, individuals first choose an identity from those images that they see around them (crucially from those portrayed in the media) prior to seeking reassurance from others (as expressed in responses to their appearance) that they are indeed who they are now claiming to be.

Now, while I would not wish to deny that traditional sources of identity and the self, especially those that are ascribed rather than achieved, no longer carry the force they once did, or indeed that, in some sense, there is a 'crisis of identity' in contemporary society, I am sceptical about the claim that individuals have no choice but to turn to media images for a source of their identity and hence that they have an inescapable need for reassurance from others concerning whatever image-identity it is they have chosen to adopt. For it seems to me that this argument fails to recognize the extent to which, in contemporary society, individuals are capable of constructing or inventing a sense of personal identity without the need to draw upon media images or depend on the attitudes or responses of others. Indeed, history rather suggests that when the institutional basis of identity becomes shaky, people do not turn outwards towards others in search of ontological security and a definition of self. Rather, they turn inwards, seeking answers in biology, psychology and in metaphysical beliefs concerning the immanent basis of identity, something that is evident in the fact that antinomian movements tend to thrive in times of social crisis (Adler 1972). Evidence that this is indeed the dominant contemporary mode of resolving the putative crisis of identity can be seen in the flourishing New Age movement, which is an area of contemporary culture where one can find an extensive literature devoted almost entirely to helping individuals resolve this crisis by helping them discover their 'true selves' (see York 1995; Heelas 1996; Hanegraff 1996). And what is noticeable about this advice is that individuals are encouraged to seek out and release this true self, not by monitoring either the media or the responses of others, but, on the contrary, by looking deep within themselves. For the basic New Age tenet is that authority lies with the self and that there is no true authority outside the self. As the New Age spokesman Sir George Trevelyan expresses it, 'Only accept what rings true to your own inner self' (Heelas 1996: 21).

However, while I would argue that this evidence suggests there is little reason to believe identity is dependent on appearance, especially as mediated via the quality of fashionability, it does not mean there is no connection between the self and the concept of taste. For what individuals discover when they search inside themselves for evidence of the nature of their 'true selves' are feelings and desires that commonly centre on responses to the world around them, while personal 'taste' is understand- ably regarded as the critical faculty accounting for the distinctive nature of these responses. What this means is that the aesthetic nature of commodities is unlikely to be a matter of indifference to consumers, particularly if they are imbued with a New Age philosophy of life. It follows that they will be especially interested in their reac- tions to products as this information will be highly pertinent to an understanding of who they really are. In other words, what a person likes and dislikes is seen as a crucial indication of the nature of his or her true self, such that individuals believe that their real individuality is manifest in their tastes or profiled in their preferences. Hence, we can conclude that, if indeed there is any real or close connection between personal identity and fashion in the modern world, it does not take the form of individuals choosing or creating an identity for themselves from images presented to them via the media, but rather that of discovering their true identity by a process of monitor- ing their responses to the various styles that are brought to their attention. If this interpretation is correct, it would mean that consumers do not so much 'buy' identity through their consumption of particular goods as 'discover' it by exposing themselves to a wide variety of products and experiences and then carefully monitoring their reactions to these as part of a process of coming to realize 'who they really are'.

OBJECTIVITY VERSUS SUBJECTIVITY IN THE MODERN WORLD

This brings me rather nicely to the last of the questions that this volume intends to address: What is the best way to preserve subjectivity in an objectifying world? Now, given that I do not believe that it is the sociologist's job, qua sociologist, to prescribe how individuals, communities or governments should act in the world,

I shall refrain from making any recommendations concerning how subjectivity might be preserved. I shall, however, comment on the implied claim that subjectivity is somehow under threat and that correspondingly the problem faced by individuals in this postmodern world is that of overwhelming objectification. For this is a claim that I believe to be easily countered with an equally convincing counterclaim along the lines of the argument outlined earlier.

I am indeed quite prepared to accept that, following the aforementioned argument concerning the decline of traditional sources of identity, individuals are increasingly likely to experience the institutions and organizations that they encounter in their everyday lives as objective if not actually as alien entities—that is to say, as not just separate from themselves and their own experience, but as actually existing over and against that experience. This, of course, is the inevitable consequence of the decline of traditional forms of belief, whether religious or secular in nature, and hence the 'legitimization crisis' that is its inevitable corollary. Yet recognizing that individuals are increasingly likely to experience the world outside the self as alien and objective does not mean that the forces of objectification are necessarily winning out over those of subjectification. For, as argued earlier, the former process actually produces its own reaction, a widespread retreat into the self that is especially apparent in the rise of that subjectivist epistemology that now underpins modern consumer society.

There are in fact two popular sayings that are intriguing pointers to the nature of this epistemology. The first is '*de gustibus non est disputandum*,' or, in English, 'there is no disputing about tastes.' This saying originally referred to the fact that it was simply a waste of time trying to convince someone, by means of rational argument, to like or dislike certain foods or drink. However, it also resonates very clearly with the point I have just made about the self-defining significance of personal taste. That is to say, consumers' tastes are unquestionably theirs in the sense that they cannot legitimately be challenged by others. By this I do not mean that a person's tastes cannot be judged by others; obviously, an individual's tastes can indeed be judged to be 'poor' or 'excellent', and so forth, according to the prevailing aesthetic canons. What I mean is that their reality cannot be challenged by others. No one can insist that I find something pleasant if in fact I don't. The second well-known, if not well-worn, saying is that 'the customer is always right.' Originally, this gained currency because it was the motto that store managers or proprietors were wont to instil in their staff so their particular retail outlet or chain could acquire or keep a reputation for good service. It was, of course, never intended to be taken literally—that is, in the sense of being a statement of epistemological principle. However, I would suggest that this is indeed precisely what it has become. Indeed, I would suggest that the assumptions embodied in these two sayings—that there is no disputing tastes, and that the customer is always right—have become the basis for a widespread and largely taken-for-granted individualist epistemology, one in which the self is the only authority in matters of truth.

We can see ample evidence to support this claim in the growing tendency to reject both the authority of tradition and that of experts in favour of the authority that individuals claim for their own wants, desires and preferences. This trend is apparent in an area like health, for example, where there has been a rapid growth of complementary and alternative medicine at the expense of more conventional medical practice (Fuller 1989). And it is clear that this development is a direct consequence of the assumption that the consumer is better placed than any so-called experts to judge which treatment is in his or her best interests. Another area where exactly the same change is apparent is religion. Here, too, the authority of the churches, in the form of the clergy, is rejected in favour of the individual's claim to select his or her own version of eternal truth; a process which has led to the development of what is often referred to as the 'spiritual supermarket' (Greenfield 1975). In effect, what has happened is that the authority of the old-style expert—that is, someone who told you what you needed and who gained his authority primarily from his institutional role—has been rejected, and his place has been taken by gurus or 'enlightened ones'—that is, someone whose role is to help you discover what it is you really want or desire. But then, of course, this is precisely what we would expect to happen in a society in which the gratification of wants has come to displace the satisfaction of needs. For when it comes to the identification of wants, the customer or consumer is, of course, necessarily always right. Always right, that is, in his judgement of what is ultimately true. In precisely the same way that it is generally assumed that no one else is in a position to tell you what you want, so too is it assumed that no one else is in a position to tell you what is true. Hence, we arrive at the popular notion of 'your truth, my truth' and the rampant relativization of all claims to veracity that accompany such a slogan. At the same time, the process through which individuals discover what is true for themselves is always and everywhere the same, and it is modelled on the manner in which they 'know' what they want. For a consumerist epistemology now prevails in which 'truth' is established in the same manner as the existence of wants—that is, through a scrutiny of one's internal emotional states. On the basis of this analysis, I would argue that subjectivity is not really in any need of preservation. Rather the contrary, in fact, for the challenge that faces contemporary Western civilization is how to find a way of preserving objectivity in a cultural environment in which—in no small measure due of the power of modern consumerism—the subjective viewpoint is now dominant.

References and Further Reading

Adler, N. (1972), *The Underground Stream: New Life Styles and the Antinomian Personality*, New York: Harper and Row.

Barbossa, L., and Campbell, C., eds. (2006), *Cultura, Consumo and Identidade*, Rio de Janeiro: Editora FGV.

Brake, M. (1985), *Comparative Youth Culture*, London: Routledge and Kegan Paul.

Campbell, C. (1987), *The Romantic Ethic and the Spirit of Modern Consumerism*, Oxford: Blackwell.

Campbell, C. (2002), 'The Desire for the New: Its Nature and Social Location as Presented in Theories of Fashion and Modern Consumerism', in Daniel Miller (ed.), *Consumption: Critical Concepts*, London: Routledge.

Davis, F. (1992), *Fashion, Culture and Identity*, Chicago, Chicago University Press.

Entwistle, J. (2000), *The Fashioned Body: Fashion, Dress and Modern Social Theory*, Cambridge: Polity.

Fuller, R.C. (1989), *Alternative Medicine and American Religious Life*, New York: Oxford University Press.

Greenfield, R. (1975), *The Spiritual Supermarket*, New York: Saturday Review Press.

Hanegraff, W. (1996), *New Age Religion and Western Culture: Esotericism in the Mirror of Secular Thought*, Leiden: Brill.

Hebdige, D. (1979), *Subculture: The Meaning of Style*, London: Methuen.

Heelas, P. (1996), *The New Age Movement: The Celebration of the Self and the Sacralization of Modernity*, Oxford: Blackwell.

Hooker, E.N. (1934), 'The Discussion of Taste from 1750–1770, and the New Trends in Literary Criticism', *PMLA*, 49/2 (June): 577–92.

Hunt, A. (1996), *Governance of the Consuming Passions: A History of Sumptuary Law*, Basingstoke: Macmillan.

McKendrick, N., Brewer, J., and Plumb, J.H. (1982), *The Birth of a Consumer Society: The Commercialization of Eighteenth-Century England*, London: Europa Publications.

Mead, G.H. (1934), *Self and Society*, Chicago: Chicago University Press.

Polhemus, T., and Proctor, L. (1978), *Fashion and Anti-Fashion: An Anthology of Clothing and Adornment*, London: Cox and Wyman.

Simmel, G. (1957 [1904]), 'Fashion', *American Journal of Sociology*, 62 (May), 541–58.

Thornton, S. (1995), *Club Cultures: Music, Media and Subcultural Capital*, Cambridge: Polity Press.

Veblen, T. (1925), *The Theory of the Leisure Class: An Economic Study of Institutions*, London: George Allen and Unwin.

Wilson, E. (1985), *Adorned in Dreams: Fashion and Modernity*, London: Virago.

York, M. (1995), *The Emerging Network: A Sociology of the New Age and Neo-Pagan Movements*, London: Rowman and Littlefield.

3 FASHION, IMAGE, IDENTITY

ANA MARTA GONZÁLEZ

> To be in fashion is a matter of taste; he who clings to custom which is out of
> fashion is said to be old-fashioned; and he who even attributes value to being out
> of fashion is an odd person. But it is always better, nevertheless, to be a fool in
> fashion than a fool out of fashion, if one chooses to brand this vanity at all with
> such a hard name, a title which the mania for fashion really deserves whenever it
> sacrifices true uses or even duties to such vanity. (Kant 1978: 245)

For centuries, intellectuals paid little attention to fashion. This disregard has been
nourished by two different influences: the platonic contempt for the world of appearances and Rousseau's rejection of the conventions of court society, to which we
could also add the Marxist critique of capitalist society. From either perspective,
fashion was regarded as a superficial, if not negative, phenomenon which prevented
people from committing themselves either to contemplative life or political action
(González 2003).

However, in recent years, fashion itself and its impact on contemporary society
have become real topics of philosophical and sociological reflection. This is conspicu-
ously the case of Gilles Lipovetsky, for whom fashion is now the characteristic way
modern democracies have found to organize a social life marked by hyperindividualism once old 'traditional identities' are no longer useful. Lipovetsky's diagnosis is perhaps overdone. Yet it is more or less shared by most of those authors who characterize
our society as postmodern, either to celebrate it or to regret it. For these thinkers,
fashion has become, for better or for worse, a way of defining one's identity—or else
a way of avoiding such definition, in the conditions of what is known as 'postmodern
society'.

It is perhaps first useful to trace an analytical distinction between 'postmodernism' and 'postmodern society.' While postmodernism can be viewed as a cultural
phenomenon, contrasted with early-twentieth-century modernism (Jameson 1991),
postmodern society involves something else: namely, a reference to the structural
conditions underlying the expansion of the postmodernist 'logic' into society. As I

show in this chapter, this logic can be described in terms of the 'de-subjectivization' of humans, which, not surprisingly, runs together with a blurring of the difference between the private and the public and, therefore, the increasing lack of proper (personal?) social space.

In this regard, a further distinction is also necessary. Up to now, the intellectual tools to critically describe the nature of postmodern culture and society in terms of de-subjectivization have been provided mainly by the philosophers of deconstruction. However, I argue that this connection is not necessary. In other words, in order to describe many phenomena of postmodern society in terms of 'objectification of the subject', there is no need to resort to the extreme versions of deconstruction which proclaim the 'death of the self', especially if we consider that not everything in our society can be properly described from this perspective. For, in spite of the increasing social implementation of postmodern ideas, people do not behave according to an all-or-nothing logic, which is the logic implied in the postmodern debate in general, and the debate about fashion in particular.

TWO CONTEMPORARY APPROACHES TO FASHION

Lipovetsky celebrates 'the empire of fashion' as the last expression and result of the modern individualization process (Lipovetsky 2002); the final episode in which, through paradox and ambivalence, the emancipation ideal of the Enlightenment has finally taken place. The emphasis on the new has entirely the traditional emphasis of the old: this is the logic of modernity (Groys 1992).

Now, it is precisely in the social scenario emergent at the end of the process of modernization where fashion may appear to have something to do with identity—or with the lack of it. In the conditions of late modernity, fashion, indeed, seems to have become one of the 'mechanisms' suggested by Giddens (1995) in order to 'mark' one's own identity.

It is apparent, however, that speaking of fashion as a mark of one's identity entails a kind of paradox. Were fashion a mark of one's (social) identity, it certainly would be a very fragile and ambiguous mark. Yet it is precisely its fragility that makes fashion so attractive to some enthusiasts of the hyper-individualism of postmodern society. Indeed, what they appreciate in the new state of affairs is the fact that the thick or substantive 'traditional identities' are gone. What they celebrate is the release from the past, the possibility of leading one's life entirely in the present.

As we know, the concept of 'identity'—and the related concept of 'identification'—was at the centre of debates in the social sciences during the 1990s. Besides the decisive influences from psychoanalysis that have helped introduce this concept into contemporary discussion, in a prima facie approach, the sudden interest in identity was also justified by the so-called crisis of (traditional) identities. By 'traditional identities', in this context, we mean the traditional ways of identifying ourselves and identifying others' place in society through references to nationality, gender and ethnicity. It is clear that the end of the Cold War, the consequent expansion of liberalism, economic globalization and massive migratory movements have all contributed to that crisis: old traditional identities are no longer a point of reference in guiding one's life.

In this context of crisis, some authors such as Giddens have proposed the development of a 'reflective identity' (1995: 15, 72). This proposal does not seem to take into account that it is actually by a quite natural process that, in critical situations, the individual reacts by focusing on him/herself. This is also the natural environment for narcissism to develop: not so much as mere egoism, but rather as a matter of survival (Lasch 1981). 'Too self-absorbed, Narcissus rejects religious commitments, abandons great orthodoxy; his attachments follow fashion; they are fluctuant, without further motivation' (Lipovetsky 1986: 67).

Apart from his positive evaluation of the contemporary boost of fashion, and merely from a sociological point of view, Lipovetsky's analysis owes much to Tocqueville's characterization of individualism as an intrinsic tendency of modern democratic societies. As the ancien régime disappears, the linking force of tradition declines and a new social scenario emerges, where the individual is the main character.

Now, Tocqueville was quite aware of the threats involved in this situation. In his reflections on American democracy, he made it clear that the natural result of a society populated by equal individuals would be 'soft despotism' (Tocqueville 2000). At the same time, however, in the young American people he detected a political culture able to balance that threat: political participation was, for Tocqueville, a way of counteracting the disintegrating effects of individualism.

However, this equilibrium has been lost since the second half of the twentieth century. Some decades ago, Richard Sennett (1977) published a book with a significant title: *The Fall of Public Man*. In that book, Sennett presented a diagnosis of present society, pointing at the disappearance of modern public space. His diagnosis had been partially set forth by Hannah Arendt, with her insistence on distinguishing 'the public' and 'the social' (Arendt 1958). As we know, Arendt claimed that the so-called social sphere was in fact a modern phenomenon, not to be confused with the classical concept of the public space.

According to Arendt, classical public space was the space of political freedom—that is, the space citizens used to interchange opinions and perform actions directly relevant to the construction of the city. Opposite this stood the classical definition of the private sphere as the space dominated by the needs of life; this space was called private precisely because it was deprived of political freedom. The private space, the space of the home, was for Aristotle the natural place of economy, understood as the administration of goods, as that which makes political life possible. It was also the natural place of labour and work.

This concept of public space underwent dramatic changes in modern times. An obvious sign of these transformations was the birth of a discipline called political economy. Its birth signified the relevance of labour and work in modern society. In other words, it signified the birth of what we nowadays call 'social'. It is worth noting, in this context, that the rise of the social realm has also been followed by the value modern society places on 'intimacy' as a way of avoiding the social levelling of people (Arendt 1958). Thus, the rise of the bourgeoisie, the development of modern cities, the industrial revolution and the modern division of labour—in short, the revolutionary transformations, which radically modified the previous way of thinking of the relationships between public and private—were also accompanied by the rise of music and poetry as ways of emphasizing man's subjectivity. Yet the emergence of the social realm somehow inverted the previous relationship between the public and the private spheres: instead of the private existing in service of the public, modernity came to think of the public sphere in terms of satisfying private needs.[1] In a further twist, contemporary society has also witnessed how intimacy has invaded the very space of the social sphere.

Arendt always resented the irruption of psychology into the public sphere, regarding it as detrimental to this sphere. In a similar way, Sennett has observed a connection between the lack of political participation and the increasing interest most people show in 'personal questions' (Sennett 1977: 27). In this regard, we need only think of the success of talk shows where people do not hesitate to reveal the most intimate details in front of the public, or the increasing value of 'authenticity' instead of 'courtesy' in social relations. The blurring of private and public entailed in these kinds of phenomena is certainly a sign of postmodernity, which, following Sennett, we might characterize as 'the fall of public man'. It is also in this sense that other authors such as Baudrillard have also concluded the 'death of the social'. In Baudrillard's view, this death is related to the transition from 'productive capitalism' to 'consumer capitalism' (Baudrillard 1998).

For Baudrillard, the boom of fashion is an essential aspect of this consumer society: objects of consumption must be ephemeral by definition; they must die quickly (Baudrillard 1999: 165). Moreover, an object of fashion is nothing other than a pure object of consumption—that is, an object deprived of its use value and reduced to its change value. While the traditional symbolic object was a mediation in a real situation and was thereby charged with symbolic meanings, the pure commodity is essentially deprived of all these connotations. This is also the condition for the personalization of objects, in the sense that people can project their desires on them.

It is because of this projection of one's desires on objects that consumption does not have a natural end (Baudrillard 1999: 224–9).

In line with his Marxist background, and unlike Lipovetsky's optimism, Baudrillard is far from celebrating this conclusion. In it he does not see a sign of real liberation, but rather the failure of real structural change—and therefore of political emancipation (Baudrillard 1999: 176). According to Baudrillard, a consumer society constitutes a new 'totality'. In this new totality, political emancipation is more difficult than ever, since the forces operating in a consumer society consummate the death of self, understood as 'the end of interiority and intimacy, the excessive exhibition and transparency of the world' (Baudrillard 1984: 196–7).

Lipovetsky and Baudrillard thus represent two different positions with regard to fashion. Lipovetsky sees fashion as a way of articulating social distinction in postmodern hyper-individualistic societies and celebrates this individualism as liberation for the human self. In contrast, Baudrillard sees fashion as a manifestation of consumer society and attributes to this society the final objectification of the human subject. Indeed, this objectification makes him unable to resist and reverse the intrinsically perverse economic system.

Likewise, both authors assume that in postmodern society, fashion has become a way of conveying some kind of social distinction, but for different reasons. Thus, Baudrillard agrees with Veblen's famous thesis of 'conspicuous consumption'—that is, social distinction comes from consumption, and, accordingly, there are different kinds of citizens depending on their different ways of consuming. By contrast, Lipovetsky insists that fashion cannot be reduced to mere economic factors, for it also entails aesthetic dimensions independent of the economy. Other theorists such as Derrida discuss the real novelty of postmodern aesthetics. Thus, the presumed aesthetic distinction is pure fiction. In consumer society we are confronted with a new 'totality', although a more indulgent one: it gives the sense of freedom but obscures true freedom.

While both approaches—liberal and Marxist—provide us with useful insights into the contemporary boom of fashion, it seems to me that both prevent us from finding a balanced approach to this phenomenon, as well as how it relates to the topic of identity. For this reason, I will now turn to the 'classical' study of Simmel, the sociologist of ambivalence, in search of a more balanced approach.

WHAT IS FASHION? A SIMMELIAN APPROACH

Ambivalence is certainly a good way of characterizing Georg Simmel's approach to modern society. This is obvious in his *Philosophy of Money*, where he unveils the double side of this privileged sign of modern society. On the one hand, money allows for a certain type of liberation of the individual; on the other, it also involves a threat of alienation insofar as it tends to generate impersonal and self-interested relationships among people, thereby also producing an impersonal society. Thus, while money enables us to lead an individual life, it also accelerates the transition from the comfortable atmosphere of traditional community to frenzied and impersonal modern society (Soldevilla 2002). However, as Lipovetsky stresses, this impersonal modern society is precisely the natural space where fashion develops.

It should be noted that Lipovetsky's link between fashion and individualism is not entirely new. At the beginning of the twentieth century, Simmel had already suggested this connection in many different ways. Like the other social theorists of his time, Simmel was interested in the main developments of modern societies, such as social differentiation and the emergence of modern individualism. However, unlike many, he also paid much attention to the small-scale phenomena of social life, in which psychology and sociology come together. As Frisby put it, 'Simmel provides us with the first sociology of modernity in Baudelaire's sense of *modernité*' (Frisby 1985: 40). Now, Baudelaire, as a poet of modern life, had defined modernity precisely in terms of the ephemeral and transitory; hence that particular affinity between 'modernity' and 'mode'—that is, fashion.

Like money, fashion is an ambivalent principle. From what he says in his essay 'Philosophy of Fashion', we can convey Simmel's definition of this phenomenon by saying that fashion is a formal principle of social assimilation and distinction (see Simmel 1997: 189). Let us clarify this.

The Formal Character of Fashion

Fashion is said to be formal because it has no particular content in itself. In principle, everything can become fashionable: tastes and clothing, words and books, places to go and hobbies to develop, even politics and religion can become fashionable—can be 'in' or 'out'.

A different matter, of course, is whether everything can become fashionable in its own terms. Indeed, to the extent that the study of science, the dedication to politics and the practice of religion involve a certain commitment, these areas cannot easily be reduced to matters of fashion. Perhaps a particular person is driven to the study of medicine because of a fashion started by a TV series; however, once he has applied himself to studying it, it is no longer a matter of fashion. To the extent it involves commitment—which, in turn, involves permanence through time—science excludes changes based on fashion. It is certainly true that we can detect fashions within science itself. It may become fashionable, for instance, to study a particular author or topic. But, again, once we commit ourselves to study that topic, fashion must be put aside: science has its own aims and methods.

On the other hand, there are things in life whose internal logic is more vulnerable to the dialectic of fashion, perhaps because they do not have a strong logic of their own and are therefore more subject to social conventions. Social conventions, indeed, are the most proper subject matter of fashion: the context in which fashion best displays its internal dynamic.

The Internal Dynamic of Fashion

The internal dynamic of fashion is also contained in the definition we have put forward: fashion is but a principle of social distinction and assimilation. In other words: fashion is a certain way of defining social affinities and, simultaneously, a way of defining ourselves as distinct among our peers. Indeed, while the impulse to create fashion follows from a desire to distinguish oneself from others, the impulse to follow fashion derives from a desire for belonging and social recognition. Since fashion involves both aspects, it represents the confluence of opposing human tendencies.

We could perhaps trace back Simmel's position to an interesting intuition of Kant's, who, in his 'Idea for a Universal History with a Cosmopolitan Intent', spoke of the 'unsocial sociability' of human beings as the motor of history and the order of society. By this, Kant understood 'the tendency to enter into society, combined, however, with a thoroughgoing resistance that constantly threatens to sunder this society'.[2] In other words, we experience the tendency to assimilate and, simultaneously, the tendency to distinguish ourselves from others. While the tendency to assimilate finds its expression in imitation of a model, the tendency to distinguish ourselves from others is demonstrated by the introduction of novelties and originality. Kant himself recognizes this tendency in the movements of fashion:

> All fashions are, by their very concept, mutable ways of living. Whenever the play of imitating becomes fixed, imitation becomes usage, and that means the end of taste. Novelty makes fashion alluring; and to be inventive in all sorts of external forms, even if they often degenerate into something fantastic and even detestable, belongs to the style of courtiers, especially the ladies, whom others then follow avidly. Those in low positions burden themselves with these fashions long after the courtiers have put them aside. Therefore, fashion is *not* properly a matter of taste (for it may be extremely antagonistic to taste), but a matter of mere vanity in order to appear distinguished, and a matter of competition in order to surpass others in it.[3]

This text contains several interesting insights that I do not want to leave unexplored.

The Fixation of Imitation Involves the End of Taste. However, Fashion Is Not a Matter of Taste

The first thesis has to do with Kant's own account of taste. As we learn in his *Critique of the Power of Judgment* (Kant 2000), what we call 'taste' is in fact a judgement—one involving the free play of faculties under the primacy of imagination. This means that in certain aspects of our lives we do not adopt the fixed rules of understanding; in addition, the primacy of imagination is also at the origin of play and novelties.

However, the second thesis posits that these novelties can be also disconnected from taste. Thus, to the extent that fashion merely has to do with novelties, it can also be disconnected from taste. It is interesting to note that this indifference towards taste is not exactly the same as lack of style: in the text, Kant speaks of 'the style of courtiers', implying that *there are tasteless styles*.

The mention of 'the style of courtiers' is also relevant for a different reason. For centuries, fashion was undisputedly a way of expressing class distinction. Thus, the bourgeoisie would try to imitate the style of the aristocracy in order to acquire social privilege; the aristocracy would respond to this by introducing a different fashion in order to keep the distance between the classes. This was also the way Simmel thought of fashion: 'fashion is . . . a product of class division' (Simmel 1997: 189).

While this latter aspect of his approach may seem controversial nowadays—for the very notion of class is under scrutiny—the intrinsic dialectic of fashion Simmel unveiled is still valid. Indeed, the trickle-down effect—from the upper class to the lower class—has perhaps been replaced by the trickle-across effect—from a certain group to another, not necessarily in a vertical direction—yet the idea of fashion as a principle of social distinction and assimilation is fully operative.

The Origin of Difference

Now, there is an aspect in which Simmel and Kant differ significantly. In the text I have quoted, Kant links the impulse to social distinction with vanity, which for him is almost inseparable from sociability. In this, Kant assumes a view of social life, prevalent in the eighteenth century, which sees vanity at the origin of cultural and economic progress—we need only think of Rousseau or Mandeville.

However, it seems to me that, unlike Kant—who links the desire for distinction to sheer vanity—Simmel would rather follow the romantics in adopting a more positive approach. For the romantics, the desire for distinction is not a matter of vanity, but rather a legitimate aspiration of individuals who recognize the value of their subjectivity, to the point that we could even speak of a requirement of self-expression.

This requirement was perhaps particularly felt in Simmel's own times. Confronted by an increasingly mechanical society, there was a real danger of human beings being reduced to mere units of industrial production. This was actually the concern shared by the modernists. Hence, perhaps, the relationship between some modernists and celebrated fashion designers, such as Elsa Schiaparelli; in these cases, fashion was perhaps tasteless in Kant's sense, but this tastelessness was precisely a way to stress personal distinction in times when urban homogenization was felt as a threat to human subjectivity.

This example also illustrates a crucial fact: the operation of fashion as a principle of social distinction and assimilation is displayed in modern cities as its natural place. Simmel's own essays are illustrative enough. I would point out two related connections: First, modern cities are the natural place of social conventions, and, as we have said, social conventions are the natural matter of fashion; and secondly, modern industrial cities populated by working individuals, who have left traditional bonds behind, are particularly anonymous and homogenizing. In such a context, fashion becomes a way of expressing one's difference. As Múgica writes in his work on Simmel, 'The hurry, excitation and vertigo of modern life constitute a certain "discharge" of interior agitation . . .; modern subjectivity is forced to perform no few defensive strategies' (Múgica and Kroker 2003a: 120). Fashion is surely one of these strategies.

As has been pointed out, social differentiation has been a common topic for social theorists since very early on. Simmel's contribution consisted in distinguishing functional differentiation (as a result of division of labour) and individual differentiation (Múgica 1999: 18). This attention to the process of individualization was also a mark of Tocqueville's analysis. However, Simmel is alone in remarking that modernization has put into place two different kinds of individualism: quantitative and qualitative individualism. Whereas quantitative individualism is a result of the intersection of social circles in which the modern individual ordinarily lives, qualitative individualism results from this intersection by setting a limit to the demands of each of those circles on the individual and leaving room for an autonomous development of his or her life (Múgica 1999: 36ss) and, thereby, for an original expression of the self.

Accordingly, Simmel characterizes the process of individualization as inheriting two influences. On the one hand is the individualism of the eighteenth century, which we can associate with the emancipation promoted by the Enlightenment—all human beings have equal rights. On the other is the individualism of the nineteenth century, which is the characteristic achievement of romanticism—every single human being is unique in kind, and true freedom also involves the expression of that uniqueness and corresponds to the aforementioned qualitative individualism (Múgica and Flamarique 2003: 72–86).

FASHION AND URBAN LIFE

Modern cities, indeed, differ greatly from small villages in that social relations are not heavily based on family, kinship or tradition. In fact, these might not even qualify as social relations in the strict sense of the term. Taken in its strictest sense, social life is precisely the kind of relationship established among people who are not too close to each other, and yet are not completely strangers. Thus, too much intimacy destroys social relations, as does too much indifference.

As Múgica observes, social space involves the reciprocal manifestation of human beings, but deprived of total interest and objective utility and of the intimate personality of every participant. Accordingly, the criteria of sociability involve the presentation of self according to a certain reservation and discernment, but also according to a certain social impulse, reflected in a desire for *being nice* (Múgica and Flamarique 2003).

The historical archetype of this social space is the French salon of the eighteenth century. This salon was, in fact, the heir of the social practices of court society. In its gestures and ways of talking and expressing emotions, the French salon was also the most conspicuous example of civilization and the social levelling power of courtesy (Múgica and Flamarique 2003). Artifice was the way of overcoming social differences within the salon.

In his account of the transformation of the public space, Richard Sennett has pointed out many strategies which have developed to adjust to a new social world. In their conduct as well as in their beliefs, the inhabitants of eighteenth-century cities tried to define what counted as public and what did not. The line drawn between the domains of private and public life was the line upon which the requirements of civility were balanced with the requirements of nature (Sennett 1977). Thus, eighteenth-century social urban life rested heavily on social conventions and, moreover, on the theatricalization of ordinary life (Sennett 1977). Social conventions—that is, social artifice—became particularly relevant in modern societies because relationships based on kinship and tradition were being lost. At all levels, the old connections had to be replaced by some kind of artifice. Thus, at the political level the social contract theories appear, and those thinkers who rejected the social contract, such as David Hume, resorted to another kind of artifice. For Hume, justice—which he understood in terms of obedience to the law—became an artificial virtue, as opposed to natural virtue. He even understood natural law as the result of a convention designed in order to keep society together.[4]

But, of course, pure law cannot hold a society together. Therefore, it is easy to understand the relevance given by enlightened authors to other social conventions. It is actually extremely telling to read how the 'worldly Kant'—the Kant of *Anthropology*—took such a great interest in questions such as deciding the most convenient number of guests at a dinner:

> If the number of participants is right, it need not be feared that the conversation will come to a standstill or that the guests will break up into small groups with those seated nearest them. The latter situation does not follow the rules of taste which are always observed when one person speaks to everybody (not only to one's neighbor). (Kant 1978)

Kant then devoted great attention in *Anthropology* to analysing the stages of the conversation during a dinner and clarifying the rules of a tasteful dinner. His concern was justified. At the end of the third book, he writes:

> No matter how insignificant these laws of refined humanity may seem, especially if you compare them with purely moral laws, then everything that furthers companionship, even if it consists only of pleasant maxims or manners, is a dress that properly clothes virtue. Such a dress must also be recommended to virtue even in a serious context. (Kant 1978)

Kant (1978) was quite aware that 'this refinement changes according to the ever-changing tastes of different ages. Thus, some twenty or thirty years ago ceremonies in social intercourse were still the fashion.' This, however, does not go against the nature of conventions: fashion consists precisely of *playing within conventions*. As such, it is necessary to human life, since these social conventions are, after all, conventional. This is why humour is so intrinsic to fashion: it is a way of showing that one is not creating absolutes from what is, to a great extent, relative to a particular culture.[5]

Social conventions, along with the fashions they generate, are regarded by Kant as belonging to humanity, and he often refers to this 'splendid misery' as one of the indirect ways whereby humankind civilizes itself and makes its way through morality. According to Kant, this process of civilization, along with all its paradoxes, entails a certain 'discipline of the inclinations' and would thereby pave the way for morality, both at the individual and the social level (González 2004).

Kant regarded his own 'an age of discipline, culture, and refinement . . . still a long way off from the age of moral training'. He was quite aware of the ambivalence of taste in regard to morals: 'Training a person to become well-mannered for his own social position will not mean as much as educating him to be morally good; but, nevertheless, the effort prepares him to please (to be liked or admired by) others in his social position. In this way one could call taste morality in external appearance' (Kant 1978). He was not alone in this approach. In his *Letters on the Aesthetic Education of Man*, Friedrich Schiller observed:

> Though it may be his needs that drive man into society, and reason that implants
> within him the principles of social behavior, beauty alone can confer upon him
> a social character. Taste alone brings harmony into society, because it fosters har-
> mony in the individual. All other forms of perception divide man, because they
> are founded exclusively either upon the sensuous or upon the spiritual part of
> his being; only the aesthetic mode of perception makes of him a whole, because
> both his natures must be in harmony if he is to achieve it. (Schiller 2001: 176)

Based on these writings, could we not qualify the eighteenth century, even more
than postmodernity, as an aesthetic age—an age really marked by the aestheticization
of ordinary life? Of course, the answer to this question will depend on what we understand by 'aesthetics', or, rather, which aesthetics we subscribe to. Kant and Schiller
were interested in an aesthetic able to preserve the classical ideal of a harmonious life.

They certainly were quite aware of the distance between their own and previous
times. Thus, in contrast to Aristotle's excellent man, who was simultaneously moral
canon and aesthetic canon, Kant and Schiller could not think of this harmony as a
natural process anymore but rather as a laborious historical and educational achievement. For them, culture had become a relatively autonomous stage between nature
and history, and its subjection to morality was not given beforehand: culture should
help the development of a moral character but could also hinder it. Indeed, following Rousseau, Kant and Schiller were quite aware that social conventions by themselves, deprived of their connection to morality, could also become hypocrisy and
thereby corrupt the heart.[6]

Rousseau's criticism of culture as artifice was in fact responsible for the break of
that classical balance. The rupture is somehow advanced, although very slightly, in an
ambiguity contained in Schiller's approach. While Kant represents a clear example of
Simmel's quantitative individualism, Schiller's case, because of his closer proximity
to the romantics, is not so clear.

Kant's quantitative individualism is apparent in that he subordinates the activity
of genius to a standard of taste developed through the communication of classes.
This standard of taste parallels, in the aesthetic sphere, Kant's own republican ideal.
It is from this perspective that we can best understand Kant's insistence on tasteful
social conventions: to the extent that the judgment of taste is potentially communicable, taste has the power to keep society together.[7]

Kant's concern with keeping society together, his concern with the consolidation
of community through the acquisition of a standard of taste, places him among the
proponents of Simmel's 'quantitative individualism'.[8] Now, it is not difficult to see
such a correct standard of taste as the aesthetic counterpart of the human race in
progress towards Kant's own republican moral ideal, up to the point that, for Kant,
genius should learn to restrain creativity according to the standard of taste.[9]

By contrast, romantic thinkers and artists exalted the idea of the genius. This can be regarded as a sign of their proximity to Simmel's 'qualitative individualism.'[10] Romanticism also involved a return to Rousseau. Against eighteenth-century aesthetic society, Rousseau proposes a 'de-aestheticization' in the name of authenticity (Múgica and Flamarique 2003: 103).

In fact, what Rousseau actually proposed was a different manifestation of self: a manifestation not determined by the artifice of civility. He wanted to overcome the expressive codes of court life, which he regarded as a kind of hypocrisy. However, as Jean Starobinski (2000) has pointed out, in Rousseau's approach there is a contradiction: if every expressive mediation is false by definition, why does Rousseau attempt to manifest his own intimacy, to write his *Confessions*, to speak out about his virtues and miseries?

The paradoxical answer to this question is that Rousseau makes subjectivity the key of a new code of expression: there must not be a social canon; the self must appear as it is, with no mediation (Múgica and Flamarique 2003: 105). Of course, one may wonder whether this rebellion against style could not become itself a certain style. From a historical perspective, this has been the case. The romantics accepted Rousseau's approach, and from then on, the romantic manifestation of the self became a mark of that 'qualitative individualism' described by Simmel.

From a cultural point of view, the Enlightenment and romanticism still define the main lines and the background of our world. Thus, we still experience the tensions between the social conventions we deem necessary for our social life and the self-expression we deem necessary for personal realization. More or less, this balance between manifestation according to social conventions and manifestation in terms of 'authenticity' was kept throughout modernity. However, in the 1960s the balance was somehow shaken. This revolution took place in the name of the subject oppressed both by social conventions and the perverted and totalitarian dynamic of consumer society, which had produced the society of spectacle (Debord 1999). Were both claims compatible? In either case, 'authenticity' became the key word.

In order to understand this reaction and how it relates to the question of identity, we have to take a detour.

THE CONTROVERSY OVER IDENTITY

The notion of identity is a modern and intrinsically problematic one. From a sociological point of view, Giddens has linked it to Western individualism (Giddens 1995: 98). While this is a reasonable approach, it obscures the fact that the contemporary controversy on identity is, in general, a rejection of the Hegelian account of identity, which is everything but an individualist proposal.

Also from a sociological point of view, but taking greater account of the philosophical roots of the controversy, Bauman has noted how the problem of identity takes different forms in modern and postmodern society. While the modern problem had to do with the construction of one's identity, the postmodern problem has more to do with the opposite task—namely, how to avoid becoming fixed in a particular identity, how to remain as a pure individual, as a minimal self (Bauman 1996: 18).

Thus, in very evocative ways, Bauman has summarized the modern notion of identity with the metaphor of the pilgrim. Pilgrims think of their life as travel with a definite goal, which gives meaning and structures their way. For the pilgrim—that is, for modern man—life is a project. Achieving one's identity is achieving the goal, fulfilling the task. By contrast, the postmodern approach cannot be summarized through a single metaphor. Its intrinsic fragmentation requires making use of several illustrating images: that of the *flaneur*, that of the homeless, that of the tourist, that of the gambler.

It seems to me that the transition from the modern problem of identity to the postmodern one cannot be adequately grasped unless we go to the roots of the philosophical controversy. Before doing that, however, I am going to take a little detour by going back to Schiller.

As pointed out earlier, Schiller stresses the need for expression that would characterize the romantic. Thus, in speaking of 'the person, which manifests itself in the eternally persisting I', he says: 'His personality, considered for itself alone, and independently of all sense material, is merely the predisposition to a possible expression of his infinite nature; and as long as he has neither perceptions nor sensations, he is nothing but form and empty potential' (Schiller 2001).

In distinguishing the person—in terms of the eternally persisting I, from the personality as the possible expression of that infinite nature—and in taking the person as 'nothing but form and empty potential' to be filled by perceptions and sensations, Schiller was also introducing the basic elements of a modern theory of identity. This theory, indeed, does not have to do with the 'empty and formal I', which Schiller, as Kant before him, took as equivalent to the rational self, but rather with the acquisition of a personality through time, which means the active involvement of the person with the world. Since these concepts are crucial in order to understand contemporary theories of identity, I will quote Schiller's (2001) whole reflection:

> [Human being's] sensuous nature, considered for itself alone, and apart from any spontaneous activity of the mind, can do no more than reduce him, who without it is nothing but form, into matter, but can in no way bring it about that he becomes conjoined with matter. As long as he merely feels, merely desires and acts upon desire, he is as yet nothing but *world*, if by this term we understand nothing but the formless content of time.

True, it is his sensuous nature alone that can turn this potential into actual power; but it is only his personality that makes all his actual activity into something that is inalienably his own. In order, therefore, not to be mere world, he must impart form to matter; in order not to be mere form, he must give reality to the predisposition he carries within him. He gives reality to form when he brings time into being, when he confronts changelessness with change, the eternal unity of his own self with the manifold variety of the world. He gives form to matter when he annuls time again, when he affirms persistence within change, and subjugates the manifold variety of the world to the unity of his own self.

The 'I', or the person, is thought of as potential power, yet this power is not activated unless it has something to act upon, namely the sensuous nature. Secondly, as long as the person is not activated—in other words, as long as sensuous nature determines the direction of one's life—the person is nothing other than *world*.[11] Third, insofar as the person acts upon his sensuous nature, he develops a personality: and it is through this personality that he can call 'his actual activity . . . inalienably his own'. Fourth, if the human being does not impart form to matter, he becomes mere world. Yet, if he does not want to remain mere form—in Schiller's terminology: if he wants to give *reality* to the form—he has to 'bring time into being'. In other words, he has to let time affect his formal being. And then, in giving form to matter, 'he annuls time again.' In this way, 'he affirms persistence within change and subjugates the manifold variety of the world to the unity of his own self.'

Looking back, it is no wonder that Hegel regarded Schiller's *Letters* as a masterpiece. In the text I have just quoted we have actually the basic elements of any theory of identity. Now, Hegel's is the greatest theory of identity produced by modernity. He was a romantic philosopher: as a romantic, he had a sharp sense of contradictions and suffered them as an inner division of the self; as a philosopher, he proposed a rational remedy for the romantic crisis—that is, he proposed philosophy as a way to overcome oppositions.

In particular, he tried to overcome the opposition between the rational and the real in an intellectual way, from within human consciousness. This overcoming took the form of a process, from an empty 'I' to a Subject. In his view, at the beginning of this process there is a pure rational element, which does not correspond exactly to reality; this lack of correspondence is due to a simple fact: while reason certainly has reality as its object, there is always something else, beyond reason—empirical reality. Now, as I have just said, Hegel is concerned with overcoming this opposition in a rational way. According to him, this can only be done through a dialectical process in which the initially empty, formal and elementary 'I' (spiritual substance) acquires experience and history until it finally becomes a self-conscious Subject identical to itself: an Absolute Subject, which does not leave anything outside of him. Thus, the

Absolute Subject consists of a Totality, which corresponds with an Absolute Concept: a concept which, so to speak, embraces all objectivity—nature and history.

In Hegel's approach, identity is the characteristic mark of 'self-consciousness'. The 'I' only becomes identical to itself at the end of the process. At the beginning of the process there is no identity, for identity requires two terms; at the beginning, the 'I' does not have anything at all to identify with: there is no 'self', no Subject. This self is something the 'I' acquires after a dialectical process. 'Acquires' means that the 'I' *contemplates* his identity. His identity can be called 'his' insofar as the 'I' contemplates it, not insofar as the 'I' produces it (Polo 1999: 193–4).[12]

Hegel's philosophy of history implies that the acquisition of Identity is always tragic because, in order to come to himself, the 'I' has to put up with falsity throughout the dialectical process (Polo 1999: 82). In spite of its abstraction, Hegel's conception of identity is a determinant of later developments and discussions of this topic. Indeed, from a philosophical point of view, contemporary discussion on identity has been regarded as a reaction against Hegel's conception of the self.

In general, Hegel's notion of identity—insofar as it is another name for Totality—is contested because it involves the inability to deal with the Other as Other. As has been pointed out, the 'I' is only open to the self; it is not open to the Other. Indeed, the only way Hegel's Subject has to deal with the Other is by assimilating it—that is, by setting aside precisely what makes the Other different from the self.

Thus, many contemporary philosophers oppose the Hegelian account for moral reasons: the concern with identity always involves the rejection of the Other as Other (Levinas 2002). Moreover, while all politics has to do with defining identities—and thereby defining, categorizing the others—Hegel's account carries this dynamic to its ultimate conclusion: Hegel's philosophy was actually at the basis of political totalitarianisms of the twentieth century. Yet the reactions against Hegel's conception of identity are very different in kind. While some attempt a complete deconstruction of the very notion of Subject, others keep this notion, though in rather unusual terms. Among those who avoid the notion of Subject is Derrida, who dissolves the subject in the text.

By contrast, philosophers like Emmanuel Levinas (Levinas 2002: 163) or, more recently, Slavoj Žižek keep a certain notion of the Subject, although from very different approaches. While Levinas's 'pure subject' (Levinas 2002: 167) draws mainly on Husserl's phenomenology, Žižek departs from Lacan's psychoanalysis. The interesting aspect of Žižek's interpretation of Lacan is that it allows for acknowledging certain parallels with Hegel (Žižek 1995). Of course, this approach should not obscure a basic fact, namely what Lacan himself realizes is an inversion of Hegel (Žižek 1995).

Just as in Freud's case, in Lacan the basic element in charge of activating the dialectical process is not reason, but rather the *libido* (Polo 1999: 255). Yet this inversion of Hegel still retains many Hegelian elements. Thus, Lacan also distinguishes between the 'I'—the *Moi*, which signifies the image the child has of itself—and the *Je*, the Subject, which is a symbolic notion. Like Freud, Lacan also assumes that the transition from the *Moi* to the *Je* takes place through a traumatic process. Particularly, the *Moi* only becomes a *Je* through the resolution of the Oedipal drama, whereby the child is introduced into the hard and demanding universe of social reality. This resolution, then, enables the *Moi* to enter into the symbolic order (Žižek 2000: 75). In some extreme interpretations, such as that of Althusser, the resolution of the Oedipal conflict involves simultaneously the acquisition of a gender identity, the subjection to the authority of the Father and affiliation to the patriarchal ideologies of late capitalism (Hall 1996: 8).

Now, according to Lacan, this traumatic process always leaves a kernel resisting entry into the symbolic realm. This kernel actually works as a 'cause' of the Subject: the so-called *objet petit a*, which Žižek characterizes as the shadow of the Subject (Žižek 1995: 59) or, in a different context, even as 'the spectral dimension which sustains the tradition' (Žižek 2000: 64). This *objet a* stands also for an impossible object which would satisfy the *plus-de-jouir* of the *Moi*. But the important thing is to note that *objet a* is constitutive of the Subject, helping define the Subject simultaneously as a drive towards subjectification which, nevertheless, can never be filled out by it. Thus, within the human subject we find a duality which can never be filled, can never be closed. Accordingly, there will be never a terminal, 'absolute subject' in the conventional interpretation of Hegel:

> Today, it is fashionable to search for one's true self—Lacan's answer is that every subject is divided between two 'true Selves'. On the one hand, there is the Master-Signifier that delineates the contours of the subject's Ego-Ideal, his dignity, his mandate; on the other, there is the excremental leftover/trash of the symbolic process, some ridiculous detailed feature that sustains the subject's surplus-enjoyment—and the ultimate goal of psychoanalysis is to enable the subject-analysand to accomplish the passage from S1 to *objet petit a*—to identify, in a kind of 'Thou Art That' experience, (with) the excremental remainder that secretly sustains the dignity of his symbolic identification . . . And it is crucial to note how this passage from symbolic identification to identification with the excremental leftover turns around—accomplishes in the opposite direction—the process of symbolic identification. That is to say, the ultimate paradox of the strict psychoanalytic notion of symbolic identification is that it is by definition a misidentification, the identification with the way the Other(s) misperceive(s) me . . . Symbolic identification occurs when the way I appear to others becomes more important to me than the psychological reality 'beneath my social mask', forcing me to do things I would never be able to accomplish 'from within myself'. (Žižek 2000: 49–50)

Just the fact that Lacan keeps the *objet a* as a counterpart of the Symbolic Subject—and moreover, that the *objet a* is constitutive of the Symbolic Subject—explains that he never renounced the notion of Subject. *Objet a* provided him with an explanation of why there may be Subjects who do not want entry into the (symbolic) world (Žižek 1995: 61–2). In other words: *objet a* also accounts for the resistance towards too much subjectification—and thereby completion of a terminal and closed identity.[13]

Now, in Žižek's hands, Lacan's de-centring of the Subject—his suggestion that the Subject cannot be merely approached from the symbolic side—has proven fertile to account for some features of so-called postmodern society:

> What happens to the functioning of the symbolic order when the symbolic Law loses its efficiency, when it no longer functions properly? What we get are subjects who are strangely derealized or, rather, depsychologized, as if we are dealing with robotic puppets obeying a strange blind mechanism. (Žižek 2000: 76)

According to Žižek, a Lacanian reading of contemporary society provides us with a reason to moderate the optimism derived from having deconstructed Hegelian identity. Žižek shows that the overcoming of a Hegelian type of totalitarianism does not necessarily lead to individual freedom; it can also lead to a different kind of totalitarianism: that resulting from the complete objectification of life.

Yet perhaps it is worth noting that this interesting theoretical achievement was somehow advanced by Simmel himself, precisely in his attention to the role of 'asceticism' in the definition of one's subjectivity and style (Múgica and Kroker 2003a: 90). In this, as is well known, Simmel is not alone. The role of asceticism in the definition of the modern individual was also one of Max Weber's contributions. Now, Simmel makes it particularly clear how the interior differentiation of the person, the possibility of a distance towards objective world, rests in that element of asceticism which puts a limit to the manifestation of the self. Moreover, according to Simmel, without that element of asceticism, there is no place for *style*.

THE POSTMODERN 'I' AND ITS AFFILIATION TO FASHION

For enthusiasts of postmodernity, the overcoming of Hegelian or traditional identities means just the happy overcoming of historical and social criteria of identification and the possibility of a complete liberation of the self—this time, with no limitations. Accordingly, there would be nothing other than pure individuals, perhaps reduced to their physical bodies and in a position to construct and deconstruct every social identity, every social fixation of their selves.

Focus on the body is certainly a mark of our age, and it is easy to understand why: from a postmodern perspective, the body, the way we mark it, the way we deal with it, can be interpreted as the remaining source of identity, once we have given up history and projects. The characteristic postmodern approach, indeed, rejects not only the pure Hegelian account of identity; it rejects the very idea of reconstructing or constructing one. Accordingly, it is opposed to any hermeneutical attempt—a Hegelian variation of reconstructing one's identity by looking back and elaborating a narrative. Yet it also rejects any modern variation, such as Giddens's, that still speaks of a reflexive construction of one's identity. The 'true' postmodern character does not want to look back or forward: she wants to remain in the present instant.[14]

Faced with pure individuals, certainly any process of identification becomes difficult. Yet this is precisely what the postmodern intends: instead of fixed social identities, he desires to preserve individual difference. This is why, for the postmodernist, identity becomes a contingent, fluid matter: a kind of game. This is also why fashion can be regarded as the best way to play the game of identities, in a kind of perpetual carnival, as Bakhtin would put it.

That game can work as long as the 'I' remains on the surface, as long as it avoids interiority and reflection—or perhaps as long as the 'I' uses reflection merely to criticize social conventions. What I call the 'Madonna-strategy'—that is, the systematic adoption of all possible identities—is a good example: this strategy is obviously equivalent to the denial of all possible identities (González 2001). What in this way emerges is a 'minimal self', almost reduced to the 'I', which incorporates one role after another. This strategy could remind us of Erving Goffman, who, in his book *The Presentation of Self in Everyday Life*, observed:

> Society is organized on the principle that any individual who possesses certain social characteristics has a moral right to expect that others will value and treat him in an appropriate way. Connected with this principle is a second, namely that an individual who implicitly or explicitly signifies that he has certain social characteristics ought in fact to be what he claims he is. In consequence, when an individual projects a definition of the situation and thereby makes an implicit or explicit claim to be a person of a particular kind, he automatically exerts a moral demand upon the others, obliging them to value and treat him in the manner that persons of his kind have a right to expect. He also implicitly forgoes all claims to be things he does not appear to be and hence forgoes the treatment that would be appropriate for such individuals. The others find, then, that the individual has informed them as to what is and as to what they ought to see as the 'is'. (Goffman 1959: 13)

As Sennett rightly observed, Goffman's depiction of social life was quite static. The individuals he represented were unable to acquire experience and to 'impersonate' the roles they take with that experience. In contrast to old theories of the world as a 'theatrum mundi', which served to express oneself in public life, Goffman's approach to roles involved a strategy of merely adjusting to social conventions (Sennett 1977: 36). Yet if we think of postmodern selves, this is perhaps the theory that best fits the object. As mentioned earlier, postmodern selves are minimal selves; they, very much like Warhol's pictures, are pure surface, for they have become like the objects exhibited in the great consumer malls of modern cities. Hence the reason for the inversion of the intimate and the social: while objects colonize intimate life, intimate confessions and naked bodies colonize ex-public spaces.

The postmodern self is, as Lasch rightly observed, a minimal self, limited to its most basic and immediate needs. It is a narcissistic self, which confuses its own reality with the image it sees reflected in the mirror of consumer society. In this way, postmodernism represents the death of the self, the celebration of contingency and superficiality. This makes it different from early-twentieth-century modernism. Early modernism was mainly an artistic movement, which, very often drawing on Nietzsche's critique of neat and orderly urban life, tried to rescue art from bourgeois taste, precisely by breaking the conventional forms which constricted life.

In spite of its often-provocative approach, it was still modern—and not postmodern—in that it proclaimed the autonomy of art, and the uniqueness of the artist. Early modernists differ from the romantics, however, because the modernist could not find subjectivity behind nature (Taylor 1989: 461ss). In fact, the modernists very often resented the romantics as bourgeois. If they were in general committed to the recovery of subjectivity and interiority, they did not expect any harmony between interior and exterior life, as was the case with the romantics, any less than they would expect a rational thread to give unity to their lives, as was the case with Hegel. Charles Taylor quotes D. H. Lawrence: 'Our ready-made individuality, our identity, is no more than an accidental cohesion in the flux of time' (Taylor 1989: 463).

We could read these words as a contrast to Hegel's conception of identity, but they also mean a reference to the flux of time, which is very common to the modernists. We need only think of Proust's attempt to recover subjective time: such an attempt clearly goes against the homogeneous and space-like conception of time proper to the mechanical society, but also against any enlightened or romantic approach to history.

Proust's narrative is entirely different from a 'traditional' narrative: in his *Remembrance of Things Past*, the flux of the experience takes the role of the 'I' in the construction of the story. Taylor sees in this the beginning of an age of decentring subjectivity (Taylor 1989: 465). Yet this decentring subjectivity was not yet equivalent to the postmodern death of the self, for the modernist still had a notion of identity, though an aesthetic one. For him, identity had become something very similar to 'style'.

As Simmel has shown, from an aesthetic point of view, this idea goes back to Nietzsche: the Nietzschean idea of 'distinction' was also one step towards the enthronement of 'style': 'the distinguished man is a strong self, a strategist of his own feelings and decisions' (Múgica and Kroker 2003a: 89). Accordingly, 'style' is a configuration of the spirit, whereby the spirit sets limits to itself and, through this distance, expresses itself (Múgica and Kroker 2003a: 88).

In postmodern society, however, style has been substituted by fashion. This corresponds to the final death of the self—hereafter reduced to a minimal 'I'. Thus, Warhol's cult of the invasion of seductive appearances and surfaces cannot be wholly understood apart from his disturbing obsession with death (Hughes 1997: 541).[15] This obsession perhaps contained that mark of postmodern society which many have conceptualized in terms of death: the death of the subject, assumed in contemporary approaches to the notion of identity.

Even Warhol's way of producing art could be viewed from this perspective. Unlike modernism, the postmodernist denies the autonomy of art; the systematic mixture of 'high culture' and 'low culture', but also the blurred frontiers between art and spectacle—the fact, indeed, that Warhol's aura was that of a movie star—is expressive of the postmodern death of the self.

Both tendencies, no less than any talk of 'ephemeral art', would have been completely strange to Proust. In postmodernism, the uniqueness of modernist art disappears. Since the self is nothing more than a creation of society, the so-called artist cannot introduce anything truly new. The only novelty he can expect is the product of *bricolage*, the more or less original interchange of elements already present in society—ultimately a game within social conventions and, consequently, nothing other than fashion.

THE NEED FOR A BALANCE

Persuasive as it is, the diagnosis of our culture as postmodern in the terms described here can only account for certain aspects of it. Not every current social conduct can be explained through this paradigm. Contemporary society is actually more complex, and the crisis of so-called traditional identities does not prevent people from still looking back at them as points of reference and trying, in turn, to reconstruct new ones.

On the one hand, the dismissal of 'old traditional identities' is not always experienced in liberating terms. Even Lipovetsky would agree.[16] From an empirical perspective, we could certify this by taking a look at the way immigrants make their way through their new environments. While they are likely to change some aspects of their old way of life—thereby, perhaps, reinterpreting their way of dealing with fashion—they do not do so without suffering (Lunghi 2003: 64–6).

On the other hand, even in the instances where the postmodern diagnosis supposedly works better—that is, in the case of traditional Western people who think of social conventions in terms of repression and postmodernity in terms of liberation—we should not think too rapidly of the death of the subject. Even those people do not live merely in the terms defined by postmodernity. It is simply not true that human beings can be reduced to mere surface. Even within a consumer society, people retain some subjective motivation to regenerate communal links (García Ruiz 2003). This impulse can be taken as a sign of the survival of the subject.

It seems to me that in both cases we are lacking a more balanced theory of subjectivity, one which can account for the different ways people act and react to social reality. For this we need an approach to the human subject that incorporates the flexibility of practical reason into social theory.

References and Further Reading

Altarejos, F. (2002), 'El problema de la identidad en la praxis social: afiliación y filiación', *Studia Poliana*, 4: 61–80.

Archer, M. (1988), *Culture and Agency: The Place of Culture in Social Theory*, Cambridge: Cambridge University Press.

Archer, M. (2000), *Being Human: The Problem of Agency*, Cambridge: Cambridge University Press.

Arendt, H. (1958), *The Human Condition,* Chicago: University of Chicago Press.

Barnard, M. (1996), *Fashion as Communication,* New York: Routledge.

Baudrillard, J. (1984), 'El fin de lo social', in *Cultura y simulacro*, Barcelona: Kairós.

Baudrillard, J. (2002), 'El éxtasis de la comunicación', in H. Foster (ed.), *La posmodernidad,* 5th ed., 187–97, Barcelona: Kairós.

Baudrillard, J. (1998), *The Consumer Society, Myths and Structures,* London: Sage Publications.

Baudrillard, J. (1999), *El sistema de los objetos,* 16th ed., Madrid: Siglo XXI Editores.

Bauman, Z. (1996), 'From Pilgrim to Tourist—Or a Short History of Identity', in Stuart Hall and Paul du Gay (eds.), *Questions of Cultural Identity,* London: Sage Publications.

Bauman, Z., and Tester, K. (2002), *La ambivalencia de la modernidad y otras conversaciones,* Barcelona: Paidós Ibérica.

Bell, D. (1979), *The Cultural Contradictions of Capitalism,* London: Heinemann.

Bovone, L., and Mora, E. (1997), *La moda della metropoli. Dove si incontrano i giovani milanesi,* Milan: Franco Angeli.

Bovone, L., Magatti, M., Mora, E., and Rovati, G. (2002), *Intraprendere Cultura. Rinnovare la città*, Milan: Franco Angeli.

Caterina, R. (1995), 'L'Abbigliamento e il sé', in Pío E. Ricci Bitti and R. Caterina (eds), *Moda, Relazioni Social e Comunicazione*, Bologna: Zanichelli.

Crane, D. (2000), *Fashion and Its Social Agendas: Class, Gender, and Identity in Clothing,* Chicago: University of Chicago Press.

Debord, G. (1999), *La sociedad del espectáculo*, Valencia: Pre-textos.

Featherstone, M. (2002), *Consumer Culture and Postmodernism*, London: Sage Publications.

Finkelstein, J. (1998), *Fashion: An Introduction*, New York: New York University Press.

Flamarique, L., Kroker, R., and Múgica, F. (2003), 'Georg Simmel: Civilización y diferenciación social (I)', *Cuadernos de Anuario Filosófico*, Pamplona.

Frisby, D. (1985), *Fragments of Modernity in the Work of Simmel, Kracauer and Benjamin*, Oxford: Polity Press.

García, A. (2003), 'La sociología de Norbert Elias', *Cuadernos de Anuario Filosófico*, Pamplona.

García Ruiz, P. (2003), 'Comunidades de marca. El consumo como relación social', *Política y Sociedad*.

Giddens, A. (1995), *Modernidad e identidad del yo*, Barcelona: Península.

Goffman, E. (1959), *The Presentation of Self in Everyday Life*, New York: Doubleday Anchor Books.

González, A. M. (2001), 'La antimoda: ¿otro estereotipo? A propósito de Madonna', paper presented at the conference on *Moda urbana*, Pamplona.

González, A. M. (2003), 'Pensar la moda', *Nuestro Tiempo*, 594: 14–27.

González, A. M. (2004), 'La doble aproximación de Kant a la cultura', in L. Flamarique and A. M. González (eds), *Anuario Filosófico*, 37/3: 679–711.

Groys, B. (1992), *Über das Neu. Versuch einer Kulturökonomie*, München: Carl Hanser Verlag.

Hall, S. (1996), 'Who Needs Identity?' in Stuart Hall and Paul du Gay (eds), *Questions of Cultural Identity*, London: Sage Publications.

Harrison, C., and Wood, P., eds (1992), *Art Theory, 1900–1990: An Anthology of Changing Ideas*, Oxford: Blackwell.

Hughes, R. (1997), *American Vision: The Epic History of Art in America*, New York: Alfred A. Knopf.

Jameson, F. (1991), *El posmodernismo o la lógica cultural del capitalismo avanzado*, Barcelona: Paidós.

Jameson, F. (2002), 'Postmodernismo y sociedad de consume', in H. Foster (ed.), *La posmodernidad*, 5th ed., 165–86, Barcelona: Kairós.

Kant, I. (1960), *Education*, Ann Arbor: University of Michigan Press.

Kant, I. (1978), *Anthropology from a Pragmatic Point of View*, Carbondale: Southern Illinois University Press.

Kant, I. (1983), *Perpetual Peace and Other Essays*, Cambridge: Hacket Publishing Company.

Kant, I. (1998), *Critique of Pure Reason*, Cambridge: Cambridge University Press.

Kant, I. (2000), *Critique of the Power of Judgment*, Cambridge: Cambridge University Press.

Kroker, R., and Múgica, F. (2003), 'Georg Simmel: Civilización y diferenciación social (II)', *Cuadernos de Anuario Filosófico*, Pamplona.

Lasch, C. (1981), *Le complexe de Narcisse. La nouvelle sensibilité américaine*, Paris: Éditions Robert Laffont.

Lasch, C. (1996), *L'io minimo. La mentalità della sopravvivenza in un'epoca di turbamenti*, Milan: Giangiamo Feltrinelli Editre.

Levinas, E. (2002), *Fuera del sujeto*, Madrid: Caparrós Editores.

Lipovetsky, G. (1986), *La era del vacío. Ensayos sobre el individualismo contemporáneo*, Barcelona: Anagrama.

Lipovetsky, G. (1999), *La tercera mujer. Permanencia y revolución de lo femenino*, Barcelona: Anagrama.

Lipovetsky, G. (2002), *The Empire of Fashion: Dressing Modern Democracy*, Princeton, New Jersey: Princeton University Press.

Lipovetsky, G. (2003a), *Le Luxe éternel. De l'age du sacré au temps des marques*, Paris: Gallimard.

Lipovetsky, G. (2003b), *Metamorfosis de la cultura liberal. Ética, medios de comunicación, empresa*, Barcelona: Anagrama.

Lunghi, C. (2003), *Culture Creole. Imprenditrici straniere a Milano*, Milan: Franco Angeli.

Lyotard, J. F. (1986), *La posmodernidad*, Barcelona: Gedisa.

Marina, J. M. (2001), *La fábula del bazar. Orígenes de la cultura del consumo*, Madrid: La balsa de la Medusa.

Múgica, F. (1998), 'La profesión: enclave ético de la moderna sociedad diferenciada', *Cuadernos de Empresa y Humanismo*, 71: 3–66.

Múgica, F. (1999), 'Profesión y diferenciación social en Simmel', *Cuadernos de Anuario Filosófico*.

Múgica, F., and Flamarique, L. (2003), 'Georg Simmel: Civilización y diferenciación social (IV)', *Cuadernos de Anuario Filosófico*.

Múgica, F., and Kroker, R. (2003a), 'Georg Simmel: Civilización y diferenciación social (II)', *Cuadernos de Anuario Filosófico*.

Múgica, F., and Kroker, R. (2003b), 'Georg Simmel: Civilización y diferenciación social (III)', *Cuadernos de Anuario Filosófico*.

Polo, L. (1999), *Hegel y el posthegelianismo*, Pamplona: Eunsa.

Russo, M. T. (2003), 'Dal corpo proprio al corpo estraneo: cultura postmoderna e immagini del corpo', in F. D'Agostino (ed.), *Corpo Esibito, Corpo Violato, Corpo Venduto, Corpo Donato. Nuove Forme Di*, 101–20, Milan: Giuffre.

Russo, M. T. (2004), 'Il corpo guardato. Autenticita' e imagine', *Segni e Comprensione*, 51: 113–21.

Schiller, F. (2001), *Essays*, ed. W. Hinderer and D. O. Dahlstrom, New York: Continuum.

Sennett, R. (1977), *The Fall of Public Man*, Cambridge: Cambridge University Press.

Simmel, G. (1977), *Filosofía del dinero*, Granada: Editorial Comares.

Simmel, G. (1986), *El individuo y la libertad. Ensayos de crítica de la cultura*, Barcelona: Península.

Simmel, G. (1997), *Simmel on Culture. Selected Writings*, ed. David Frisby and Mike Featherstone, London; Thousand Oaks, CA; New Delhi: Sage Publications.

Simmel, G. (2002), *Cuestiones fundamentales de sociología*, Barcelona: Gedisa.

Soldevilla, C. (1998), *Estilo de vida. Hacia una teoría psicosocial de la acción*, Madrid: Entimema.

Soldevilla, C. (2002), 'Triálogo: aproximaciones teóricas a la sociología del consumo', *Revista Vivat Academia*, 32.

Starobinski, J. (2000), *Remedio en el mal. Crítica y legitimación del artificio en la era de las luces*, Madrid: La balsa de la Medusa.

Taylor, C. (1989), *Sources of the Self: The Making of the Modern Identity*, Cambridge: Cambridge University Press.

Taylor, C. (1992), *The Ethics of Authenticity*, Cambridge: Harvard University Press.

Taylor, C. (1993), *Hegel and Modern Society*, Cambridge: Cambridge University Press.

Tocqueville, A. (2000), *Democracy in America*, trans. H. Mansfield and D. Winthrop, Chicago: University of Chicago Press.

Touraine, A., and Khosvokhavar, F. (2002), *A la búsqueda del sí mismo. Diálogo sobre el sujeto*, Barcelona: Paidós.

Žižek, S. (1995), *Hegel mit Lacan*, Wien: Die deutsche Bibliothek.

Žižek, S. (2000), *The Fragile Absolute—Or Why Is the Christian Legacy Worth Fighting For?* London: Verso.

Žižek, S. (2004), *Conversations with Žižek*, ed. Slavoj Žižek and Glyn Daly, Cambridge: Polity Press.

4 IDENTITY AND INTERSUBJECTIVITY

ANN MARGARET BRACH

The relationship between fashion and identity is a common theme in the literature on fashion. There is no clear consensus on the nature of this relationship, except that it is characterized by ambiguity, if not conflict. There is a sense—sometimes implicit, sometimes explicit—that individual or personal identity and social identity are at odds with each other. Fashion is seen as a particular area in which the conflict between the two is played out visually. Some writers focus on social identity, one's relationship to a group or groups; others emphasize the creation and portrayal of one's individuality, one's unique identity; in many cases, the theme is the opposition between these two aspects of identity or at least the ambivalence of fashion with respect to both aspects.

For Simmel, conflict is the essential driving and harmonizing force of society; opposition is necessary and, in the end, creative (1971 [1908a]).[1] Lipovetsky sees the 'reign of the ephemeral' (fashion) as a positive development of democracy and individualism: the constant change of fashion is a kind of triumph over the conformities imposed by authorities or social groups; it produces a 'peaceful relativism' (1994: 236) or tolerance that holds together a heterogeneous society. Within the apparent despotism of fashion is both a rebellion against stable forms imposed by tradition and, according to Lipovetsky, ample room for personal choices within any fashion of the moment.

If association with a group implies a conformity that threatens the individual, then it may seem that the only way for the individual to triumph is to reject such group identification. But as long as human beings live a social life, the problem of conformity is unavoidable. However small or nonconformist the group, there will always be something that binds the group together and which can be interpreted as conformity. The nineteenth-century dandy, in his rejection of the fashions of the times, instituted a fashion himself (Breward 2003). Subculture rebellions against mainstream fashion, represented in hippies, punks and other groups, eventually become grist for mainstream advertising and commercialization (Breward 2003) and merely add to the complexity and diversity of fashion (Lipovetsky 1994). To the extent that fashion itself imposes a kind of conformity, this can only be met with an unending series of fashion changes, however small, so that at least the conformity is a serial conformity, with each new style undermining its predecessor. Changing the factors of conformity (the external styles and manners of thinking and behaving) as rapidly as possible generates the illusion of newness, creativity and uniqueness that results from the emphasis on the present that characterizes rapid change.

If identity is permanent and unchanging and fashion is characterized by frequent change, there seems to be an even deeper threat to identity from fashion than from traditional social groups. This may reflect the postmodern project, a flight from identity achieved through the rejection of anything permanent. Perhaps there is a hope that if the process of change moves fast enough, it will spin off the individual, as if by centrifugal force, with an identity entirely detached from any style, fashion, group or any external thing at all.[2] But can there really be identity detached from everything, especially from other subjects?

To address this question, I begin with a phenomenological account of fashion that looks at the ways that fashion and clothing in general are disclosed to us: what we intend when we do or do not consider something to be fashion and what the objective correlates of our intentionalities are—the various forms of clothing. Then I look at identity and its intersubjective constitution. Third, I explore the relationship between identity, fashion and image and the objectifying influence of the image-making industries on the subject.

FASHION AND CLOTHING—A PHENOMENOLOGICAL ACCOUNT

There is a certain ambiguity in the use of the word *fashion* in English. Fashion can refer in a general way to styles or to a manner of doing something, or it can refer specifically to a style or manner that is most current or up to date. *Mode* in French or *moda* in Italian and Spanish are more often used for the latter sense of fashion, so when they are translated into English as *fashion* there can be some confusion as to what exactly is intended by an author.[3] For clarity, I will use the word *style* to refer to the broader meaning of fashion and the word *fashion* to refer to the narrower meaning. Both style and fashion are formal,[4] admitting of any number of different contents in a wide variety of cultural domains: interior design, technology, ideas and behaviours can have styles, some of which may be 'in fashion' at a particular moment. The most common domain in which fashion is discussed is that of clothing, which will be my main focus here as well.

When we speak of fashion in clothing, we become aware of certain assumptions and distinctions. To begin with, there is assumed as the horizon or context for fashion in clothing the overall phenomenon of clothing itself. To understand what constitutes fashion in clothing, we will also want to understand what does not constitute fashion and see if we can clarify what distinguishes these in a purely formal way, independent of what any particular fashion happens to be. There is also a broader context for clothing, including all kinds of body adornments and modifications (Eicher, Evenson and Lutz 2000), which will not be addressed here.

The fact that some items or styles are 'in fashion' implies that there are others that are 'not in fashion' or are 'out of fashion'. In either case, fashion is thematic, whether by its presence in a particular item or style or by its absence. However, there are also clothes which are neither in fashion nor out of fashion, clothes for which fashion is not thematic at all. Police uniforms, traditional ethnic dress, and religious vestments are not, in themselves, in or out of fashion. The question of fashion is not operative in these cases.

So what, then, is essential when fashion is the focus of our concern? Newness, ephemeralness, change and aesthetic creativity have all been associated with fashion. Newness and aesthetic creativity or 'aesthetic fancy' (Lipovetsky 1994) often characterize fashion, but they do not seem to be quite essential. Some fashions are more or less direct reincarnations of older styles or are borrowed from clothing types that do not fit into the theme of fashion. What makes them new is that as the current style they differ from the previous fashion. Aesthetic fancy is no doubt an important part of fashion, though fashion can be strongly influenced by other factors, such as wartime scarcity of resources or social opposition to the use of fur.

Fashion as changing or ephemeral, coming into being and dissolving quickly without leaving a trace, points to something more essential about fashion. The matter or content of fashion must change for fashion to exist at all. However, change alone is not sufficient, since the styles of non-fashion items also change. It is the frequency and often the discontinuity of the change that leads to fashion being characterized as ephemeral. Fashion is experienced as the style that belongs to the present moment. It is about what is acceptable now. It has no tie to the past, unless such a tie is itself in fashion, and it does not point to the future, unless such an indicator is also fashionable.[5] This is true regardless of the actual length of fashion cycles, which have become much shorter over the last century or so. I would sum up this characteristic as the 'nowness' of fashion.

For fashion to exist, there must also be some arbiter that determines what is fashionable now. The arbiters of fashion may be found in a variety of places: a social elite, whether the wealthy, pop entertainers or supermodels; the fashion industry, couturiers or fashion magazines; or a subculture of some sort, such as hippies, punks or teenagers. The arbiters of fashion can also be some combination of these—for example, a pop star may introduce a fashion, but it must be picked up by a set of teenagers with influence over their peers and sufficient discretionary income to create an attractive market for clothing manufacturers. The material details (source, complexity, process) of fashion arbitration have changed over time, but its essential characteristic is still that some relatively small and influential group sets the fashion.[6] One person does not do so, at least not alone, nor is fashion determined by a large number or majority of people (Simmel 1971 [1904]). Fashion becomes fashion before the majority pick it up. By the time a large number do acquire the fashion, some new fashion has incubated.

If any particular style remains in fashion for a long time or is adopted by too many people, it ceases to be fashion. It may become traditional garb, uniform, or simply the ordinary, unremarkable clothing or tools that everyone is expected to have. Ordinary blue jeans, for example, are not really a fashion any longer as much as a kind of standardized clothing. To be fashionable, jeans must possess the colour, cut, rips, or fading pattern deemed to be current.

Given the essential characteristics of 'nowness' and arbitration by a fashion elite, one can investigate the sociological factors and roles of fashion. To be consistently in fashion implies being connected somehow to the fashion setters or to the means of communication and indicators of fashion (countless magazines promise to keep their readers up to date on fashion, though different magazines cater to people in various relationships to the fashion curve). Being 'in the know' implies something about one's connections, one's taste or one's ability to discern emerging trends. Being on top of fashion also requires certain financial means. How far into a trend one picks it up and how long after the trend one maintains it also places one socially. In some social and professional sectors, the fact that one eschews fashion is also significant—being unfashionable or rebellious against fashion can be sociologically thematic as well. Now, let's move to the clothing types in which fashion is not thematic.[7] These clothes are not taken as being particularly current ('now'), nor does one look to some kind of fashion arbiters to determine the style of these clothes. They may have remained in use for a long time or may point to a past tradition; they may be dictated by a formal authority or have arisen as a kind of social habit. Perhaps the first clothing of this type that comes to mind is the *uniform*. Uniforms are what the word implies: a single form or style worn by a number of people. They typically identify a more or less stable aspect of a person's life, an aspect pertaining to membership in a well-defined group: a profession, a school, a branch of the military or the incarcerated. Uniforms signal rights, duties and/or restrictions associated with the status. They are connected to institutional authority because the uniformity of the style must be specified by such an authority. Fashionable elements are generally considered to be inconsistent with a uniform. People who wear uniforms, in school or in the military, for example, are usually prohibited from wearing anything in the way of jewellery, accessories or hairstyles that could be taken as fashion.

While uniforms are associated with a fairly stable status as a member of an institution or well-defined group, *ritual vestments* pertain to a particular act or task. A ritual act has a meaning or is part of a system that transcends the person who performs it. For example, a judge wears special robes when sitting at the bench to administer justice as prescribed by the law of the land; a religious minister wears special vestments when performing liturgical acts that represent the beliefs of the religious community; the president of a university or the dean of a college wears academic robes when officiating at graduations and other formal academic events.

A *dress code* is similar to a uniform in that it is required by an authority, but it is less prescriptive and therefore does not immediately identify a stable aspect of the wearer. Dress codes define a certain more or less restricted universe of clothing that is permitted or not permitted, based on what is considered by the authority to be reflective of a particular group: a law firm, a country club, a restaurant. The idea is to project a particular image and create a particular environment. Dress codes can be more or less restrictive and more or less explicit. Some dress codes specify what must be worn (tennis white, jacket and tie); others specify what may not be worn (shorts, tank tops). They can pertain to casual, business or formal attire.

Another category of clothing that bears some resemblance to uniforms and dress codes, but that also has its own distinctions, is *standardized clothes*. Crane includes among 'standardized clothes' or 'standardized costumes' such items as smocks or overalls, used by manual workers, or the common men's attire of suit and tie (2000: 26). This type of clothing seems to fall between a uniform and a dress code, both in formality (requirement) and in specificity (actual uniformity). Standardized clothes are not strictly required by an authority (when they are, they become a uniform or a dress code). T-shirts and blue jeans may be very common among a group of young people, but no one explicitly requires such uniformity of the wearers of these clothes. Standardized clothes may function as a foolproof way of adhering to a dress code. At certain business meetings calling for 'business casual', nearly all the men will be found wearing golf shirts and chinos, though a business-casual dress code could conceivably include a wider range of options.

Some clothes are referred as *classic* in style. This seems to constitute a distinct form of clothing, though it may also overlap with standardized clothes. Simmel finds that classic items are less susceptible to fashion, though sometimes they are 'fashionable'. 'The nature of the classic is determined by a concentration of the parts around a fixed centre; classic objects possess an air of composure, which does not offer so many points of attack, as it were, from which modification, disturbance, destruction of the equilibrium might emanate' (Simmel 1971 [1904]).

Costumes for theatrical presentations seem to be yet a separate category. Even if they reflect the fashion of a particular time, they are not taken as fashion, as acceptable to wear now, but as reflective of a fashion of some time. Theatrical costumes are probably the most obvious use of clothing to communicate: time period, culture, ethnic group, age, character and emotional state can all be conveyed through appropriate costuming. As such, they provide the most explicit connection between fashion and identity, which would not work in the theatre unless it had some basis, however vague, in our ordinary experience of clothing.

Traditional or ethnic costumes are clothes that represent the largely standardized styles used in times and places where fashion was not operative. When such dress was actually worn as everyday attire, it would identify the wearer as outside of the fashion process. Today, this type of clothing is frequently used for theatrical or dance costumes or as a kind of ritual dress worn for public events; in either case, the costume refers to a tradition that the wearer wishes to evoke and possibly keep alive despite the changes of fashion.

Particular articles of clothing can move from one category to the other. Style elements from non-fashion-thematic areas can become thematic as fashion: schoolgirl uniform skirts, Scottish kilt patterns or military camouflage can be incorporated into current styles. But as soon as this occurs, these instances of the style are no longer uniforms—they are fashions. One form can gradually change into another: some school uniforms, for example, are becoming dress codes as a range of options are made available for certain elements of the uniform (for example, a particular skirt may be mandatory but the shoes may be any style as long as the heel is no more than one inch high, and sweaters in a specified array of colours may be worn). Even before school uniforms were relaxed into dress codes, schoolgirls often tried to vary their uniforms—that is, to institute some sort of fashion at least within the context of the social setting of the school by adjusting the uniform itself or attempting to wear prohibited items. Joseph also indicates that some nonconformity among an elite segment within an otherwise uniformed group may be a sign of the elite status of the segment (Joseph 1986: 85–8).

The various ways that we can use these categories or types of clothing points to the multitude of purposes we can have for clothes. Clothing can protect one from the natural elements or from man-made dangers (radiation in a laboratory, welding sparks, asbestos). Clothing is used to promote beauty or aesthetic ideals, including creating illusions of beauty or proportion that one may not actually possess (wider shoulders, narrower hips). It can be used for modesty or for seduction. Clothing can be used for dramatic portrayals, spying and other instances of depicting oneself as someone else or projecting certain images—of authority, respect, competence, motherliness, and so on—with what we wear. We use clothing to control others and to rebel against their control, to signify our individuality or our belonging to a particular group. We may even use clothes to demonstrate solidarity with a group to which we do not actually belong (wearing green on St Patrick's Day even if one is not Irish). We choose some clothing to help us perform better at athletic or military feats (or to give the impression that we are more athletic than we are).

These various purposes are distinct from the array of clothing forms presented earlier: fashion, uniforms, ritual garments, dress codes, standardized clothes, dramatic costumes and traditional costumes (and any others there may be). Each of these categories represents a fairly stable form which can have any content. Some of these forms can apply to other cultural objects besides clothes: technologies and behaviours can be uniform or standard or regulated by broader norms akin to dress codes (such as etiquette in the case of behaviour and standards of interoperability in the case of technologies). Each form may arise in a given circumstance in response to particular needs. Uniforms of domestic staff in the late nineteenth century may well have been instituted to enforce visible social class boundaries (Crane 2000), or they may have been instituted in twentieth-century private schools for the purpose of minimizing visible social-class boundaries. Dress codes may be introduced in a country club to maintain a certain social impression or in public schools to reduce gang identification and consequent gang violence. Social sciences help us understand the purposes and functions of clothing: the way that fashion mediates between the desire for individuality and the desire to belong to a group (Simmel 1971 [1904]); the use of clothing by one group as an instrument of social control over another or as a means of resisting such control (Crane 2000); or the role of fashion in bringing about particular social and political conditions (Lipovetsky 1994).

However, once the form exists, it has a kind of independence from individual purposes, an identity and an internal logic of its own. A uniform, because it is a uniform, is always taken as signifying membership in a formal group. It can be worn by someone who is not a member of the group; this does not make the uniform less of a uniform, although it may create a conflict between the stable purpose or end of the uniform and the purpose of the individual wearing it. The person may wear a uniform to infiltrate enemy lines or to portray a police officer in a movie or to mock religion. However, the wearer's purposes depend on the stability of the uniform's end—the individual's purpose is played off against the end of the uniform. He cannot successfully spy in enemy territory unless the uniform he wears is taken to be sign of membership in the enemy's military. The one who mocks religion by wearing a religious habit inappropriately is only successful because the habit is a sign of the religious institution. One cannot pass as a member of a country club by conforming to the club's dress code unless the dress code is taken to reflect the social class the club wishes to attract. It is in the realm of purposes that types of dress can be used in ways that may differ from their usual employment. Nazi prison camp uniforms can be used to remind people of a historical atrocity, and traditional ethnic dress can be used to celebrate and keep alive one's heritage.

We can change the matter associated with these forms and use them for purposes that may be orthogonal to their ends, but we always exercise this creativity against the backdrop of the stability of the forms. This is what is reflected in the observations that even 'anti-fashion' rebellions have often given rise to fashions. Once the form of fashion becomes thematized, it retains some permanence—an identity—even in its negation or in its alteration. These examples bring out the intimate relationship between the objective forms in clothing and our taking these to be what they are.

The distinction between the ends of clothing forms and the multiple purposes to which we can put them suggests a contrast between our use of clothing (and other body adornments or modifications) and the displays of animals. A peacock can spread his tail to attract a peahen. Other animals can enhance their size to intimidate a predator or modify their colour to better camouflage themselves. But there are important differences between these behaviours and the human use of clothing. Although animals' appearance can change over time in response to the forces of natural selection, they are always limited at any moment to what nature has afforded them. They can never have fashion in the sense of the creative changing of styles. Fashion is a particularly human endeavour. But not only fashion—all the other forms of clothing discussed earlier are human creations. Despite their relative stability, we can use them for a multitude of purposes. So our use of appearance differs from that of animals in at least two ways: our ability to invent new styles and forms and our ability to use even stable forms of clothing for purposes distinct from the ends implied in those forms. For animals, appearance and display only function as means to natural ends of self-preservation and reproduction. Human rationality allows us to creatively use appearance for purposes—such as political, artistic and religious—beyond these natural functions. We can choose how we wish to display ourselves and why we do so. It is the element of choice and creativity that makes the relationship between fashion and identity so complex.

IDENTITY, IMAGE AND FASHION

Identity is what allows us to recognize a thing as the same thing despite the passage of time, the manifold of different perceptions of the thing and the changes that may occur in it. Identity applies to physical objects, persons, places, activities, ideas, imaginings and fictional creatures. The identity of a person includes the recognition of oneself as the same subject of various experiences, changes, actions, perceptions and choices over time.

Each aforementioned clothing form helps disclose some aspect or attribute of the wearer: occupation, ethnic background, favourite sports team. How well any particular article of clothing captures something genuine about the wearer depends on a number of factors. The forms in which fashion is not thematic tend to communicate more clearly, with uniforms generally being the most unambiguous form of communication by dress (Joseph 1986) and fashion being more ambiguous since its contents change so frequently. No single type or article of clothing can be taken alone as an indication of identity, though. Most people wear different types of clothing for different occasions, each of which relates to only one aspect of who they are. Patterns of dress over time would need to be observed: a person who dresses fashionably every now and then may be choosing fashions that happen to appeal to her, in which case the fashionable dress may reveal personal taste rather than concern for fashion per se; someone who always dresses fashionably, regardless of the style, shows that he has knowledge of fashion and the interest and means to act on that knowledge. The personal and social context in which clothes are worn is important: is the person ill, did he lose his suitcase in travel, is she interacting with a new social milieu that has different standards of dress? The intention of the wearer is also relevant: is the uniform worn on duty, in a parade, or in protest? The identity of a person cannot be reduced to a single aspect, certainly not to a single type of clothing. All these elements, plus many other non-sartorial aspects, are manifolds in which the identity of the wearer can be known.[8] However, within the realm of clothing, fashion, as the least prescriptive and least standardized type, may reveal more about a person due to the greater scope for choice it allows. With this in mind, I will explore how fashion is related to identity and also to image.

Of all the things that can have identity, only persons can have images and fashions. Only a person can take himself or another as an image: an image of glamour or of confidence, of a good mother or a heroic citizen. And only a person can fashion clothing, customs, speech, interior design and technology to create and communicate these images. A person's identity remains constant even when the images of that person (to herself and to others) change. As a teenager she has the image of an insecure girl or a rebel; as an adult her image is one of self-confidence or bureaucratic conformity. At work he is the aggressive, competitive businessman; at home he is a caring father and cooperative husband. Fashion and other forms of clothing provide ways of communicating these images; thus, fashion is linked back to identity in a less immediate way than image: the rebel wears black or pierces her nose; the ambitious businessman joins the elite country club or carries the latest model of personal digital assistant. The relationship between fashion and image can also vary with time and culture: a nose stud is not rebellious on an Indian girl, and more young women (and men) sport them as a sign of individual style rather than rebellion; the elite country club may become so popular that the elite move on to another club, as sometimes occurs with bars, restaurants and vacation spots. The relentless development of technology challenges the most technologically savvy person to keep up with the latest gadget.

In this description, identity has a certain priority over image, as does image over fashion. When this order is maintained, fashion can communicate images that reflect the deeper characteristics of a person, such as his fundamental values, which are more closely associated with identity because of their greater stability or permanence. This three-stage process is fraught with dangers because each transition—from identity to image and from image to fashion—can be weak, superficial and even false. When the order is reversed, fashion is meaningless and superficial.

An example of the relationship among identity, image and fashion can be seen in the area of etiquette. Etiquette is not exactly a fashion, although it is a style of behaviour that can change along with other cultural changes. It is an important element of communicating an image of social status and education, which was thought at least to reflect deeper character and values that are part of one's identity. But if it becomes more formalistic and detached from deeper moral and social values, etiquette becomes rooted only in image—the image one wishes to project to be acceptable in society. Eventually, it becomes an end in itself and, as such, a mask of one's identity rather than a manifestation of it. This can lead to a rejection of etiquette as superficial at best and at worst false, hypocritical and an impediment to self-realization. Etiquette that is rooted in identity rather than mere image would not fall into this trap. One would know when following accepted norms of etiquette was appropriate and when it was not. For example, etiquette may indicate that one does not speak about certain issues in particular situations, but there may occur a situation in which justice or charity requires one to speak up despite the prohibitions of etiquette. A person whose etiquette is well rooted in his or her character and identity will know when and how to 'violate' etiquette appropriately. People who violate etiquette merely to protest it only show the shallowness of their own understanding of etiquette.

INTERSUBJECTIVE CONSTITUTION OF IDENTITY

In much of the discussion about fashion and identity there is an implicit, sometimes explicit, sense that an individual's personal identity is in conflict with identity involving groups. In this section I explore some approaches from two thinkers in the phenomenological tradition to suggest a resolution of this conflict, albeit at a philosophical level, rather than a psychological or sociological level.

Edmund Husserl describes how the identity of an ideal object (a mathematical structure in his case) is established through an intersubjective process. The process is based on one's ability to recall the ideal geometric object (the Pythagorean Theorem, for example) as the same object whose evidence was experienced at an earlier time. This involves a memory of one's own knowledge, one's own subjective experience, at an earlier time. The ability to reawaken one's earlier subjective experience or insight (and thus establish the identity over time of what was experienced or understood) points to the ability to achieve identity with other subjects besides oneself—that is, we can all share the same Pythagorean Theorem (Husserl 1970c). While Husserl focused on the ideal structures or objects of mathematics, this process may be applied to other shared identities. Identity is established or constituted by the subject who is capable of recalling something previously experienced or known and recognizing it as the same thing. The ability to share these identities opens up the possibility of real communication about the world, ideas and selves. Thus, other persons can be viewed

> as co-subjects, with whom one forms a community in experiencing, in thinking, in acting, with whom one has common praxis in the surrounding world even though each one still also has his own . . . A first step is explicitly to be vitally at one with the other person in the intuitive understanding of his experiencing, his life-situation, his activity, etc. From there one proceeds to communication through expression and language, which is already an interrelation of egos. Every sort of communication naturally presupposes the commonality of the surrounding world, which is established as soon as we are persons for one another at all. (Husserl 1970a: 328)

Establishment of the identity of something over time also occurs with the self: I identify my current writing self with the remembered self who rode the bus yesterday and the imagined self who will have dinner with friends tonight. This ability to achieve identity regarding myself as well as regarding other things entails what Sokolowski calls a displacement of self: when we remember, there is a remembering self and a remembered self; similarly, when we imagine, there is an imagining self and an imagined self. This displacement of self in the achievement of identity is already a kind of intersubjectivity—and ability to communicate between subjects. Husserl states that 'subjectivity is what it is—an ego functioning constitutively—only within intersubjectivity' (Husserl 1970b: 172).

> A central role in bringing about the self-differentiations that are possible and necessary for us is played by the imagination . . . [I]t is a possibility of displacement,

of *Versetzung*, which helps actualize the self. In imagination we become distinguished into an imagined self and an imagining self . . . We appreciate ourselves (as imagined) at some distance to ourselves (as imagining), and 'the self' is that which is the same in both dimensions, the imagining and the imagined. The same structural displacement occurs in memory, except that repetition instead of projection dominates. (Sokolowski 1992a: 79)

The self is the kind of being that can enact such displacements without losing its identity; in fact, its identity as a self is developed and maintained precisely in such self-differentiation, not only in imagination but also in remembering, recognizing, repeating things, understanding other persons, and the like. (Sokolowski 1992b: 294–5)

If personal identity is seen as either affiliation with traditional social groups or classes or as differentiation from these groups, both presuppose that there is something communicable about identity, some kind of intersubjectivity at work. Sokolowski's analysis suggests that the dichotomy between identity as affiliation and identity as differentiation is resolved because 'identities . . . are the other side of distinctions' (Sokolowski 1992a: 82); both are needed to establish our identity in a process that occurs in relationship with other persons throughout our lives. If one denies identity, one must also deny relationship.

We achieve self-identification, and correlatively self-differentiation from others, at all stages of life, early and late . . . Amid the assimilation, the urge to distinguish asserts itself and this urgency is concerned not with objects we deal with but with our own selves.

This assimilation and distinction is always going on . . . As we grow older, all the identities the self achieves through the stages of life are simply the other side of differentiations it accomplishes within assimilations it has been undergoing.

. . . And when we are said to assimilate the behavior of others, we do not merely imitate but also react on our own to a tone and pattern they set, and then we see how they react to our reactions. In this give and take we internalize other people. But the time always comes when we have to differentiate ourselves from what we assimilate; what we differentiate as ourselves contains, in turn, what we differentiated earlier in other assimilative matrices, and the style of earlier distinctions persists in modifying the tone of those we are making now. (Sokolowski 1992a: 77–9)

The unique status of the person or subject, whose identity is established in intersubjective relations, makes the person vulnerable to attack on his or her identity as a subject through attacks on intersubjectivity. To remove or weaken identity one must de-subjectify the person, which can be accomplished by reducing the possibility of intersubjective constitution of identity, especially the identity of the subject herself. A healthy identity of oneself as a subject will more likely take place through relationships with other well-formed subjects. When personal identity is established through interaction with objects or with persons portrayed, and therefore taken as mere images, one's own identity is likely to resemble an object or image. This leads us to look at images and image-making.

IMAGE-MAKING AND IDENTITY AS IMAGE

The intersubjective nature of images can be seen in Sokolowski's description of picturing:

> It occurs when something is taken as a picture of something else: there must be an object taken as the picture; there must be something appreciated as pictured; and there must be somebody who takes the object as a picture. Picturing occurs at the intersection of these three elements . . .
>
> The maker of a picture is a fourth to the three elements. (Sokolowski 1992b: 6)

The picture Sokolowksi has in mind is a visual (or auditory or dramatic) representation of something: a photo, painting, play or mime that is physically distinct from the thing pictured. The images discussed in this chapter include these as well as persons taken as images. To the extent that a person is taken as an image, he is taken as an object, not a subject. We can take a person as an image of an institution, a social class, a character trait like heroism or a lifestyle like the glamorous lifestyle of a celebrity. The individual taking the person as an image can be anyone else and even the person himself, which indicates the intersubjectivity of pictures or images, not just of identity. The fourth element, the making of the picture, can refer to the image-making industries: fashion, television, radio, movies, music recording, news media and advertising.[9]

All these image-making industries are relevant to discussions of fashion and identity. Fashion—in clothing, behaviour, technology and other objects—is communicated through these media. They provide the framework that supports the complex network of actors who function as arbiters of fashion, and they announce the styles currently considered fashionable; they may even fulfil these functions simultaneously.

The influence of the image-making industries is pervasive. A media professor in Washington, D.C., assigned her students a very difficult task: to go without mass media—television, radio, the Internet—for one week and write about the experience. The reaction of most students was disbelief, if not horror. Those who successfully completed the assignment achieved a higher degree of awareness of the influence of the media on their lives. One student wrote about the assignment as a turning point for him, as it was the first opportunity he had taken to be alone with his own thoughts. More than learning something about media, he learned about himself: what he really thought and valued.

This student had not previously realized the extent to which his constant interaction with the image-making media was affecting his sense of himself. What happens to the identity of a person when intersubjective relationships—even one's relationship with oneself—are increasingly replaced or mediated by interactions with objects, specifically with images? Is it possible that the objectification of persons is at least in part a process by which we form our own identities as objects or images by interacting more with objects than with other subjects, or with subjects that have been reduced to images? If we are interacting so frequently with things and with images that may not have a close relationship to subjective identities, might we not develop our own identities to be more like objects or images?

The development of the image-making industries is a good example of Simmel's ideas about objectification. For Simmel, objectification refers to what happens when objective culture takes on its own intrinsic logic without regard for subjective culture—the cultivation of the person. His formulation points to a correlation between subject and object that moves in both directions. The subject produces cultural objects and in turn is cultivated in his use of or interaction with those objects. Simmel's concept of objectification has both a positive and a negative aspect. The positive aspect refers to the way that a cultural product transcends its creator to become something capable of cultivating others: 'The more separated a product is from the subjective spirituality of its creator, the more it is integrated into an objective order—the more distinct is its *cultural* significance and the more suited it is to become a general means for the cultivation of many individual souls' (Simmel 1971 [1908b]: 233). On the other hand, there can be an objectification of the subject when objects of culture pursue their own internal logic, without regard for the cultivation of subjects and ultimately to the detriment of subjective culture (Simmel 1968). Technologies and economic methods like division of labour, for example, can be pursued and applied in ways that treat the person as an object.[10]

While no one can deny the obvious benefits of media and communication technologies, they do seem to have developed in some ways that threaten genuine subjective culture. For example, the frequency with which we interact with technologies, exclusively or as mediators for human interactions, is stunning. In cases where technology enables human interactions that might otherwise have been impossible, it can be counted as a blessing. But frequently, technologies have become substitutes for persons or provide access to an image rather than to persons.[11] People on television and in ads are not other subjects, other selves; they are images. There is no give and take and no empathy, as would be the case in true intersubjective relationships. There is only the absorption and reflection of image. In place of a dialogue between subjects, there is a relationship between a person and an image. Even when technologies appear to provide access to real people, it is sometimes only to images of those people. This is the case with online 'romances' in which people portray themselves as younger, better looking or richer than they really are. An image without a real subject—without subjective identity—is a mere object.

The entertainment media delivers highly artificial images that are offered as real. Explicit sex and graphic violence only make the realities of sex and violence appear artificial and change people's expectations of the real world. The overexposure of celebrities and the images they portray provide a false sense of closeness to people who are actually very far away—socially, economically and often morally. The so-called reality television shows are often more artificial than the scripted programs. Much of the news media is now referred to as 'infotainment' due to its increased focus on creating and projecting images. The prevalence of media has spawned a whole industry that trains businesspeople, public officials and advocates of every cause on how to project the right image and deliver the right message in TV and radio interviews. Substance—identity—is often left on the cutting-room floor.

The ability we have to put the images provided by the image-making industries in proper perspective—the perspective of subjective culture—is developed, I believe, in relationships with real subjects who have reasonably well-developed identities. Our ability to see and to see through the images of the image-making industries is threatened by the breakdown of relationships: family, friends, colleagues, social peers. I think this breakdown is due to the lack of empathy that results from inadequate human interaction. This is an example of how subjective culture can be unable to assimilate and properly challenge objective culture.

In contrast to the hierarchy described earlier, in which identity is reflected in images that are communicated through fashions, the process of objectification of persons works in the opposite direction. Fashion (through the image-making industries) develops ephemeral images that fail to contribute to a stable identity. This may account for the prevalence of images of youth and of street culture in fashion today; the young have little past to speak of and often little concern for the future—they exemplify living in and for the moment. Taken on their own, outside of the context of a whole life cycle, their perpetual experimenting with identity, image and fashion can become an end in itself rather than a process of self-discovery and self-development leading to a stable identity. This influence of street culture in fashion is seen in outfits that are purposely torn, faded or soiled; clothes that do not fit—too tight or very baggy—as if they were cast-offs never intended for the wearer; and clothes that a few decades earlier would signal the wearer as a product on sale. Magazines often show models photographed in makeup resembling bruises and black eyes and with sullen, dejected looks, if the face of the model is even shown. These images are reminiscent of homeless people, runaways and prostitutes—people who are often socially invisible, anonymous: unidentified and unrelated.

CONCLUSION

These reflections suggest a broader perspective from which to view the relationship of fashion and identity. Despite the prevalence of fashion in many areas of modern culture, there are always aspects of culture in which fashion, per se, is not thematic, as shown in the example of clothing discussed here. Fashion can be seen as one of a variety of means through which identity can be disclosed, including both material objects and chosen behaviours. These aspects of the subject are not actually the person's identity, but identity is manifested and known through them, when genuine intersubjective relationships are not replaced with images.

References

Breward, C. (2003), *Fashion,* Oxford History of Art Series, Oxford: Oxford University Press.

Craik, J. (1994), *The Face of Fashion: Cultural Studies in Fashion*, London, Routledge.

Crane, D. (2000), *Fashion and Its Social Agendas: Class, Gender, and Identity in Clothing,* Chicago: University of Chicago Press.

Davis, F. (1992), *Fashion, Culture, and Identity,* Chicago: University of Chicago Press.

Eicher, J., Evenson, S. L., and Lutz, H. A. (2000), *The Visible Self: Global Perspectives on Dress, Culture, and Society,* New York: Fairchild Publications.

Entwistle, J. (2000), *The Fashioned Body: Fashion, Dress and Modern Social Theory,* Malden, Massachusetts: Polity Press.

Husserl, E. (1970a), 'The Attitude of Natural Science and the Attitude of Humanistic Science. Naturalism, Dualism, and Psychophysical Psychology', in *The Crisis of European Sciences and Transcendental Phenomenology,* trans. David Carr, Evanston, Illinois: Northwestern University Press.

Husserl, E. (1970b), *The Crisis of European Sciences and Transcendental Phenomenology,* trans. David Carr, Evanston, Illinois: Northwestern University Press.

Husserl, E. (1970c), 'The Origin of Geometry', in *The Crisis of European Sciences and Transcendental Phenomenology,* trans. David Carr, Evanston, Illinois: Northwestern University Press.

Joseph, N. (1986), *Uniforms and Nonuniforms: Communicating through Clothing,* New York: Greenwood Press.

Lipovetsky, G. (1994), *The Empire of Fashion: Dressing Modern Democracy,* trans. C. Porter, forward by R. Sennett, New French Thought (series ed. T. Pavel and M. Lilla), Princeton, New Jersey: Princeton University Press.

Rubenstein, R. P. (1995), *Dress Codes: Meanings and Messages in American Culture*, Boulder, Colorado: Westview Press.

Simmel, G. (1968), 'On the Concept and the Tragedy of Culture', in K. P. Etzkorn (trans. and intro.), *George Simmel: The Conflict in Modern Culture and Other Essays*, New York: Teachers College Press, Columbia University.

Simmel, G. (1971 [1908a]), 'Conflict', in D. N. Levine (ed. and intro.), *On Individuality and Social Forms*, Chicago: University of Chicago Press.

Simmel, G. (1971 [1904]), 'Fashion', in D. N. Levine (ed. and intro.), *On Individuality and Social Forms*, Chicago: University of Chicago Press.

Simmel, G. (1971 [1908b]), 'Subjective Culture', in D. N. Levine (ed. and intro.), *On Individuality and Social Forms*, Chicago: University of Chicago Press.

Sokolowski, R. (1992a), 'Making Distinctions', in *Pictures, Quotations, and Distinctions*, Notre Dame, Indiana: University of Notre Dame Press.

Sokolowski, R. (1992b), 'Picturing', in *Pictures, Quotations, and Distinctions*, Notre Dame, Indiana: University of Notre Dame Press.

PART II FASHION AS COMMUNICATION

5 FASHION, IDENTITY AND SOCIAL ACTORS

LAURA BOVONE

Most of us have relatively little to do with fashion designers' suggestions, high fashion images or prêt-à-porter purchases. For all of us, clothing is a duty; for some of us, a pleasure; and for many of us, a problem. This duty/pleasure/problem may sometimes receive a solution from a glossy magazine, but more often we make our decisions when we open our full-to-overflowing wardrobes. We all live in a world of consumption, and yet what has long been considered fashion—fashion that every year brings new prescriptions, rules that are temporarily accepted by everybody, or lately, design fashion—is affecting our behaviours less and less. Conversely, the cultural fashions of the moment—and our personal stock of clothes—have achieved greater importance, imposing slacker standards on us than before, but leading us in various different directions.

In order to understand how fashion affects our lives—our identity, our way of presenting ourselves and, consequently, of socially shaping our bodies—this chapter first considers the overall problem of clothing by identifying its peculiarity in the wide world of material goods consumption.

Secondly, as this approach deals only partly with the theme of identity, and neglects the particular relationship between our identity and our way of clothing ourselves in order to appear, we then consider the connections and gaps between clothing and identity. The two ends of this problem may be connected if we consider our body—and, unavoidably, our dressed body—as a basic element of our identity.

Thirdly, I try to frame the cultural and economic dynamics underlying the fashion system in order to determine in some way the responsibilities of the actors involved in this process and examine the question in terms of both production and consumption. The fashion system is an economic and cultural system that repeatedly finds in the market an opportunity to achieve, albeit provisionally, a definition of the meaning of its objects. From this point of view, the responsibility for what is happening in the field of fashion is much more widespread than appears at first sight.

Finally, this consideration gives us the opportunity to question one of the unquestioned keynotes of contemporary culture, the aestheticization of everyday life (Featherstone 1991b), of which the excessive power of fashion dictates seems a countercheck. If we succeed in keeping away from stereotypes and pay attention to some recent tendencies, we perceive that even in the inveterate fashion consumer, new interests/values, which up to now had been considered in decline in the postmodern age, are in fact emerging.

A methodological premise is worth mentioning: the sociological approach of this work requires us to support our theoretical reasoning with empiric references. Where available, I provide some examples drawn from research carried out in Milan by the Center for the Study of Fashion and Cultural Production of the Università Cattolica del Sacro Cuore.

FASHION AND CLOTHING

When we consider the relationship between fashion and identity, how fashion expresses our authentic individual identity or how, instead, it is able to eliminate authenticity from our lives, we clearly refer to clothing and not to fashion in itself. We refer to our clothing consumption, which is nourished by the large and extremely articulated fashion system but only indirectly connected to fashion production in the narrow sense. It would be advisable to start by concisely defining what we mean by fashion and then examine clothing and associated consumption. Based on a considerable amount of literature, Entwistle effectively summarizes the most acknowledged use of the word *fashion* as follows:

> 'Fashion' is a general term which can be used to refer to any kind of systemic changes in social life, in architecture or even academia; the 'fashion system' as it pertains to dress refers to a particular set of arrangements for the production and distribution of clothing . . . , a special and unique system for the production and consumption of dress that was born out of historical and technological developments in Europe. (Entwistle 2000: 45)

In the clothing field, fashion provides cyclical proposals of change. This is where the concept of fashion needs to be inextricably linked to the concept of consumption, in its social and communication dimensions and in terms of the evolution of consumption through the different stages of modern and postmodern society.

Modern society, based on industrial production and market requirements, has always worked towards innovation; change for the sake of change seems even today to be the only motivation capable of inducing to consumption those who already have everything. Consumption always depends on the spending cap. individuals. Thus, while in a society of scarcity it apparently concerns only the classes, consumption becomes an interesting matter for sociology in a society of opulence, where it seems to affect the lifestyle of the majority of the population. Consumption becomes increasingly interesting in general (and particularly as regards clothing) in a society in which there is room for mobility and imitation. Simmel (1911) skilfully highlighted the pendulum movement of differentiation and imitation as the core of fashionable behaviours, where the periodical clothing renewal of an elite may be extended also to larger population segments.

Fashion becomes a widespread interest in clothing from the late eighteenth century, when a first 'consumer revolution' is recorded in Europe (Entwistle 2000: 97, who also refers to Campbell 1989), together with greater purchasing power and a considerable development of urban life. The first clothing explosion concerns the new middle classes—the leading bourgeois actors in the French and industrial revolutions—which now have the possibility to defy the privileges and prohibitions of the courts. The second explosion occurs in the second half of the last century, when the privilege of Paris, the acknowledged world leader in the fashion of the year, begins to stagger due to the fashion designers of London, New York and, lately, Milan. Finally, it is the turn of the street styles, minority juvenile styles, developed in the 1970s by a limited number of graduates from the English fashion schools and later acknowledged as the basic inspiration sources for a large part of contemporary production, that constitute the third and most recent explosion.

As Lipovetsky (1987) remarks, modern fashion, in the true sense of the term (fashion of the 100 years ranging from the mid-nineteenth to the mid-twentieth centuries), which has its centre in Paris, is still a perfectly bipolar production and distribution system. Haute couture creates new trends and produces a few articles of clothing made to measure, and industrial production then tries to imitate it; they refer to two clearly differentiated classes. This centralized fashion is still essentially a women's fashion, since men's fashion has not yet achieved a comparable system, neither in terms of famous designer names nor in terms of investments.

According to Diana Crane, today we have

> three distinct categories of fashion—luxury design fashion, industrial fashion, and street styles. These three categories are weakly interconnected: street fashion has some influence on luxury fashion and vice versa, and both have some influence on industrial fashion. (Crane 2000: 166)

Luxury design fashion not only includes high fashion, but also prêt-à-porter, which today has actually become its prevailing and ruling form. The big clothing manufacturers, who particularly in Italy deal very much with luxury prêt-à-porter, have a high stake in understanding where consumers want to go and in systematically observing and studying them. As a matter of fact, at least in Italy, the links between these three subsystems are perhaps closer than Crane suggests (Volonté 2003a).

It is therefore clear that the mainspring of fashionable behaviours is not exclusively emulation—that is, the attempt of lower classes to imitate the style of the upper class. Fashion does not only spread from the top with a 'trickle down' effect (Fallers 1961, but also Baudrillard 1970). There are also 'bottom up' pressures involving other causes of this process, other non-economic variables or variables not connected to class position. The gender variable, for example, which was already emerging in the pioneering theorization of classical authors, did not then play an independent role, since it was overwhelmed by different priority demands and, most of all, did not escape the prejudice of that age: namely, that women had enough time and opportunity to devote themselves to fashion (Simmel 1911) and through their dress display the wealth of their husbands (Veblen 1953). These great theoreticians did not go as far as placing clothing within everyday life practice, explaining one's choices and motivations as such, which is the only level at which we can sound out the meanings we give to the objects we buy and use.

In order to properly analyse fashion consumption, it is necessary, on the one hand, to pay attention at the micro level—that is, to examine the situated and incorporated practices involved through the sociological approach. On the other hand, it is necessary to reassess the interactive dynamic of the actors involved in the mechanisms of the production of meaning, and here cultural studies becomes the dominant context. This approach, which I dwell on in the third section, shows us the complexity of the fashion phenomenon, which cannot be simply considered as a vector starting from either top or bottom, or explained based on single factors—such as class, gender, age or ethnic group. It should be understood, instead, as the result of a negotiation between individual and collective actors provided with different economic and symbolic power—starting from their actual position in terms of class, gender, age or ethnic group—but with a similar ability to give meaning. Through empiric research (which, as Entwistle [2000] repeatedly points out, is scarce), it is possible to understand how the combination of these variables plays a role in individual situations. The sociologist, as Goffman (1983) correctly remarks, should remain tied to the situation because only from this starting point of a microanalysis can we understand the importance of macro variables: a dress, a consumer object,

> is the very arena in which culture is fought over and licked into shape . . .
> Choices express and generate culture in its general sense . . . Ultimately, they

are moral judgments about what a man is, what a woman is. (Douglas and Isherwood 1979: 57)

So the objects we choose are not only fundamental to understanding aesthetic sensitivity, but also, in general, the system of values (McCracken 1990). Therefore, they are not the tools of a generic expressiveness or a generic submission to production dictates, of authenticity rather than conformism, but rather opportunities to place ourselves socially via a situated practice, to communicate to the outer world our belonging or exclusion, or even our ambivalence and instability.

IDENTITY AND APPEARANCE

The problem of identity is not a problem of appearance. However, I can only approach another person and his/her identity through appearance—words, actions, glances or dress, which, to some extent, might also be considered as personal narratives, or accounts of the self (Davis 1992; McCracken 1990)—and the other person will know me in the same way.

Schultz's phenomenological analysis is unequalled in illustrating the progression of comprehension, the attribution of a 'center of spontaneous activity' (Schutz 1964: 82) to the other I meet in my everyday life:

> The physical object 'the Other's body,' events occurring on this body, and his bodily movements are apprehended as expressing the Other's 'spiritual I' towards whose motivational meaning-context I am directed . . . To be sure, everyone has only his own experiences given in originary presence. But by the intermediary of events in the outer world, occurring on or brought about by the Other's body, especially by linguistic expressions in the broadest sense, I may comprehend the Other by appresentation; . . . a communicative common environment is thus established, within which the subjects reciprocally motivate one another in their mental activities. (Schutz 1962: 314–15)

Schutz makes a clear distinction between what I can empirically capture of that identity and the 'spiritual I' to which I turn without being able to draw it in its concreteness, but only through an 'appresentation'—that is, by referring the world of my experience to another world provided with a different order. However, corporeity, more than a perceptive limit, should be considered—according to the phenomenological perspective—as a perceptive horizon, that is, like a window, unique and personal, which opens out onto a possible/assumed immateriality.

According to Goffman (1961: 152), both in common-sense and in social-science tradition, 'the sacred part' of identity 'has to do . . . with what an individual is "really" like underneath it all . . . the obligatory world of social roles.' However, about this invisible authenticity, free from the forms and rules of society, Goffman is not able to say anything; if he mentions identity, he does it only to consider its visible effects, its manoeuvres aimed at defending its territory or its definition (Bovone 1993).

On the stage of everyday life, the performer declares what he is, he risks his own 'face', his image is at stake and he is involved in a continuous negotiation with his fellow performers and the audience. To do this, he provides himself with complex equipment ranging from the furniture of his home to his clothes. Among all other objects, what fits to our body—the dress and its accessories—has, however, a particular status:

> The individual ordinarily expects to exert some control over the guise in which he appears before others. For this he needs cosmetics and clothing supplies, tools for applying, arranging, and repairing them, and an accessible, secure place to store these supplies and tools—in short, the individual will need an 'identity kit' for the management of his personal front. (Goffman 1968: 28–9)

Fashion choices, in particular, are linked to the fragmented identity and strategies of the performer, who is always obliged to cope with a variety of characters. It is an opportunity for distancing oneself from one's official role, for giving the other roles an opportunity to emerge. Clothing is a basic element of the particular 'situated system of activity', of the peculiar interaction moment in which the actor establishes the character he will play, makes his choice for one of his 'multiple self-identifications' or, better, decides which self-identification he should privilege in a particular situation. Fashion choice is a means for reflecting on oneself, for recovering one's independence with respect to an ultra-socialized model of oneself to which should correspond an ultra-socialized way of clothing oneself. Our obsession for changes, our desire to differentiate ourselves from the others, but most of all from what others would more obviously expect from us, is, according to Goffman, the actual sense of fashion, which provides us with the tools for controlling the image others will have of us. 'Role distance is to role as fashion is to custom' (Goffman 1961: 151–2).

On the other hand, the outward appearance and the clothes of the other run up to us even prior to his words, and we must rely on them to start any kind of relation.

> When an individual enters the presence of others, he will want to discover the underlying facts of the interaction, that is, the actual outcome of the activity of the others, as well as their innermost feelings concerning him. Paradoxically, the more the individual is concerned with the reality that is not available to perception, the more he must concentrate on his appearance. (Goffman 1959: 249)

If Goffman abandons a precise hypothesis concerning the self that stays behind the actor and the character, contemporary sociological theories, from the postmodernist debate to cultural studies, are still focused on socially situated manifestations of the self. For example, 'cultural identity' for Hall and du Gay (1996) is an accounted social identity, that which an individual reveals through words and behaviours. The term refers, to some extent, to exteriorized cultural productions, without, however, saying that this would exhaust the completeness of an individual or that an individual is totally determined by his or her roles. This does not allow us to judge the authenticity of productions and behaviours, their freedom and spontaneity, but rather invites us to observe their manifestations and listen to their accounts.

Therefore, we can conclude (with Alvira 2004) that if we are to distinguish between outer and inner identity, it is also true that any inner identity becomes social, relates and communicates itself through the outer identity. If I cannot have but very partial access to identity through appearance, then the body is the basic means for drawing the interiority or the thoughts of the other, and it is impossible to leave out clothing and consider it as an irrelevant accessory. Today, the body-clothing-identity connection is not only acknowledged, but also considerably treated in specialized literature: 'Fashioning the body becomes a practice through which the individual can fashion a self' (Finkelstein 1998: 50).

We are generally aware that there is a form of gestural, theatrical communication of the body, which is as important—as Goffman (1959) again has taught us—as the contents of communication, or what is actually said. Clothing takes part in our complex communicative staging, but among the number of objects surrounding us, through which we build our interaction with the other, it plays a special role. Among the different non-verbal language modalities, clothing is the most typically human one because it belongs to any age and culture and is practically absent in all other living beings. We usually present ourselves to others, and even to ourselves, dressed. Therefore, clothing becomes a part of our bodily identity and, consequently, of our social identity. But whereas the body is mostly a fact, dress is the result of a choice. A choice that in many periods and circumstances had seemed almost unavoidable, but actually has always had some interesting margins of discretion, as the most attentive historians have remarked (Wilson 1992).

We are aware that in premodern society, and partly also in modern industrial society, identity was taken for granted: in the former, it was established by family status, geographic origin and community with its institutions, and in the latter, by work position and related social class (Bauman 1996). Clothing was once either a noble dress (in all its shades and varieties within the different courts) or a peasant dress (a durable costume, though regionally varied). Later came bourgeois attire—rigidly conceived for businessmen or housewives, as an everyday dress, a Sunday dress or a worker dress. In any case, until recent years, for the majority of the population the stable elements in one's dress far outnumbered those systematically subject to change. Most clothes passed almost intact from one generation to another, as if they still were al-most premodern society costumes. In this way, too, in modern industrial society, one generation passed on a good-citizen model to the following one, a tradition which only entered into a serious crisis starting in the final decades of the past century.

The problem of identity is a problem of indeterminateness, which begins when identity is considered as something to be achieved—not a fact, but a task. In this sense, it is both a modern and postmodern problem, although not the same problem in the two epochs, as Bauman clearly states:

> If the *modern* 'problem of identity' was how to construct an identity and keep it solid and stable, the *postmodern* 'problem of identity' is primarily how to avoid fixation and keep the options open. (Bauman 1996: 18)

The modern individual is a moving individual, a rising bourgeois, a worker who wants to improve himself in comparison with his parents. In any case, the modern individual remains 'a pilgrim', as Bauman (1996) writes, and achieves his socially acknowledged goal without the mind being diverted by glittering things and op-portunities. Modern identity is not stable, but its mobility is oriented. The process of identity individualization is only starting.

The choices of the postmodern individual—which Bauman compares to a restless tourist or a gambler—are provisional and deliberately partial because the lack of a new organic model induces us to keep any opportunity open to avoid final choices. It is, today, the problem of a 'homeless mind' (Berger, Berger and Kellner 1973), which does not know where to anchor its choices, nor does it want to.

Fashion is 'the empire of the ephemeral': Lipovetsky (1987) applies this definition to the whole vast world of fashions, cultural industry in its traditional mass-media sense and the urban economy which relies on those fashions. We explore all of our choices concerning fashion without rejecting any of them. Avoiding classification, dressing like nobody else, as Polhemus (1995) remarks, is the only way to feel authen-tic. As a matter of fact, just as with identity, even the choice of dress is increasingly less legible 'in contemporary, fragmented societies . . . where lifestyles, age cohorts, gender, sexual orientation and ethnicity are as meaningful to people as social class in constructing their self-images and in their presentation of self' (Crane 2000: 2).

The key actor in the capitalistic postmodern society is no longer the worker but the consumer (Bauman 2002a). Today, the labour market provides increasingly fewer regular jobs, encourages experimentation, leads people to accumulate expe-riences that often cannot be clearly ascribed to work or to the expressive area and causes satisfaction with any job that provides money for leisure and consumption. We have moved far from the ethics of work, from work as a vocation, such as Weber (1919) theorized.

The gender variable, too, enters the matter of identity and fashion in different ways. In the modern age, the true citizen was the man, educated by the family and the school to be a hard worker, a productive individual useful to the progress of the nation. Gregarious was the role of the housewife (that is, a woman without a status of her own), and fashion reflected the undisputed division of tasks in the married couple. Fluegel (1930) explains 'the great masculine renunciation' of suits as ornaments with the new demand for practicality coming from the men of the rising bourgeoisie. During the last decades, women have been able to aspire to (although they cannot always reach) the top of the labour ladder, and work is no longer the core activity in postmodern men's lives, or the social anchorage of men's identity. Then dealing consciously with one's own clothing is no longer considered a typical female matter or even as something particularly effeminate. Consistently, the most conspicuous growth in menswear styles derives from leisure time. It is also true that fashion is produced more for young people who wish to distinguish themselves from older generations rather than from the lower classes.

> The postmodern construction of non-occupational identities through clothing appears most strongly among the young and among racial and sexual minorities, whose members view themselves as marginal or exceptional in relation to the dominant culture. (Crane 2000: 198)

This rather transgressive and definitely informal fashion—that is, not characterized by precise and univocal rules—is mostly championed by the new elites of creative jobs, by those men or women who work in an independent or subordinate way in the symbolic/cultural/experience economy (du Gay and Pryke 2002; Caves 2000). On the one hand, one of the elements strikingly characterizing those organizations that attract the new creative classes is actually the informal clothing style. On the other hand, this new creative class is characterized by an interpenetration of work time and leisure time (Florida 2002; Bovone, Magatti, Mora and Rovati 2002).

This 'relaxed' fashion not only derives from a desire for comfort, but it is also related to the decline of the sources of established authority (perhaps the most striking heritage of the cultural revolution of the 1960s and 1970s) and to the individualization process of contemporary society. The unconditional admiration for upper-class styles and the connection between clothing and social hierarchy disappear together with the inner hierarchy of our personal wardrobe and Sunday dress (Lipovetsky 1987).

For many people, the body becomes the object of the same cares and conscious efforts that in the past were devoted to one's spiritual edification or, more frequently, to one's career. In an image society, the body becomes a project, a basic requirement for achieving any success or pleasure (Featherstone 1991a). Clothing takes part in this project, and even becomes osmotic with the body itself (more evidently if we refer to permanent marks such as piercing, tattoos, etc.); it contributes to the dignity of the self, avoids embarrassing situations and mediates among different social solicitations. According to Davis, dress is

> a kind of visual metaphor for identity and, as pertains in particular to the open society of the west, for registering the culturally anchored ambivalence that resonates within and among identities. (Davis 1992: 25)

Not by chance, those who most deliberately make use of the opportunities provided by clothing to distinguish themselves are first the feminists and lately marginal minorities (referring to ethnic or sexual belonging). Their identity and clothing become more consciously problematic when there is the possibility/need to confront themselves. In this regard, Wilson (2003) talks about an 'oppositional dress'.

Some meaningful examples of accepted versus antagonist fashion, as well as their relationship to individual identity, may be drawn from research carried out in Milan in the mid-1990s (Bovone and Mora 1997; Bovone 2003). We examined, through in-depth interviews and focus groups, about seventy sixteen- to thirty-year-old Milanese in their clothing choices. They were high-school students attending the last years of school and members of spontaneously aggregated groups. Some of these groups (such as the football team, the bar group, the choral ensemble and the parish group) had been chosen for their quiet continuity with adult culture, whereas the other groups (such as hooligans, graffiti artists, frequenters of a social centre, rockers and ravers) for their evident discontinuity.

The image cult, typical of the prevailing mentality, seems to have become an integral part of the lifestyle of our interviewees, but with a range of such different modalities that often it is hardly recognizable to adult eyes. The young students think it is appropriate to take care of one's appearance, not only because it is expected in contemporary society, but also because image is clearly considered a way of establishing communication, sending messages. Clothing style for some girls can be a privileged means for expressing the most secret part of themselves that they are not able to put into words. There are those who dress to fit in and those who dress to stand out. The ravers and the rockers dress up to 'disguise'.

Clothing also mediates between their mood and group requirements, without excluding anything and without totally embracing anything. The alogical structure of image allows trespassing of all boundaries. There is always the possibility to turn things to one's own advantage; errors are never irreparable or devastating, and the true self will never be directly confronted. As Maffesoli remarks, unlike rational thought, which creates precise distinctions and antinomies, image creates bridges:

It is a sort of 'mesocosm,' a world which is placed halfway between the macro- and the microcosm, between the universal and the solid, between the species and the individual, between the general and the particular. Hence, its effectiveness. (Maffesoli 1993: 140)

A little unexpectedly for us, the young interviewees frequently connect the theme of image with the theme of authenticity. Image brings to the surface what they have inside: 'Clothing actually reflects the thoughts of a person' (group from the social centre); 'Clothing, talking, music tastes, the places where one goes . . . are expressions of a way of feeling' (football team). In young people's conversations, authenticity does not actually seem an entity, but rather a changeable relation both with themselves and with others. The changeability of authenticity makes temporary removal from it absolutely bearable; on the other hand, authenticity may be concealed to others just through the image ('Sometimes I feel sad and I do not want others to see it, so I wear bright colours,' a female tourist-institute student reports). The relevant thing is the awareness of what is intentional in juvenile clothing: a T-shirt is not enough to guarantee one's political belonging; it is necessary to understand whether or not an idea corresponds to a particular way of clothing because the person who dresses without any awareness is a 'puppet' (social-centre group).

Ultimately, in order to understand how dress is used, the use needs to be verbalized. But the same may be applied to the body and to identity. Identity comes to us through its incorporated manifestations and needs to be expressed. Therefore, image/dress acts as an intermediary between authenticity and other people's expectations, between a reflexive-critical attitude (which relates to one's own interiority) and homologation (conforming to social rules). The balance is extremely unstable, although in general nobody seems to make an absolute choice either in favour of individual ethics or in favour of generally accepted norms.

The most interesting and significant explanation is provided by the young interviewees of the rave group, who openly declare two social identities and two kinds of morality referring to two different worlds: the night—that is, the world of 'inner freedom'—and the day—that is, the world of 'everyday rules'. Two social identities mean two images, two ways of dressing—namely work attire and a 'costume' for the rave corresponding to the 'freedom from customs'. But they also mean a shamelessly declared duplicity, authenticity theorized as parting from rules without any feeling of guilt. Normality has nothing to do with norms any more; it is made to measure. 'In conclusion, this is not even transgressive, it is normal. This term has lost its sense . . . it is alternative life, outburst of fancy, freedom . . . perhaps inner freedom which is brought out as freedom from customs' (rave group).

The contemporary debate on identity, to which I referred at the beginning of this section, provides some appropriate categories that can summarize young people's behaviours. Their acknowledged and well-managed ambivalence hovers between social rules and borderline authenticity. Identity is an offered image and an account, a non-planned process: it is neither something taken for granted nor something built starting from a shared good-citizen model, the product of successful socialization, functional to living together in society. According to Giddens (1991: 5), 'reflexive biography' is what gives unity to an individual: 'The reflexive project of the self . . . consists in the sustaining of coherent, yet continuously revised biographical narratives'; therefore, it is not a modern a priori life project, but a way to provide unity to non-reflective and partial choices, and rationalize and give them a sense a posteriori. Stuart Hall, relating to cultural identity, summarizes as follows:

> Because identities are constructed within, not outside discourse, we need to understand them as produced in specific historic and institutional sites within specific discursive formations and practices. (Hall 1996: 4)

This means that we are not able to sum up the problematical postmodern identity; rather, we are left with its collected narratives or accounts.

WHO DRESSES OUR IDENTITY? THE SUBJECTS OF CULTURAL PRODUCTION

The connection between freedom and fashion is often expressed in negative terms: fashion may either reduce freedom or provide suggestions of endless transgression. Even the double life of the ravers can be stigmatized in this way.

The aesthetic concern that characterizes fashion consumption is often explicitly labelled as a non-rational or non-moral concern. This opinion is in some way the result of the typical intellectual distance kept by Marxist criticism, ranging from the school of Frankfurt to Baudrillard (1972), towards the consumption of culture-industry products considered frivolous and passive pastimes. More generally, the central circuit of the culture industry lived—and is still living—an evident contradiction (already underlined by Horkheimer and Adorno 1947) between the term *culture* (which is traditionally conjugated with creativity and freedom) and its standardization and commoditization. This ultimately implies a contrast between those who (freely?) produce it, who are in possession of the key/codes of culture, and its likely passive users, the consumers.

However, this theme may be dealt with in a quite different manner. We can consider fashion from the producers' point of view as an endless search for the new aimed at gaining consumers' interest. From the consumers' point of view, we can see fashion as access to an inexhaustible market of appearance, in which one can buy elements of sociality, layers in which to wrap oneself before establishing contact with others.

In the coming paragraphs I examine the freedom/constraint dialectics in parallel with the analogous production/consumption dialectics, keeping in the background the increasingly aesthetic character of contemporary goods production. I would like to focus my reasoning on the communicative possibility of fashion as cultural production, while trying to break any monolithic framework we may apply to the analysis of the fashion market and the relations between producers and consumers.

In my opinion, we can make a significant step forward if we consider fashion goods in terms of 'material culture' (as for example Dant 1999) instead of using the probably worn-out term 'culture industry'. Material culture is neither related exclusively to industrial/serial productions nor refers particularly to mass-media intangible productions—words, music, images. It refers, instead, to the numerous artefacts we use in our everyday life, which mostly have a function connected to our needs—namely subsistence, home, work—but that are specifically chosen and appreciated by us because they enrich our lives by giving them meaning. As I previously remarked, the economic link between demand and supply at least partly confirms the cultural link between a meaning proposal and its acceptance (Appadurai 1986). Obviously, many subjects contribute to this link to make these goods interesting for the purchaser by adding socially acknowledged symbolic elements. It is therefore clear that when we refer to the meaning of objects, our intention refers to a variety of meanings, a string of meanings only partly shared by the actors involved. As a matter of fact, the broader concept that frames this way of considering consumption is 'popular culture' (Griswold 1994), which is the most suitable for pointing out a large-scale encounter between producers and consumers, which in no case can be completely passive, nor can it wipe out the interests of either party. As Fiske (1991) explains, culture is a construction to which everybody contributes.

If the first and most important application of popular-culture theory concerned media culture, today it is clear that material objects (things, material culture), as soon as they are considered in their involvement in transactions and discourses, also become a part of this popular culture. The more complex, rich and refined a society is, the less the variety of material goods can be explained through their material use. Clothes are meant to cover us, but this does not obviously justify the quantity of clothes produced and purchased. This variety may instead be explained by the immaterial content these objects have acquired. The cultural component, the meaning, becomes prevailing and explains our choice for one dress or another. Furthermore, culture as a whole, even mediated culture, is no longer considered exclusively in the hands of the ruling class or its acknowledged experts, but rather as a never-definitive elaboration of meanings. Meanings themselves are considered hidden, many-sided or floating (Appadurai 1986).

This mass-production and mass-consumption society works precisely because goods are continuously reformulated in more interesting or attractive ways, in forms associated with other forms, recalling something else or, better, other persons, consumer or producer categories or even social groups we wish to approach or from which we want to depart (Douglas and Isherwood 1979). This is really a peculiarity of some sectors, such as fashion, where products have a market value (or an added value, in comparison with similar products) not because of the sophisticated technology they employ or the amount of work involved, but mostly because they succeed in selling an idea, an experience, as well as an opportunity to signal this intangible possession to others. Just because the hierarchy of signs is not always evident and the uncertain postmodern subject is in search of anchorage, what we want to sell/buy is not so much a status or a 'distinction' symbol (as the classical authors, Baudrillard 1970 and Bourdieu 1979, also maintained) but, in general, an identity element providing one of the possible self-identifications or images of the self that the postmodern individual collects (Bovone 2003). Mass production also shares this need for differentiation, for an increasingly sophisticated formal research or a communication that can add to it in an evocative way all the aesthetic characteristics necessary for becoming competitive (Lash and Urry 1994).

As regards clothing, it is difficult today to determine who establishes what is fashionable, and only empiric research gives us some ideas on the complex flow of meanings. Both enterprises and fashion designers have to cope with numerous obstacles; they are obliged to negotiate with a particularly endless sequence of gatekeepers who, as Herbert Blumer (1969) analytically showed, filter the trajectory from production to consumption. The cultural-communicative circuit is evidently entangled (Barnard 1996).

Today, it is absolutely clear that fashion designers, entrepreneurs, professionals introduced in the different production stages, photographers and journalists, agents, distributors and retailers contribute in different and never-definitive ways to the composition of meaning (Ruggerone 2001; Volonté 2003a; Mora 2006). Finally, in order to be in a position to talk about popular culture, it is necessary that products be transferred—that is, understood, contested, changed, contaminated—to the everyday life of many persons and that they ultimately take root there.

Therefore, in a broader sense, the subjects of cultural production are not only those who make it coincide with their economic activity—designers, manufacturers, communicators, retailers—but also consumers, those who are called by de Certeau (1990: XLV) 'non-acknowledged producers'. These are those who unpredictably react to the different products offered by the macro- and microcircuits of cultural production and contribute in their own way, by opposing, accepting or cunningly reshaping the meanings provided by the market.

> A rationalized, expansionist, centralized, spectacular and noisy production is confronted with a production of a completely different nature called 'consumption,' marked by its tricks, by its fragmentation connected to opportunities, by its poaching, by its secrecy, by its unceasing murmuring, which make it almost invisible, because it does not distinguish itself in any way through its own creations, but through the art of using what is provided for it. (de Certeau 1990)

Today these tactics are increasingly studied and considered within corporate strategic calculations, particularly face to face with the large investment of mass production. From this point of view, even market research (and particularly the strategic use of young, cool hunters sent to the four corners of the Earth) may be considered a communication channel for feedback.

Quite different is the production-consumption relation and the communicative interaction established at a small-enterprise level, at least in the particular Milan context, which in the late 1990s became our object of study: a 'cultural quarter' (O'Connor 1996; Montgomery 2003), a fashionable neighbourhood (Bovone 2005), a concentration of the symbolic economy on which the postmodern city lives.

Cities have been hotbeds for fashionable consumption in every age (Simmel 1911; Lipovetsky 1987), as well as centres of gravity for industrial production. Nowadays, production structures are reconverted to consumption. The urban economy promotes distribution. Thus, commercial and service activities, entertainment places and restaurants come together in some quarters to form an integrated system, a postindustrial district dedicated to consumption. In Milan, this transformation has particularly gravitated around the fashion system, though relying in practice on a local multiform entrepreneurial tradition.

I am particularly referring to research we carried out focusing on the small cultural entrepreneurs based in the Ticinese quarter of Milan (Bovone et al. 2002). We dealt with microenterprises, mostly family-run, operating in the different areas of cultural production, such as communication and entertainment, fashion, tourism, design and furniture, food and in the service, trade and manufacturing segments.

This quarter has a varied population, due to several waves of immigration—workers from Southern Italy after the war, students and artist-bohemians during the 1970s and, in recent years, in an already partly gentrified quarter, professionals, entrepreneurs and middle- and upper-class citizens. It is a traditionally tolerant quarter that still loves diversity, just as a creative quarter is supposed to (Florida 2002). Cultural entrepreneurs do not belong exclusively to any of these waves. They are old artisans working for decades in the quarter or brilliant aesthetes of the last generation.

Our in-depth interviews revealed that the entrepreneurs who operate in this circuit, which involves one-third of Milanese enterprises, certainly behave according to market logic, but in a different way compared to the central circuit of the mass cultural industry. They have found their place in the market and in the city in a rather spontaneous and casual way, as most often happens in subcultural urban circuits and in small artistic-artisan productions, where the boundaries between producers and consumers seem to vanish (Crane 1992). It is urban, non-centralized, but not even de-territorialized production.

They are, in general, culture producers who do not seem segregated in an antagonistic way—that is, with radically different interests—in comparison with consumers and territory. Interviews reveal the entrepreneur's ability to connect different worlds of meaning, to lay, through the cultural object, a bridge linking a variety of subjects: family members, assistants, suppliers, as regards production; customers, friends, neighbours, again family members, as regards consumption. Some of these subjects may carry the quarter's deep-seated ideas, competences and values, sometimes for decades or centuries.

If in almost any entrepreneur of this quarter the motivation to work combines an economic component with an aesthetic/symbolic one, these two spurs do not have the same weight for all. Not all the entrepreneurs interviewed have the same ability to manipulate significant objects, the same awareness and the same desire to use them to establish relations. In particular, two kinds of entrepreneurs have clearly emerged: those who, having invested in a total, 'identitarian' way of doing business, act as if they sold elements that were useful to build their customers' identity, and those who are aware of working on meanings for precise market needs (Mora 2002).

The first entrepreneur may be a pure creative, one who invents products (ecological handbags) or services (an innovative models agency) or who has stored up objects made by others (a woman who collects ethnic textiles). In this case, we are witnessing an expert in laying bridges of taste ('those who come to my shop like what I choose') who puts the economic side of his or her work between brackets, or does not recognize this facet as determining.

The second entrepreneur seems to develop with greater ease by focusing and even making a strength of the ambivalence between economic and aesthetic-cultural motivations. In particular, the economic motivation demands finding a suitable relation with the market and, consequently and unavoidably, with the enterprises that dominate it. Market requirements may even indicate the opportunity to make heterogeneous choices compared to the trend established by the big cultural corporations—that is, the opportunity to exploit one's originality, the originality that only small businesses are able to cultivate. If the first entrepreneur is the one who is more typically 'identitarian,' the one who, as I wrote at the beginning, deeply identifies with his or her product and, using it as a medium, tries to hand over/sell to customers some elements of his or her own identity, the second entrepreneur, who is particularly aware of being a basic articulation between elite culture and mass culture, can be called an 'entrepreneur-articulator' (in the sense given by du Gay and colleagues [1997] to the verb *to articulate*).

This complex dialectic between local production and global market also concerns the production-consumption virtuous circle which is a peculiarity of this quarter. A part of the goods and services produced in the quarter are locally consumed by those who live and work in it, another part is similarly consumed locally by persons in transit (tourists, businesspeople, young people from Milan and Lombardy) and a third part is exported. Cultural entrepreneurs work on meanings in order to resell them; they transfer them from one context to another and adapt them to different publics.

As real cultural intermediaries, they manipulate meanings, and, as expert consumers of goods and lifestyles, they personally test and exhibit (Bourdieu 1979; Bovone 1994). They are immersed in consumption culture and promote it. As it is a typically 'drenched in meaning' culture (Lury 1996: 226), they are the main reference group for that meaning, both in terms of consumption and production. As Bourdieu has stated, they believe so much in what they do that they are the first ones to try it. They wear the clothes they want to sell, both in their work hours and in their leisure time; they enjoy working and promote themselves in their free time. But, contrary to what Bourdieu theorized/remarked on, their cultural production seemed to be aimed more at elaborating connections than barriers, identitarian passages rather than demarcation standards. This may confirm that their aesthetic-social involvement prevails over their economic involvement, thus foreshadowing the possibility of overcoming the typical producer-consumer antagonism.

To some extent, business size, its products and its rooting in the territory are the elements that make it possible to confront or even pour out identities: if the cultural product is the major medium of this practice, the still-available 'traces of community' (Bagnasco 1999) are important as well. The quarter is the stage on which identitarian performances take place, where negotiations of meaning can be carried out in an atmosphere nourished by reciprocity and trust.

In conclusion, fashion is clearly both an aesthetic and an economic phenomenon; it is an economic world using aesthetic elements, proposing aesthetic solutions. It is a consumption phenomenon, which does not necessarily oppress individual identity but usually provides it with resources and sometimes-alternative spaces. Fashion in clothing is a proposal aimed at dressing our body, the way in which we socially present ourselves. More than other objects we choose, buy and use, it seems to involve our social identity; like many other objects, it communicates something inner to the outer world, makes values and affiliations concrete.

Criticism of postmodern production aesthetization, particularly feminist criticism, highlights the excessive aesthetization of the body, particularly the female body, and of the commoditization of women (Wilson 2003; Davis 1992; Ruggerone 2006). But the debate on postmodernity has also allowed us to consider clothing as a typical expression of popular culture in which each consumer becomes the main character.

On the other hand, the dynamics of economic interests and consumption are not anonymous. On the contrary, as sociologists, we are committed to bringing out the social subjects involved, the social identities that confront each other. We are engaged in dealing with production and consumption together (Ruggerone 2001; Entwistle 2000; Crane 2000).

OTHER KINDS OF CONSUMPTION AND ALTERNATIVE FASHIONS: AESTHETICS AND ETHICS

We need to continue examining the distinction between modern and postmodern culture. Modern culture includes the account of progress. It is a partisan culture and prepares interesting events, including new fashions, which definitely seem better than the previous ones and have the authority to replace them. Postmodern culture is a fence-sitting culture; it waits and sees, does not judge, observes the different styles—from the stylists or from the street—and the fragmented show of the world. Postmodern culture seems totally dedicated to image, interested only in appearance, fascinated by aesthetics. But in principle it does not exclude anything or choose any option. It is a conciliatory culture where any cultural object can be taken seriously.

Care for one's appearance, aesthetics and body ornamentation have always been the guiding principles in the choice of clothing, when such a choice has been possible. However, the different meanings we may attribute to clothing are not only of an aesthetic nature. Clothing is a domination and constraint tool, but it may also become a rebellion or subversion tool; as mentioned earlier, it is an important corner of the cultural arena in which we fight to define a situation. From this point of view, aesthetic research may be instrumental for other purposes; dress covers our appearance, and it can be exclusively based on aesthetic standards, but again, it depends on which form of beauty we are looking for in a particular circumstance. Wilson writes:

> Socially determined we may be, yet we constantly search for the crevices in culture that open moments of freedom . . . fashion is one among many forms of aesthetic creativity which make possible the exploration of alternatives. (Wilson 2003: 244–5)

As we noticed in our interviews with young fashion consumers, the society of image has produced sophisticated users of figurative symbols who are able to explain their choices very precisely. They evaluate whether or not, or how much, their search for an image depends on individual or group standards, on their need to conform to standards considered ineludible or, instead, on their desire to express their own authentic nature and, consequently, on standards they personally perceive as moral, even though they are labelled by others as deviant. If fashion fragmentation has been related to identity fragmentation, as though it were partly responsible for it—and after all, Goffman too considered it as the possibility to make room for different parts of the self—we should say, instead, that for some minority groups, from juvenile cohorts to ethnic groups, clothing operates in the direction of strengthening identity. Wilson (1992) even suggests that the different statements made on the fragmentation of the self and the crisis of identity are actually projections made by academic researchers of a self-evident crisis of white-male identity or, more in general, a signal of the definitive failure of a rationalistic explanation of behaviours, whose sense should otherwise be described.

Alberoni (1964) wrote many years ago that 'consumption is an action provided with a sense', no less than the productive, rational and moral action on which modern sociology has focussed, from Weber to Parsons. Today we know that consumption has always been an action provided with a sense in any age and in any culture (Douglas and Isherwood 1979). But what is its sense in a society in which consumption plays a prominent role, since the role of the citizen is established in terms of consumption instead of production (Isin and Wood 1999)?

Talking about a postmodern culture has never excluded the survival or revival of previous cultural stratifications. It has been argued (Bauman 1992; Bovone 1994) that usually those who follow postmodern culture are particularly developed fringes of the population, new intellectuals, new cultural intermediaries in a position to reflect both on themselves and on society, spokespersons of the social reflexivity characterizing our age. These individuals, such as for example the cultural entrepreneurs I mentioned at the end of the previous section, might surely express the most innovative cultural trends, become the privileged interpreters or, better, the codifiers of contemporary culture. However, this reflexivity is not necessarily or exclusively based on aesthetic competence and awareness.

According to Inglehart (1997), postmodern values are post-materialist values: if, due to generally higher standards of living, a smaller number of individuals are concerned about their material subsistence, the consumption race may be read as a search for meanings and experience, as proposed in the latest sociological theory. Up to now, it was the aesthetic side of this search that had been emphasized the most, and therefore, I dwelt on this aspect in depth in this chapter. As I mentioned at the beginning, 'aesthetization of everyday life' (Featherstone 1991b) is one of the set phrases which seems to express the spirit of postmodern culture. But probably the most interesting feature of postmodern culture—because it is more open to different declinations in the future—is, instead, a more generic and all-inclusive ambivalence, an inability to set something aside for something else, a desire—about which Bauman (1996) talks—not to deny oneself anything. It might seem, again, a form of hedonism, as the search for one's pleasure/interest. The tourist's attitude trains us to hope for the possibility of enjoying in a rapid sequence (or even simultaneously) different landscapes able to give us an inexhaustible experience of all the positive things we are not able to find in our usual landscape. But it is, at the same time, a never-ending exploration. According to Bauman, 'postmodernity can be seen as restoring to the world what modernity, presumptuously, had taken away; as a re-enchantment of the world that modernity tried hard to dis-enchant' (1992: 10).

Disenchantment, in the Weberian tradition (Weber 1919), is the rationalization process of the world that began as a result of modernization. The modern age acted in the name of reason, subordinating the world and nature to a carefully calculated economic progress, and thus brought everybody under the same moral imperatives, primarily the work ethic.

Therefore, the passage from modern disenchantment to postmodern re-enchantment can be considered as an abandonment of (shared) morality in favour of (individual) aesthetic/hedonistic evaluation standards, or an exaggerated reaction to modern ethics that seems to repeat the ancient swing from Protestant ethics to the romantic spirit (Campbell 1989). But both passages are probably less radical and definitive than their critics would maintain. According to Bauman, the postmodern age gives back individual responsibility to everybody and restores a more varied possibility of judging without the limiting umbrella of rational calculation and universal values.

'Individualization', 'the compulsion to lead a life of one's own' (Beck and Beck-Gernsheim 2002), induces people to cast doubt on old categories and dichotomies, to choose à la carte fashions, and to combine them à la carte.

More specifically, in modern/class society, dress items were 'closed texts, with fixed meanings', whereas, in the fragmented/postmodern society, these items are 'open texts', represented in different ways by different social groups (Crane 2000: 243). The item providing us with the interpretation key of the modern age is the hat, a closed and compulsory text par excellence; the key item in postmodern fashion is the T-shirt, open text par excellence, a never-ending text that everyone is able to write.

Bauman, in fact, reappraises the postmodern experimenter attitude and decides that a positive attitude towards others may consist of acknowledging and maintaining their diversity:

The 'pleasure collector' develops . . . an interest aimed at keeping unchanged . . . the difference of the other and its right of being different, . . . and finds its pleasure just in the freedom of the others and by shouldering the responsibility for their peculiar uniqueness. (Bauman 1999: 124–5)

In this way, the positive attitude towards the other—the responsible, moral attitude—becomes compatible with personal pleasure. The choice between a moral-modern standard and an aesthetic-postmodern standard, between modern austere disenchantment and postmodern hedonistic re-enchantment, seems to correspond to radically making up one's mind between being and having, between one's edification and consumption. However, Bauman (2002b) continues, the choice between being and having is a choice that we cannot, or do not, want to make today. None of these options seems particularly attractive or possible today. Being is a choice for achieving a stable identity through, for example, a permanent job or place, a final partner. Having is a choice for accumulating goods, ballast to take with us. Therefore, it is better to accumulate 'sensations', which in fact replace the idea of stable happiness that modernity related to the idea of progress.

But here, perhaps, in this breaking away from being and having, new combinations may become available. Consumption may then turn into critical and responsible consumption (regarding one's health, the health of others and the planet, the welfare of far-away manufacturers fighting for their profit to the detriment of big-organization profits, etc.). But responsible consumption does not mean saying goodbye to pleasant feelings and experiences; surely it is not irreversible, such as a vow of poverty. It is an additional experience—one which may help us accumulate a little less, which comforts us if we shop too much or get tired of shopping—because the clothes we buy are manufactured ecologically without exploiting the labour force of the South (see the Clean Clothes campaign against fashion corporations). These clothes sometimes have a fashionable, exotic aspect and may contribute to making different cultures compatible with one's own culture.

We are not obliged to make a drastic choice between ethical and aesthetic options. The choice for what is beautiful is not necessarily a selfish choice. Consumption, the new frontier of citizenship, may not only help us reassure ourselves, provide us with new experiences or anchor our shaky identity, but may also help us find a new way to relate to others, a new sociality and a new morality.

Postmodern consumers' ability to combine is enhanced, as a cosmopolitan tendency, which seems indispensable for coming out of the deadlock affecting the development model of Western society. As Latouche (2003) maintains, we need to 'decolonize the imaginary'. And Beck talks about an indispensable 'cosmopolitan perspective':

> Cosmopolitanization means that the key questions of a way of life, such as nour-
> ishment, production, identity, fear, memory, pleasure, fate, can no longer be
> located nationally or locally, but only globally or glocally . . . Dialogic imagina-
> tions presuppose . . . imagined presence of geographically distant others and
> worlds. (Beck 2002: 29–31)

The fact that sociological theory focuses on the imaginary is a clear sign of a
tentative process, based more on suggestions than indications and projects, typical
of the postmodern mentality. But it is also an invitation that significantly involves
both producers and consumers and which acknowledges the considerable weight
of consumers in orienting consumption but, either implicitly or explicitly, invites
producers to take them into account.

It is possible to create virtuous circles. For example, in the field of clothing, the
strong return of furs among fashion wear must certainly be related to the action
taken by furriers and their associations aimed at showing that their industry has adopted in practice many of the ecologists' claims that had succeeded in cornering the
industry in the first place (Skov 2005). This phenomenon is even more evident in
alternative circuits than in large-scale retail. Fair trade shops, second-hand retail and
artisans who use environmentally friendly commodities represent the other side of
the coin of responsible consumption. As with the other urban cultural entrepreneurs
mentioned earlier, these entrepreneurs try to sell products in which they believe to
consumers like themselves, they circulate identitarian products and form with their
customers and distributors a city-centric cultural circuit in which production and
consumption overlap and get mixed up (Lembi, Montagnini and Mora 2004).

Some inhabitants of postmodernity seem no longer satisfied—perhaps because they
are saturated—with the enchantment of forms and colours. They look for, propose and
spread consumption patterns and fashions that are both beautiful and fair. Responsible
consumption has become a growing phenomenon everywhere and doubles every year
in Italy: a recent survey on 1,500 representative sample cases shows that in 2005, 45 per
cent of Italians purchased fair-trade goods (Bovone and Mora 2007). It is not surprising
that these consumers were mostly well-educated women with a middle-to-high income,
who have perhaps bought too much in recent years and wanted to buy something different (see also, for international data, Micheletti 2003; Micheletti and Stolle 2006).

Fair consumption costs as much as other less fair kinds of consumption and sometimes even more. Fair consumption is placed in the medium-to-high price segment,
the difference being no more that 'quid' of design, which constitutes the added value
of all the goods we possess in numerous copies. It is not an aesthetic difference, but
a moral one. It becomes moral consumption, which can pass throughout our life,
from food to clothing and leisure time, from the essential to the superfluous, thus
characterizing our whole lifestyle.

Individualization leads us to provide individual answers to the problems and fears of the new century, but for the first time it is clear that we cannot solve our personal problems or satisfy our desire for beauty if we do not consider others, if we do not consider that there is a convergence between private interest and public interest. Others are in any case an awkward, and today absolutely disquieting, presence. But are we able to defend ourselves from the fear of terrorism by properly choosing among the consumption options offered by the market? Maybe not, but if we are not able to identify a political solution to the macro-dilemmas of our time, if we are not able to engage ourselves in it, fair trade and boycotting campaigns against large-scale retail may give us the impression that we are in some way contributing to the global cause we obscurely understand to be connected to terrorism. Today, we make an attempt; tomorrow, we will make another attempt: the logic of fashion does not demand an exclusive and final choice; as tourists, we can experiment even with good deeds, but we are not in a position to definitively decide their hierarchy.

CONCLUDING REMARKS

A fragmented society does not provide certainties, but rather provides new consumption opportunities, which we have to take into account whether we are rich or poor. But a fragmented society does not lend itself well to monolithic criticism. Its culture, and also—and particularly—its material culture, as de Certeau (1974) has taught us, should be read 'in the plural' by casting light on all its actors. We should consider ourselves its actors because otherwise it would be as though we handed it over to hands that are not ours. What mainly distinguishes the most recent approaches to consumption and fashion from the classical ones is that the contemporary sociologist is no longer an external critic of material culture or serial culture, an aristocratic moralist who keeps herself out of it. A typical example is the harsh and rationalistic criticism of the theoreticians of the Frankfurter school, who did not see any possibility of contamination between their culture and the mass culture produced by the cultural industry, between art for the intellectual and entertainment for the masses. The intellectual understood differences, made choices and did not bother with more popular elements except to critique and stigmatize them. Today, we know that even the intellectual takes part in consumer society, takes part in the fashion system, contributes to its reproduction, makes use of it and so on. Compared to others, the intellectual only has some additional or different encoding and recoding tools at her disposal. Therefore, we are far away from the certainties of the past.

The uncertainty of our age and our discipline makes it more and more difficult to talk about culture in the abstract, to attribute values and ideas or declare them in a credible way without the support of empirically describable objects. Ideas and images must become words and narratives, but also, if possible, material documents which, for a while, fix their meaning (Crane 1994: 2–4).

Based on her history studies, Crane (2000) argues, in addition, that a non-verbal symbolic language and, consequently, material culture—and in this case particularly the language of things and clothing—change before becoming aware of their change, and hence before a verbal account of such change can be formulated. We can draw two important conclusions from this idea, one concerning common-sense awareness and the other concerning the possibilities of scientific research:

1. Fragmentation and the swift sequence of fashions, which are often accused of having harmful effects on consumers' consciousness, have perhaps always encouraged confrontation and its rationalization at a later stage. However, today fashions change at a faster rate than they did in the modern age. This might be a direct cause for the stronger reflexivity of the postmodern consumer, increasingly able to reflect upon the occasions and the tools he or she can use to enhance his or her identity.

2. Similarly, observing fashion and its changes would allow the social scientist to make some better-grounded remarks on developing values, to find their sociological account even before a complete discourse at a common-sense level could be circulated.

References and Further Reading

Alberoni, F. (1964), *Consumi e società,* Bologna: Il Mulino.

Alvira, R. (2004), 'Modernidad y moda', in M. Codina and M. Herrero (eds), *Mirando la moda,* Madrid: Ediciones internacionales Universitarias.

Appadurai, A., ed. (1986), *The Social Life of Things,* Cambridge: Cambridge University Press.

Bagnasco, A. (1999), *Tracce di comunità,* Bologna: Il Mulino.

Barnard, M. (1996), *Fashion as Communication,* London and New York: Routledge.

Baudrillard, J. (1970), *La société de consommation,* Paris: Denoel.

Baudrillard, J. (1972), *Pour une critique de l'économie politique du signe,* Paris: Gallimard.

Bauman, Z. (1992), *Intimations of Postmodernity,* London: Routledge.

Bauman, Z. (1996), 'From Pilgrim to Tourist—or a Short History of Identity', in S. Hall and P. du Gay (eds), *Questions of Cultural Identity,* London; Thousand Oaks, California; New Delhi: Sage.

Bauman, Z. (1999), *La società dell'incertezza,* Bologna: Il Mulino.

Bauman, Z. (2002a), *Il disagio della postmodernità,* Milan: Bruno Mondadori.

Bauman, Z. (2002b), *Society under Siege,* Oxford: Polity Press.

Beck, U. (2002), 'Cosmopolitan Society and Its Enemies', *Theory, Culture and Society,* 19: 1–2, 17–44.

Beck, U., and Beck-Gernsheim, E. (2002), *Individualization*, London; Thousand Oaks, California; New Dehli: Sage.

Berger, P., Berger, B., and Kellner, H. (1973), *The Homeless Mind*, New York and Toronto: Random House.

Blumer, H. (1969), 'Fashion: From Class Differentiation to Collective Selection', *Sociological Quarterly*, 10: 275–91.

Bourdieu, P. (1979), *La distinction*, Paris: Editions de Minuit.

Bovone, L. (1993), 'Ethics as Etiquette: The Emblematic Contribution of Erving Goffman', *Theory, Culture and Society*, 10/4: 25–39

Bovone, L., ed. (1994), *Creare comunicazione. I nuovi intermediari di cultura a Milano*, Milan: Angeli.

Bovone, L. (2003), 'Clothing: The Authentic Image? The Point of View of Young People', *International Journal of Contemporary Sociology*, 40/2: 205–18.

Bovone, L. (2005), 'Fashionable Quarters in the Postindustrial City: The Ticinese of Milan', *City and Community*, 4/4: 359–80.

Bovone, L., Magatti, M., Mora, E., and Rovati, G. (2002), *Intraprendere cultura. Rinnovare la città*, Milan: Angeli.

Bovone, L., and Mora, E., eds (1997), *La moda della metropoli. Dove si incontrano i giovani milanesi*, Milan: Angeli.

Bovone, L., and Mora, E., eds (2007), *Tra individualismo e responsabilità. Il potenziale dei consumi critici*, Rome: Donzelli.

Campbell, C. (1989), *The Romantic Ethic and the Spirit of Modern Consumerism*, Oxford: Basil Blackwell.

Caves, R. E. (2000), *Creative Industries: Contracts between Art and Commerce*, Cambridge, Massachusetts: Harvard University Press.

Codina, M., and Herrero, M., eds (2004), *Mirando la moda*, Madrid: Ediciones internacionales Universitarias.

Crane, D. (1992), *The Production of Culture*, Newbury Park, California: Sage.

Crane, D. (1994), 'Introduction: The Challenge of the Sociology of Culture to Sociology as a Discipline', in D. Crane (ed.), *The Sociology of Culture*, Oxford, UK, and Cambridge, Massachusetts: Blackwell.

Crane, D. (2000), *Fashion and Its Social Agendas*, Chicago: University of Chicago Press.

Dant, T. (1999), *Material Culture in the Social World*, Buckingham and Philadelphia: Open University Press.

Davis, F. (1992), *Fashion, Culture and Identity*, Chicago: University of Chicago Press.

de Certeau, M. (1974), *La culture au pluriel*, Paris: Uge.

de Certeau, M. (1990), *L'invention du quotidien 1. arts de faire*, Paris: Gallimard.

Douglas, M., and Isherwood, B. (1979), *The World of Goods*, New York: Basic Books.

du Gay, P., and Pryke, M., eds (2002), *Cultural Economy*, London: Sage.

du Gay, P., Hall, S., Janes, L., Mackay, H., and Negus, K. (1997), *Doing Cultural Studies: The Story of the Sony Walkman*, London; Thousands Oaks, California; New Delhi: Sage.

Entwistle, J. (2000), *The Fashioned Body*, Cambridge, UK: Polity Press.

Fallers, L A. (1961), 'A Note on the Trickle Effect', in S. M. Lipset and N. J. Smelser, *Sociology: Analysis of a Decade*, Englewood Cliffs, New Jersey: Prentice Hall.

Featherstone, M. (1991a), 'The Body in Consumer Society', in M. Featherstone, M. Hepworth and B. Turner (eds), *The Body: Social Process and Cultural Theory*, London: Sage.

Featherstone, M. (1991b), *Consumer Culture and Postmodernism*, London; Newbury Park; New Delhi: Sage.

Finkelstein, J. (1998), *Fashion*, New York: New York University Press.

Fiske, J. (1991), *Understanding Popular Culture*, London and New York: Routledge.

Florida, R. (2002), *The Rise of Creative Class: And How It's Transforming Work, Leisure, Community and Everyday Life*, New York: Basic Books.

Fluegel, J. C. (1930), *The Psychology of Clothes*, London: Hogarth Press.

Giddens, A. (1991), *Modernity and Self-Identity: Self and Society in the Late Modern Age*, Cambridge: Polity Press.

Goffman, E. (1959), *The Presentation of Self in Everyday Life*, New York: Doubleday Anchor.

Goffman, E. (1961), *Encounters: Two Studies in the Sociology of Interaction*, Indianapolis, Indiana: Bobbs Merril.

Goffman, E. (1968), *Asylums*, Harmondsworth, UK: Penguin Books.

Goffman, E. (1983), 'The Interaction Order', *American Sociological Review*, 48: 1–17.

Griswold, W. (1994), *Cultures and Societies in a Changing World,* Thousand Oaks, California: Pine ForgePress.

Hall, S. (1996), 'Introduction: Who Needs "Identity"?' in S. Hall and P. du Gay (eds), *Questions of Cultural Identity*, London; Thousand Oaks, California; New Delhi: Sage.

Hall, S., and du Gay, P., eds (1996), *Questions of Cultural Identity*, London; Thousand Oaks, California; New Delhi: Sage.

Inglehart, R. (1997), *Modernization and Postmodernization: Cultural, Economic and Political Change in Forty-Three Societies*, Princeton, New Jersey: Princeton University Press.

Isin, E. F., and Wood, P. K. (1999), *Citizenship and Identity*, London; Thousand Oaks, California; New Delhi: Sage.

Lash, S., and Urry, J. (1994), *Economies of Signs and Places,* London: Sage.

Latouche, S. (2003), *Décoloniser l'imaginaire. La pensée créative contre l'économie de l'absurde,* Paris: Parangon.

Lembi, P., Montagnini, E., and Mora, E. (2004), *Esplorando i mondi del consumo critico. Una lettura sociologica*, forthcoming paper.

Lipovetsky, G. (1987), *L'empire de l'éphémère*, Paris: Gallimard.

Lury, C. (1996), *Consumer Culture*, London: Polity Press.

Maffesoli, M. (1993), *La contemplation du monde*, Paris: Grasset.

McCracken, G. (1990), *Culture and Consumption*, Bloomington and Indianapolis: Indiana University Press.

Micheletti, M. (2003), *Political Virtue and Shopping: Individuals, Consumerism and Collective Action*, New York: Palgrave Macmillan.

Micheletti, M., and Stolle, D. (2006), 'The Gender Gap Reversed: Political Consumerism as a Women-friendly Form of Civic and Political Engagement', in B. O'Neill and E. Gidengil (eds), *Gender and Social Capital*, New York: Routledge.

Montgomery, J. (2003), 'Cultural Quarters as Mechanisms for Urban Regeneration. Part 1. Conceptualising Cultural Quarters', *Planning Practice and Research*, 18/4: 293–306.

Mora, E. (2002), 'Imprenditori di cultura, produttori di identità', in L. Bovone, M. Magatti, E. Mora, and G. Rovati, *Intraprendere cultura. Rinnovare la città*, Milan: Angeli.

Mora, E. (2006), 'Collective Production of Creativity in the Italian Fashion System', *Poetics*, 34: 334–53.

O'Connor, J. (1996), 'Popular Culture, Cultural Intermediaries and Urban Regeneration', in S. Hall and P. Hubbard (eds), *The Entrepreneurial City: Geographies of Politics, Regime and Representation*, Chichester: John Wiley.

Pine, B. J., and Gilmore, J. H. (1999), *The Experience Economy: Work is Theatre and Every Business a Stage*, Boston: Harvard Business School Press.

Polhemus, T. (1995), 'Sampling & Mixing', in G. Ceriani and R. Grandi, *Moda: regole e rappresentazioni*, Milan: Angeli.

Ruggerone, L., ed. (2001), *Al di là della moda*, Milan: Angeli.

Ruggerone, L. (2006), 'The Simulated (Fictitious) Body: The Production of Women's Images in Fashion Photography', *Poetics*, 34: 354–69.

Schutz, A. (1962), 'Symbol, Reality and Society', in *Collected Papers, i*, The Hague: Martinus Nijhoff.

Schutz, A. (1964), 'The Problem of Rationality in the Social World', in *Collected Papers, ii*, The Hague: Martinus Nijhoff.

Simmel, G. (1911), 'Die Mode', in *Philosophische Kultur*, Leipzig: Klinkhart.

Skov L. (2005), 'The Return of the Fur Coat: A Commodity Chain Perspective', *Current Sociology*, 53: 1, 9–13.

Veblen, T. (1953), *The Leisure Class*, New York: New American Library.

Volonté, P., ed. (2003a), *La creatività diffusa*, Milan: Angeli.

Volonté, P. (2003b), *Moda e stile: dall'egemonia del ciclo al cross dressing*, in P. Volontè (ed.), *La creatività diffusa*, Milan: Angeli.

Weber, M. (1919), *Wissenschaft als Beruf*, Munchen-Leipzig: Duncker and Humblot.

Wilson, E. (1992), 'Fashion and the Postmodern Body', in E. Wilson and J. Ash (eds), *Chic Thrills. A Fashion Reader*, Berkeley, Los Angeles: University of California Press.

Wilson, E. (2003), *Adorned in Dreams: Fashion and Modernity*, London: Tauris.

6 THE PROLIFERATION OF FASHION AND THE DECLINE OF ITS CODE OF MEANINGS

ALEJANDRO NESTOR GARCÍA MARTÍNEZ

Fashion is a multifaceted phenomenon that can be discussed from various perspectives in that it refers to many aspects and social institutions. It is also connected with the construction and representation of personal identity. It is, in this regard, what Marcel Mauss called 'total social fact': these facts bring into play the totality of society and its institutions because the problems that they present 'are at the same time juridical, economic, religious and even aesthetic and morphologic'. They are a 'whole, complete social system' (Mauss 1979: 258–60). This characterization of fashion as 'total social fact' is especially evident in contemporary societies, where it has spawned a growing amount of study and increasing relevance. The hypothesis that guides these reflections is the following: promotion of the general phenomenon of fashion in contemporary societies must be understood within the general civilizing process. This process brings transformations in terms of structure and human subjectivity and is interrelated with the emergence of the process of individualization in different societies.

As we will see, since the world of fashion is at the same time an economic industry, an aesthetic referent, a way of social self-assertion before others, a way of communication and a vehicle of definition of personal and social identity, it calls for multidimensional reflection. In order to give an account of its increasing importance in contemporary societies—in relation to correlated tendencies connected with the civilizing process—it is first necessary to clarify the multiple significance of the concept of 'fashion' and the most useful perspectives that have been developed for its explanation and understanding.

NOTES ON THE CONCEPT OF FASHION

The concept of *fashion* refers to constancy in invention or in change when making a choice between a variety of options (Squicciarino 1998; Barnard 1996). In Spanish, the word for fashion (*moda*) comes from the Latin word *modus*, which served to mean, in a wide sense, a choice—or regulated system of choices—according to certain criteria, or taste. In English, the etymology of the word *fashion* follows its Latin origin of *factio* and the verb *facere*, so it indicates the attribute of election for action. Besides, in this sense, the concept of fashion is related to that of style: in Spanish, to say that something is 'in fashion' (*está de moda*) is synonymous with saying that something 'is in style' (*se estila*); and similarly, the English noun *fashion* can be considered a synonym of *way* or *manner* (in terms of a way or manner of speaking, which also corresponds to the French expression *façon de parler*). Although 'being in fashion' (*estar de moda*) and 'being in style' (*estilarse*) may coincide in their meanings, it is possible to separate the concepts of *style* and *fashion* precisely because we understand that fashion has a short-lived and temporary character. So, while the concept of *fashion* represents particular options that change without difficulty and that are subject to continuous innovations, the concept of *style* makes reference to a *stable* system of elections. These conditions of duration and stability that characterize the concept of *style* will be useful for us in later reflections.

For the moment, it is useful to indicate another issue in relation to the concept of fashion: its link, insofar as it is an *election*, to human action. What we call fashion is, at the same time, some objects and some conducts referred to these objects. In principle, it seems reasonable to maintain that the important thing is not the object as such, but the conduct referred to the object. What is 'in fashion' is not a specific style of dress or a club or a particular artist or some recurrent words or habitual greetings used in specific contexts; but, on the contrary, to *get dressed* in a particular way, to frequent one place or another, to appreciate an artist and his work and to talk or behave in a certain way. Nevertheless, the divorce between object (an expression, a style of dress, a location, etc.) and conduct is, as we will see, not only possible, but one of the characteristics that has encouraged the proliferation of fashion in contemporary societies, and it has added a notable complexity to its interpretation.

THE LANGUAGE OF FASHION

From the perspective of semiotics, the possibility of noticing in fashion a language through which meaning is expressed has been pointed out. In this way, clothing or a buzzword may have a meaning, even if it does not have a communicative intention. All this is part of those significative non-verbal signs that Erving Goffman calls 'body gloss' (Goffman 1994) and that authors such as Barthes (1971) and Eco have considered part of the object of semiotics. As Eco explains, 'semiotics has to do with whatever may be conceived as a sign. A sign is everything that can be understood as a significative substitute for something' (Eco 1977: 18).

In this way, although limiting the concept of fashion to clothes and corporal trappings, Alison Lurie (1994) offers an interpretation of dressing forms (colours, textiles, etc.) and meanings related to age, sex, occupation and social status. Her work takes on the psychological perspective of the significance of the clothing and corporal ornamentation supported by Flügel (1930). In fact, Lurie goes so far as to affirm that the visual language of clothes holds its own grammar, syntax and vocabulary. It is similar to what Marshall Sahlins (1976) indicates from a structuralist perspective about the colour, tone or texture of clothes: they are useful for expressing distinctions in terms of sex, age, occupation and ethnicity. However, and without going to such extremes, the fertile perspective from semiotics of clothing analysis, shared by Barthes and also by Lévi-Strauss (1964), has recognized, in general, that the codes of inherent meanings related to clothing and personal decoration are ambiguous due to their fluidity and change: the meanings are unstable and depend on various circumstances or even on the body posture that people assume and the way they act. In short, even though fashions 'speak', it is not clear what they say (Davis 1992).

What can be highlighted regarding these semiotic approximations of fashionable phenomena is the crucial fact that the signifier is required to have what we can call 'communicative context' in order to have a meaning. In this communicative context, the emitter and receiver share a code that makes the meaning and its interpretation possible. It is good to remember that all communicative processes occur in a social context in which it is possible to understand and interpret signs. In other words, only thanks to some 'pre-judgements' or 'implicits' shared by emitters and receivers can a common code exist, and it is this that produces the complicity between the emitter and the receiver. In short, for a shared code of understanding in the communicative context, it is necessary for encoding and decodification to correspond sufficiently. Schmidt describes it by saying that 'in systems of communicative presuppositions between A and B, enough integrating common elements must exist if you want a successful communicative action' (Schmidt 1991: 99).

Thus, the social context makes possible a common code and a set of tacit understandings and significances that a social group shares and that provide a more or less unitary world vision. That is what Elias and Bourdieu refer to with the concept of *habitus* (Elias 1982, 1994a; Bourdieu 1990; Bourdieu and Wacquant 1992): some structures of general orientation learned in the social context and which also describe our definition and understanding of reality. Weber also uses this same term to label the set of beliefs and inherited habits that are shared generally by a human group (for example Weber 1969: 423); Simmel, for his part, suggests the idea of a 'veil' from which people consider each other and from which they understand reality (Simmel 1977a: 45); George Herbert Mead (1993) refers to the internalization of socially organized attitudes (*the generalized other*); in a closer sense to communicative action, García Amilburu uses the term 'common sense' (1996: 143), Schmidt refers to the 'communicative presuppositions' (1991: 99), Jauss talks about 'structures of previous understanding' (1987: 79) and Even-Zohar uses the concept of 'pre-knowledge' (1990: 39); and finally, to point out only one more example, Katz and Lazarsfeld (1966: 48ss.) dedicate a great deal of attention to the opinions shared by a social group precisely because the 'shared' condition confers on an opinion its 'social reality'.

In light of all the previous observations, the weakening of that shared code implies a loss of significance: the signifier is reified and becomes autonomous without the possibility of being used for human communication (taken as the understanding by the receiver of the intentional significance of the emitter). In this sense, the weakening of the shared code supposes a vision of fashion like a universe of significant vacuum of meanings. If, on the contrary, the understanding of the significance expressed by the emitter in his conduct of fashion is possible thanks to a common shared code, the issue becomes basically about the functions that these fashionable conducts perform according to the meaning attributed by the social actor and understood as such by others.

It is important at this point to bear in mind that fashionable behaviours take place in a social context, which means an interpretative context. In this regard, we should distinguish between the intentionality of a particular behaviour and the understanding or interpretation that others give to that conduct. In fact, we can consider the social context (within which behaviours take place) as a big stage in which there are meanings, intentions, understandings and interpretations. The interpretation given to a particular behaviour may not correspond to the intended meaning. In any case, the interpretation (fitted to the intended meaning or not) has real effects because we are immersed in a social context that is a communicative context. Although we cannot affirm that any behaviour (a way of dress, for example) has 'a' meaning, it is possible to say that it 'is meaningful' because others are interpreting and understanding that behaviour in some way. Therefore, if I wear all black, for example, people might not understand my intention of playing (I can do it just for fun), but they are still interpreting my conduct according to some common (or not so common) system of values or meanings given to that colour; and then they behave according to that interpretation of my behaviour.

In accordance with the foregoing, a weakening of the shared code of meanings in favour of a progressive reification of fashionable objects would obscure for others the meaning intended by the social actor in his conduct. This direction makes sense in terms of the general process of emergence of individuality that characterizes the civilizing process and that gives an account of the relevance and profusion of fashion in contemporary societies.

FASHION AS A SIGNIFYING UNIVERSE

At first, the conducts of the members of a social group are directly linked to their conditions of existence. The precarious ornamentation that can be noticed in our historic forefathers obeyed basically a magic function in the activities of hunting. Only when certain abundance and security were guaranteed did ornamentation with a more purely aesthetic sense appear. At a later time, as indicated by Squicciarino (1998: 153ss.), Curtius and Hund (1971) have shown that certain conducts of ornamentation had another social function: to distinguish various levels of status or social attributes, such as commitment and authority. However, because it was a *stable* system of symbols, it cannot be considered properly as fashion.

Fashionable conducts like those described (that is, with their character of short-lived new behaviours relating to a scope of conduct) can be found without difficulty in societies with notable division and social stratification. At that point, the performance of fashionable practices is used to identify a social actor with a social group that is differentiated from the rest and with whose members the individual shares that exclusive conduct. The short-lived character of the conduct arises from the possibility of other groups imitating the conduct in order to become equal to the differentiated group; once the conduct has been extended, it no longer distinguishes between groups, and, in consequence, it has to be renewed or replaced with a new one.

The previous proposal is in the foundation of various authors who have studied the distinction and social assimilation functions of fashionable conducts. This is the case, for example, of Spencer, Veblen, Simmel, Elias and Bourdieu. For Herbert Spencer, fashion is understood to be a strategy of the lower social classes to aspire to social equalization; these classes imitate the behaviour and fashionable conducts of the upper classes (Spencer 1947). Veblen's (1953) idea on the vertical diffusion of fashion according to criteria of distinction and social assimilation is continued by Simmel and Norbert Elias. In Simmel's arguments, this idea is integrated in his well-known ambivalent characterization of the human being as being-for-himself (*für sich sein*) and as being-for-the-society. With this characterization, the functions of fashionable conducts are three and are intimately related: that of distinction or social assimilation; the definition of personal individuality; and the satisfaction of aesthetic expression.

Concerning the first function, it is useful to point out that the opposite of intentionality of differentiation is, in Simmel's words, assimilation, which also could be called 'identification with the group': it is, above all, a mode of identification with members of a given group and, as a consequence, of distinction from others, and it responds to a psychological need for group linkage and personal self-assertion. The second important function of the conduct of fashion is that it contributes to the construction of personal identity and individuality: the psychological needs suggested by Simmel correspond to the being-for-himself of the human being, with his/her individuality. However, for Simmel, the two terms of ambivalence can never be considered separately. That is why he affirms almost simultaneously that fashion is a badly conceived plan of social needs or, better, of 'purely formal psychological needs': the individual cannot be-for-himself without being-for-the-society (Simmel 1986).

Finally, the latter feature of fashionable conducts indicated by Simmel is the indifference in relation to its contents, its detachment from reality in accordance with a certain aesthetic consideration. This seems coherent with the fact that objects and distinctive behaviours have to do with nonessential realities for survival: in our most basic needs, we all act in a similar way and make use of similar strategies. But insofar as the means of satisfying a need become more interchangeable and admit more heterogeneous solutions, a deeper differentiation of conduct is possible. That is why, at the top, the conducts most susceptible to differentiation or personal expression are those that have less relation with some basic aspect of survival or reality. This idea is, in coherence with Curtius and Hund's (1971) or Thiel's (1991) arguments on the need for social differentiation and a consequent differentiation of conducts, for fashionable phenomena to appear.

Norbert Elias discusses the interrelated ideas of distinction/assimilation and also the idea of definition of personal identity in his civilizing theory and his study on court society (Elias 1993a,b), although the aesthetic consideration of fashionable conducts is highlighted much less. According to these ideas, fashionable conducts (in one's way of dressing, behaving at table, talking, etc.) are adopted by the upper classes to distinguish themselves from the lower ones and to define their own social status. Since the lower classes want to become equal to the upper classes in order to realize their prerogatives and 'power opportunities', the fashionable conducts are gradually spread throughout all classes. The propelling force of this process, as mentioned, is the equalization of living conditions that implies increasing human interdependences and the division of functions; all these tendencies require and foment increasing reserve in the individual and a stricter regulation of his behaviour and his emotions. Nevertheless, according to Elias, a purely rectilinear and vertical tendency in this process of diffusion of fashionable conducts does not exist. He distinguishes between two phases in this process: a first phase of colonization or assimilation, and a second of rejection.

The first phase (diffusion and assimilation of fashionable conducts) is originated in a socially reduced circle, where the lower classes are dependent on the upper ones. These upper classes manage to impose, whether consciously or unconsciously, their behaviour, in part as a means of distinction and maintenance of their social status against the aspirations of the new groups, which are on the increase. Therefore, in this phase of assimilation, a progressive equalization takes place from the top down, but the influence and dominance of the upper classes are maintained. In the second phase, the phase of rejection, as the social position or status of the new groups has become strengthened, and after a progressive equalization and weakening of contrasts, a class consciousness is consolidated between the new groups that tends to show and preserve their differential character contrasted with the models of the previous upper classes, now weakened in their status and influence (Elias 1993a: 514ff.). This also means that ways of behaving are not only transferred from above downwards; rather, with the change in the social centre of gravity, the conducts are transferred from the bottom up and horizontally. This can be noticed, for example, in the rise of the bourgeoisie, where the code of aristocratic behaviour lost much of its rigidity and the forms of contact and social cohabitation became more flexible, and even vulgarized.

We can find similar ideas and arguments in the work of Pierre Bourdieu: he has indicated in his well-known work on social distinction (Bourdieu 1991) that the definitions made by the members of a social group in their conducts and choices are useful for distinguishing themselves, as well as for identifying themselves with the social group. According to Bourdieu, certain groups are in a better position to impose upon others a definition of 'proper' conduct, of what is 'culture' or even 'beauty'. They are the 'established' groups indicated by Elias (1994b), who can impose their definitions and preference upon the 'outsiders'.

There are two relevant aspects of these symbolic impositions of some groups upon others: on the one hand, they can impose the meaning of various signifiers (to wear one suit or another means something, or to frequent particular places means something); and, on the other hand, they have to do with a form of domination that often goes unnoticed by the dominated because it is symbolic domination. Thus, in fact, if the dominant group manages to impose a definition of 'quality literature' and a 'cultured person', then those who want to be regarded as such have to accommodate themselves, sometimes unknowingly, to a definition that comes, in a manner of speaking, as an inheritance. They have not contributed to defining it, but it is in fact transmitted within that general system of orientations referred to earlier as *habitus*. Thus, for example, Hintzenberg, Schmidt and Zobel (1981) have suggested that the concept of 'literature' depends on instances of socialization, and Casas affirms that the person observes 'certain rules that individuals learn socially and that authorize the approval of what is aesthetic or what is literary' (Casas 1994: 256).

It is interesting, in order to support the function of social distinction and symbolic domination of certain social groups, to focus on the change in the legitimacy of social distinction when the conducts of several social groups become progressively equal: the legitimizing of social distinction in these cases is no longer based on particular conducts, more and more rapidly imitated by other groups. On the contrary, the legitimizing is then based on style, on dignity, a sort of interior quality that distinguishes between the 'truly civilized' and the imitators or newcomers. With this, a division in uses of *fashion* is established, as an apparent conduct and concrete choice founded on taste is set apart from the more or less *stable* style or interior quality that sustains those conducts and preferences. Put in another way, fashion, as a way of symbolic domination, has also been presented as the manifestation of a style, of some interior quality that differentiates one person from others.

This argument conforms to the concept of stratification which has predominated in human history, in which those with virtues (of several sorts: martial, philosophical, of command, etc.) are differentiated from the rest, and those that lack them constitute the majority. This habitually implied a social differentiation also supported by social status accompanied by particular rights and privileges. In this way, the upper classes or leading elites, in general, managed to assume some qualities that served to distinguish themselves from the rest of their fellow citizens. When these supposedly superior qualities were questioned, their legitimacy (and the resulting inequality or social differentiation) had to be maintained in other ways, lest the social order should collapse, as Tocqueville pointed out in his analysis on the collapse of the Ancien Régime in France (Tocqueville 1982).

In short, there exists a long chain of reflections that link the phenomenon of fashion and the attributed significance of fashionable conducts to three fundamental functions: the identification with the group or the separation from others, the definition of personal position and identity according to that significance and the expression of some aesthetic preferences. Of course, fashionable conducts, because they maintain a shared significance which is accepted by the members of a group, can be considered from the perspective of other social and individual functions. Thus, for example, König has understood the tendency to decorate oneself, the attraction of the new or even human fancy, as the foundation of the conducts of ornamentation (König 1969). Also, from a perspective of sexuality, Elster maintains that fashion is determined by the erotic relation between man and woman and has its foundation in the human need for erotic variation (Elster 1925). Finally, many authors have drawn attention to the economic function of fashion and its particular importance in a consumer society for the maintenance of the system (Rivière 1992).

With the previous definition of the concept of fashion and some of its functions, we can now try to answer the question that has given rise to these reflections: Why do fashionable phenomena have such prominence and relevance in contemporary societies?

FASHION AS AN EMERGING PHENOMENON OF THE CIVILIZING PROCESS

We have pointed out that fashionable conducts are more apparent in differentiated societies. Using the Durkheimian distinction between differentiated and non-differentiated societies (Durkheim 1986), it is clear that in non-differentiated societies, individuality and the need for distinction were reduced due to the homogeneity and similarity of their members. This process of social differentiation is at the foundation of the increasing prominence of fashion in contemporary societies and, also, of the changes or overlaps that are noticeable in its manifestations and functions. All this can be included, generally speaking, in what we call 'the civilizing process'.

Norbert Elias has dedicated a great part of his work to understanding the civilizing process (Elias 1993a). His basic thesis is that there are changes in the structures of the personality (*habitus*) of the members of a community in the direction of greater self-restraint of impulses; this thesis corresponds with various ideas and arguments present in a long tradition of sociological thought. In fact, the link that Elias establishes between these changes in the *habitus* and transformations in social structures or *figurations* can be related to Simmel's, Durkheim's and Mead's theses on the 'emergence of individuality' that happens within the process of social differentiation. The lengthening chains of interdependence (Elias), social differentiation (Simmel) and the *division du travail* (Durkheim) are multifaceted processes in which individuality emerges (Mead) in relation to an increasingly dense framework of human relations. The individual progressively *becomes distant* in the course of these processes in relation to his conduct: the immediacy between *stimulus* and consequent conduct is deferred or delayed. Individuality appears in that mediation.

The problem the individual must confront in this context of progressive social differentiation (and, in consequence, of progressive individualization) has been categorized in several ways that lead to the same idea: the overload of individual consciousness. Durkheim is drawn to this idea with his concept of *anomie*, according to which the regulation and integration of non-differentiated societies (which have a strong collective consciousness) have turned into a pathology that regulation and integration are insufficient to prevent. This is so, in Durkheim's opinion, because *adequate* regulation no longer depends on a common, shared moral standard, but rather on the norms that emanate from the *integration of functions*. In other words, in Durkheimian thought, the dissolution of the collective type and the weakening of social links based on similarity, which are correlative to the necessary implantation of the division of labour because of material and moral density, constitute only one aspect of that general process of civilization in which a differentiated and definable subjectivity emerges. This differentiated subjectivity is linked to other ones because of the differentiation and interdependence that the division of labour implies. Thus, the individual person, because of the weakening of common morality, is forced to elucidate his conduct by himself. The individual lacks sufficient regulation of his own behaviour; that insufficient regulation implies an overload of individual consciousness; this overload makes the implementation of creative solutions and choices necessary in several situations of action.

Similarly, in his findings, Simmel considers that life in modern societies is 'highly stimulative' (Simmel 1986), which also means an overload of individual consciousness. The reaction of those who live in a large city is, then, of 'indolence': he suggests that modern cities generate conditions which predispose individuals to be reserved in their relationships with others. The size of cities and the increasing number of people who live in cities make people protect themselves against this 'intensification of nervous stimulation'. To do so, individuals engage in a process of *intellectualization*. Individuals use their 'head rather than their heart' in their interactions with others. To explain this, Simmel points to the contradictory aspect of city life: a *physical* proximity to hundreds of other individuals yet a *social* distance from those same individuals. The city forces us to repress our emotional involvement with others and instead to use more logical and formal criteria in our interactions with them. Intellectuality is thus seen to preserve subjective life against the overwhelming power of metropolitan life, which would otherwise overload individual consciousness.

A last example on this issue is Norbert Elias. This sociologist points out the issue of the 'informalization' of conducts, though he develops it insufficiently: this 'informalization' is connected with the idea of the overload of individual consciousness confronted with the need to determine the course of action in a specific situation. As Elias affirms: 'Informalization brings with it stronger demands on apparatuses of self constraint, and, at the same time, frequent experimentation and structural insecurity. One cannot really follow existing models; one has to work out for oneself a dating strategy as well as a strategy for living together through a variety of ongoing experiments' (Elias 1997: 37). In short, all these ideas point to what has been called the 'process of deinstitutionalization' of action in the phenomenological theory of action (Luckmann 1996): since individual conscience is limited, social institutions are those habitual solutions, learned in society, that can be used to solve problems without the need for conscious effort. When deinstitutionalization of action is observed in a field of conduct, consciousness becomes overloaded, and a conscious effort is necessary to choose the course of action that could solve the situation.

This overload of consciousness, therefore, is a consequence of the general human civilizing process in the direction of a progressive separation between the stimulus and the conduct in response to it, and it is connected with the processes of informalization (Elias) and the weakening of social institutions (Luckmann) or, in Durkheim's words, the collective conscience that is present in differentiated societies. There are two consequences of this general process followed by contemporary societies, in the direction of progressive social differentiation, of an increasing emergence of individuality and, as a culmination, of the appearance of processes of informalization and weakening of the collective conscience. In the first place, there is a weakening, in parallel, of that 'communicative context', of that shared code that made the intentional significance of a conduct of fashion possible and understood as such; and, secondly, is the appearance of conducts that are not institutionalized but that have a highly distorted significance, that are ephemeral and constantly changing.

All this makes sense in terms of the personality of members of Simmel's differentiated society, who hold an enthusiasm for adventure. This venturesome spirit of contemporary personalities who live in differentiated societies is due to the 'choky sentiment of tension and disorientated nostalgia' (Simmel 1977b: 611) that life in the metropolis provokes in human subjectivity. This leads people to look for new experiences to suffocate that unrest and dissatisfaction of the spirit. In Simmel's words, 'the absence of something definitive in the centre of life leads people to look for a momentary satisfaction in excitations sensations and brand-new activities' (Simmel 1977b: 612). This quest for novelty that characterizes the citizen's venturesome spirit is started by the social structure in which it is developed.

The weakening of the shared code of significances (or, as it is also called, the de-institutionalization or informalization of action) and the quest for novelty are, as we have noted, processes which emerge within the general civilizing process. New postmodern interpretations of fashionable phenomena can be placed in this context. Thus, the weakening of the shared code which allows fashionable conducts to 'talk' and communicate preferences (preferences through which a person defines himself within a social group) also weakens some of the social functions habitually indicated in reflections on fashion. This has also meant a sharp break between the 'object of fashion' and the 'conduct of fashion' (which we distinguished at the beginning of this chapter): fashion no longer involves 'getting dressed' in a specific way and the meanings associated with it, but rather that a simple object (an article of clothing, for example) has become reified and can take on multiple meanings. In this context, efforts to consolidate a symbolic domination by defining specific meanings to several objects are increased with renewed force; of course, the definition of identity is not the only interest in this symbolic domination: commercial and economic purposes also play their part. The virulence of this fight for symbolic definition is possible because an emptying of the significance of fashionable objects has occurred, and they have been disassociated from the conducts that were giving them their meaning.

Baudrillard's affirmation that fashion is arbitrary, transient, cyclical and unrelated to the intrinsic qualities of the individual (Baudrillard 1998: 100) relates to all these concepts. In his diagnosis of consumer societies where fashion phenomena take place, there is room only for appearance, extroversion without content and the blurring of personal identity (Baudrillard 1990). Thus, Baudrillard considers that the complete emptying of significance, capable of constituting an object as a pure object of fashion, takes place when such an object has been reduced to a pure consumer good. This is what makes it possible to distinguish an engagement ring from a simple ring. The first, as long as it retains a precise symbolic connotation, cannot be considered an object of fashion. The second could be considered as such. In this sense, an object is in fashion because it has become an object of pure consumption—meaningless. Based on this argument, and operating on structuralist presuppositions, the world of culture is considered a semiotic system in which each cultural product, once reduced to a pure consumer good, has at the same time been reduced to the condition of a meaningless sign. Therefore, the significant force of these meaningless signs consists of referring to the remaining signs of the system.

However, although the weakening of the common code of significances that has resulted from the process of civilization, and the social differentiation and emergence of individuality, may be carried to extremes as illustrated by Baudrillard, it seems reasonable to consider that the weakening of fashion phenomena is only that—a weakening and not an absolute dissolution of the shared code and symbolic communication. If so, it is possible to propose a different diagnosis (different from Baudrillard's), like that proposed by Lipovetsky. He sees in all these processes a liberation of individuality and a triumph of a completely differentiated identity (Lipovetsky 1993). For him, fashion, though never without ambiguities, constitutes one of the most interesting aspects of pleasure-loving contemporary culture. Thus, according to his judgement, this has to do with the revitalization of the care of the 'I' and becomes the moral and aesthetic concern with self-realization; so fashion constitutes in general something like a catalyst of the modern process of individualization and merits a globally positive assessment. On the other hand, consideration of the weakening of the shared code instead of its complete dissolution also gives rise to other interpretations and analyses of the phenomenon of fashion, such as those of Bell and Giddens, who propose an understanding of this phenomenon as a way of expression or construction of personal identity (Giddens 1995; Bell 1987).

Moreover, this interpretation of the partial, never complete weakening of the shared code in the process of informalization (or deinstitutionalization) remains in use along with the other social functions of fashion that were previously mentioned in this work.

CONCLUSION

To understand why the phenomenon of fashion has become so evident nowadays, we should consider its connections with the general civilizing process. This process implies structural transformations and changes in individual personality. Therefore, besides progressive social differentiation, the lengthening chains of interdependence, the division of labour and the development of the monetary economy, it is possible to detect parallel changes in the *habitus* of people in the direction of greater detachment, greater intellectualization of life and a progressive reserve of subjectivity that results in an interest in novelty and adventure. Simultaneously, all these processes are correlated to what many sociologists have called 'the process of emergence of individuality'. All these social changes and transformations of subjectivity, which take place in the civilizing process and in the process of emergence of individuality, also imply a tendency towards the informalization or deinstitutionalization of conducts—that is, at heart, a weakening of the common code or the collective conscience of members of society.

Reflections on the phenomenon of fashion should be placed in the context of this process. Since it is a context where structural changes and transformations of subjectivity can be observed simultaneously, it is necessary to undertake the study of fashion from both a micro-sociological and a macro-sociological perspective. The persistence of significance in common codes of communication might, in fact, be at risk. Should these common meanings disappear, the significance of fashion would get relegated, like some have suggested, to a mere game of appearances and a struggle for symbolic domination, or a mere game for the economic profit of consumer societies.

References and Further Reading

Barnard, Malcolm (1996), *Fashion as Communication,* London/New York: Routledge.

Barthes, Roland (1971), *Elementos de semiología,* Madrid: Corazón.

Baudrillard, Jean (1990), *La transparencia del mal,* Madrid: Anagrama.

Baudrillard, Jean (1998), *The Consumer Society,* London: Sage Publications.

Baudrillard, Jean (1999), *El sistema de los objetos,* Madrid: Siglo XXI Editores.

Bell, Daniel (1987), *Las contradicciones culturales del capitalismo,* Madrid: Alianza.

Bourdieu, Pierre (1990), *El sentido práctico,* Madrid: Taurus.

Bourdieu, Pierre (1991), *La distinción,* Madrid: Taurus.

Bourdieu, Pierre (1993), *The Field of Cultural Production,* Cambridge: Polity Press.

Bourdieu, Pierre, and Wacquant, L.J.D. (1992), *Réponses. Pour une anthropologie reflexive,* Paris: Éditions du Seuil.

Casas, Arturo (1994), 'Pragmática y poesía', in Darío Villanueva, *Avances en Teoría de la Literatura,* 229–308, Santiago de Compostela: Universidad de Santiago de Compostela.

Curtius, M., and Hund, W. D. (1971), *Mode und Gesselschaft,* Frankfurt: Europäise Verlagsanstalt.

Davis, Fred (1992), *Fashion, Culture and Identity,* Chicago: Chicago University Press.

Durkheim, Emile (1986), *De la division du travail social,* Paris: Presses Universitaires de France.

Eco, Umberto (1977), *Tratado de semiótica general,* Barcelona: Lumen.

Elias, Norbert (1982), *Sociología fundamental,* Barcelona: Gedisa.

Elias, Norbert (1990), *La sociedad de los individuos,* Barcelona: Península ideas.

Elias, Norbert (1993a), *El proceso de la civilización. Investigaciones sociogenéticas y psicogenéticas,* México: Fondo de Cultura Económica.

Elias, Norbert (1993b), *La sociedad cortesana,* México: Fondo de Cultura Económica.

Elias, Norbert (1994a), *Teoría del símbolo. Un ensayo de antropología cultural,* Barcelona: Península.

Elias, Norbert (1994b), *The Established and the Outsiders,* London: Sage Publications.

Elias, Norbert (1997), *The Germans,* Cambridge: Polity Press.

Elster, Alexander (1925), 'Mode', *Handwörterbuch der Staatswissenschaften,* 4 (Jena): 603–14.

Even-Zohar, Itamar (1990), 'Polysystem Studies', *Poetics Today,* 11.

Flügel, John Carl (1930), *The Psychology of Clothes,* London: Hogarth.

García Amilburu, María (1996), *Aprendiendo a ser humanos. Una Antropología de la Educación,* Pamplona: Eunsa.

Giddens, Anthony (1995), *Modernidad e identidad del yo,* Barcelona: Península.

Goffman, Erving (1994), *La presentación de la persona en la vida cotidiana,* Buenos Aires: Amorrortu.

Hintzenberg, D., Schmidt, S. J., and Zobel, R. (1981), *Der Literaturbegriff in der Bundesrepublik Deutschland,* Braunschweig-Wiesbaden: Vieweg.

Jauss, Hans-Robert (1987), 'El lector como instancia de una nueva historia de la literatura', in J. Mayoral (ed.), *Estética de la recepción,* 59–85, Madrid: Visor.

Katz, Elihu, and Lazarsfeld, Paul F. (1966), *Personal Influence: The Part Played by People in the Flow of Mass Communications,* New York, London: Free Press.

König, René (1969), *Sociologie de la mode,* Paris: Payor.

Lévi-Strauss, Claude (1964), *El pensamiento salvaje,* México: Fondo de Cultura Económica.

Lipovetsky, Pilles (1993), *El imperio de lo efímero. La moda y su destino en las sociedades modernas,* Barcelona: Anagrama.

Luckmann, Thomas (1996), *Teoría de la acción social,* Barcelona: Paidós.

Lurie, Alison (1994), *El lenguaje de la moda: una interpretación de las formas de vestir,* Barcelona: Paidós.

Mauss, Marcel (1979), *Sociología y antropología,* Madrid: Editorial Tecnos.

Mead, G. H. (1993), *Espíritu, persona y sociedad: desde el punto de vista del conductismo social,* Buenos Aires: Paidós.

Rivière, M. (1992), *Lo cursi y el poder de la moda,* Madrid: Espasa.

Sahlins, Marshall (1976), *Culture and Practical Reason,* Chicago: University of Chicago Press.

Schmidt, Siegfried J. (1991), *Fundamentos de la ciencia empírica de la literature,* Madrid: Taurus.

Simmel, Georg (1977a), *Sociología. Estudio sobre las formas de socialización,* Madrid: Revista de Occidente.

Simmel, Georg (1977b), *Filosofía del dinero,* Madrid: Revista de Occidente.

Simmel, Georg (1986), *El individuo y la libertad. Ensayos de crítica de la cultura,* Barcelona: Península.

Simmel, Georg (2002), *Cuestiones Fundamentales de Sociología,* Barcelona: Gedisa.

Spencer, Herbert (1947), *Principios de Sociología,* Buenos Aires: Revista de Occidente.

Squicciarino, Nicola (1998), *El vestido habla: consideraciones psicosociológicas sobre la Indumentaria,* Madrid: Cátedra.

Thiel, Esnard (1991), *El lenguaje del cuerpo revela más que las palabras,* Barcelona: Elfos.

Tocqueville, Alexis de (1982), *El Antiguo Régimen y la Revolución,* Madrid: Alianza Editorial.

Veblen, Thorstein. (1953), *The Theory of the Leisure Class: An Economic Study of Institutions,* New York: New American Library.

Weber, Max (1969), *Economía y sociedad,* México: Fondo de Cultura Económica.

7 HOW SUCCESSFUL IS COMMUNICATION VIA CLOTHING? THOUGHTS AND EVIDENCE ON AN UNEXAMINED PARADIGM

EFRAT TSEËLON

This chapter analyses the issue of sartorial communication by drawing on the disparity between the diversity of looks and meanings in ordinary people's wardrobes and the homogeneity of dressing meanings that have been observed in scholarship on fashion communication but that also pervade popular culture notions of fashion as a language-like code with clear, transparent and shared meanings. The notion of the homogeneity of the cultural meanings of objects that is reported in much of fashion research and that is ubiquitous in popular representations of fashion advice programs and columns, I argue, is a research artefact which results from a disproportionate focus on occasion wear instead of wardrobe research, communication of visual information (e.g. style) and structural information (e.g. occupation, lifestyle) to the detriment of experiential aspects of meaning conveyed by clothes which my own research found as just as important, if not more. As a result, experimental findings and theoretical elaborations have been engaging in reifying 'the stereotype approach' based mostly on paper-and-pen methodology. As an alternative, I provide a paradigmatic logical and empirical test of the 'linguistic code' thesis by comparing intentions with interpretations of 'real people' in interaction. This type of research addresses the question of the accuracy and reliability of clothing communication by avoiding the fallacy of stereotype elicitation that cognitive social perception desk research has generated.

> Is clothing meaning clear cut and straightforward or is it variable and contingent (language like)?

In order to examine this question, the chapter is divided into two parts. The first part analyses the assumptions underlying the existing paradigm for the study of communication through clothing. The second part offers a critique of the current paradigm and provides a theoretical and empirical alternative paradigm.

THE CURRENT PARADIGM FOR STUDYING AND UNDERSTANDING SARTORIAL COMMUNICATION

I want to start this chapter by referencing two examples from contemporary culture that happened in April 2010. The first was an exhibition and an accompanying book (Clark and Phillips 2010), *The Concise Dictionary of Dress,* at the storehouse of reserve collections (including costumes) of the Victoria & Albert museum (see http://www.vam.ac.uk/collections/contemporary/artangel/index.html).

It examines the nature of dictionaries, archives and dress curatorship through a display of eleven interventions, each made of a pairing of definitions and installations. The definitions—by the psychoanalyst Adam Phillips—commonly associated with attributes of clothing are of an unconventional, sometimes intriguing kind: they remind us of the store of meaning hidden in the folds even of habitual clichés. Each definition was paired with an artistic installation, utilizing the storehouse space and architecture as well as existing exhibits in the archive. The installations were produced by the curator Judith Clark. For example, the definition of Conformist consists of

1. A state of essential simplification; safe in numbers;
2. Recipient of an unnoticed demand, complicit; choosing not to choose; compliant, and therefore enraged; unwitting double agent;
3. Blended into a selected background;
4. Committed to difference, and by it; horrified by the idiosyncrasy of desire; uniformly agreeable;
5. Accurate, diligent; wired for surprise; mourning variety;
6. Consensus as spell; idealist. (Clark and Phillips 2010)

It is paired with a William Morris ornamental wallpaper design in pale coordinated colours produced on a fabric dress. Positioned against each other, the mannequined body draped in the patterned dress next to the wallpaper of the same design, the identity between the wall and the wearer almost lends meaning to the expression 'fading into the background' while also recalling a wallflower. Plain—which is defined as (1) Nothing special where nothing special intended; (2) Hiding to make room—is materialized by a series of covered dresses each wrapped differently in the white material used by conservators to preserve textile goods, poised as if waiting to be unveiled, each a potential source of attributed meanings which until and unless the dresses are unveiled are a property of the viewer, not the objects. Tight is displayed in a dark, narrow, constricted larder, with viewers having to squeeze in one at a time and observe through a narrow gap a burgundy Victorian jacket with nothing but a projected erotic photograph of a naked woman bent over backwards for a skirt. Here, the meanings of the viewing conditions as well as the garments correspond, while the erotic image speaks of cultural conventions and expectations, or of hidden desires. Measured is defined as: (1) Against chaos; a way of thinking about disarray; calculated excess; (2) The fitted as fitting; (3) Proportion as the mother of virtue; (4) The milder ecstasies of the considered; (5) Contained by the idea of containment. It is illustrated with an early-nineteenth-century kid glove embroidered with little hunchback figures and musicians and is stored in a hidden cabinet that used to house a water tank. Here, the form provides both elegance and constriction as suggested by the ornamental hunchbacks, the social convention of wearing gloves and the constrained and hidden space. Desire and vitality are hinted by the cabinet's former use to contain water.

The second example refers to a popular culture phenomenon.

A news article in the *Times* reported that an eighteen-year-old youth 'faced an antisocial behaviour order (ASBO) which included a ban on "wearing trousers so low beneath the waistline that members of the public are able to see his underwear"'. It also prohibited him from wearing any clothing 'with the hood up' in public. However, the bans were withdrawn after a discussion before a hearing at Bedford Magistrates' Court on April 27, in which District Judge Nicholas Leigh-Smith said: 'Some of the requirements proposed struck me as contrary to the Human Rights Act.'

But the *Times* headed this news as 'Judge rules Asbo on low-slung trousers illegal' (see http://business.timesonline.co.uk/tol/business/law/article7116303.ece). Other articles referred more explicitly to the attribution to wearers of such fashion (using the term *yobs*). The *Daily Mail* said 'Yob wins right to wear trousers that show his underpants after judge said Asbo ruling would "breach human rights"' (see http://www.dailymail.co.uk/news/article-1271851/Judge-says-Asbo-ruling-low-slung-trousers-breach-human-rights.html), while the *Daily Telegraph* insinuated that such criminal behaviour requires other forms of punishment: 'What boys with sagging trousers need is a good belt' (at http://www.telegraph.co.uk/

comment/columnists/bryonygordon/7683057/What-boys-with-sagging-trousers-
need-is-a-good-belt.html).

Whether or not 'fashion policing' is a useful or desirable act of social control, the
judge was referring to a series of transpositions of meaning with the certainty com-
manded by well-established stereotypes. The trend apparently originates in the US
prison system, where the practice of taking away prisoners' belts to prevent them
from hanging themselves forces them to walk around with sagging trousers. From
there, it was borrowed as a trend by US rappers and then travelled overseas to their
fans and other disaffected or fashion-conscious youth.

Jumping to conclusions about character and behaviour, however, seems to be
quite a leap. And yet it shows the depth of credibility that sartorial stereotypes
hold. Sartorial stereotypes are not necessarily class or gender related, as is sometimes
claimed. In May 2010, the public was notified that 'a fashion faux pas by Yukio
Hatoyama, the embattled Japanese prime minister, has caused his popularity to dive
further in the polls.' The offensive item turned out to be a colourful a 1980s-style
checked shirt designed in large blocks of red, blue, yellow, green and purple. A fashion designer, Don Konishi, criticized the ill-advised sartorial choice as being indicative of more serious shortcomings, saying, 'This shirt comes from the '80s or '90s.
His ideas and philosophy are old. Japan is facing a crisis and we can't overcome it
with a prime minister like this' (http://www.telegraph.co.uk/news/worldnews/asia/
japan/7719194/Fashion-faux-pas-costs-Japanese-PM-popularity-slump.html).

Clothing research and sartorial reality produce quite different pictures. Clothing
research and costume history have traditionally concentrated on the unanimous and
the convergent, on 'pockets of homogeneity' with regards to clothing rules and their
meanings. In contrast, the reality of wearing clothes appears far more fragmented,
random, fluid and idiosyncratic, where rules are not the biggest players, where no
clear code is followed by all, where divergent frames of reference can be brought to
bear upon the same clothing signals. This split between the rather 'over-organized'
and the rather 'under-organized' pictures inspired the work reported in this chapter.

The idea that clothes communicate is bound up with another idea: that they
draw on a shared pool of meanings applicable to clothes. It also presupposes that the
meanings—even if shared—are unambiguous, or if ambiguous that there are agreed
ways, say in the manner of rules of dressing, that instruct us how to interpret one's
appearance. Yet even a cursory examination of the dynamics of clothing signification
reveals a contradictory cultural attitude. On the one hand, there is an underlying
implicit assumption about unity of meaning, the meaning of certain looks. Whether
we examine fashion media or general media, we note that fashion meanings are represented as rigid, self-evident and rather stereotypical. There is also a related implicit
assumption about the 'right' measure of doing something (for example, the meaning

of over- and under-engagement in appearance work—e.g. being either 'fashion victim' or 'frumpy' are equally disapproved of), and about 'right' and 'wrong' ways of presenting oneself. Such assumption explains the popularity of fashion makeover programs, or newspapers and magazines' fashion advice columns framed within a rather judgemental discourse where self-styled fashion experts or fashion gurus analyse ordinary people's bodies and wardrobes and advise them on how best to display their assets and downplay their shortcomings.

In contrast to this tendency for operating as if there is a shared consensus about meanings and manners, an opposite academic discourse operates with an implicit assumption of diversity of meaning, which regards sartorial meaning as contextual, complex and contingent and negotiated within a context. In sum, there is a split between 'meaning as negotiated' research practice and 'meaning as fixed' everyday practice. In the popular discourse (e.g. media fashion talk), stereotypes are alive and well, even as they are becoming politically incorrect in theory. In scholarly discourse, theorists go out of their way to argue that an article of appearance cannot in and of itself convey predicted meaning and that far from being rigidly defined, clothing carries ambivalent meaning which is interpreted in a context.

Rather paradoxically, as the following examples illustrate, when popular discourse tries to appear open it still ends up being prescriptive, and when it tries to capitalize on a rigid system, it doesn't quite measure up.

The first example comes from Trinny and Susannah's *What Not to Wear for Every Occasion* (Constantine and Woodall 2003), which accompanies the successful BBC makeover series *What Not to Wear*. At one and the same time it aims at liberating women from conventional notions of how to dress nondescriptly for particular occasions as well as inscribing them in a whole set of new rules called 'be yourself'. And the tone is just as prescriptive when they warn that learning how to 'hide the body's faults' can be 'utterly obliterated if you are dressing inappropriately for the occasion'. They go on to undermine the reader's confidence by warning her that 'sad though it is, there is no getting away from the fact that, these days, we are still judged by the way we look' and 'remind' her that 'nearly all women understand the horror of realising that you are wearing the wrong clothes'. They make it sound like dressing 'with an individual flair' is just another fashion trend. But there is help at hand from the two self-styled experts who aim at 'guiding the misguided'. Ironically, they claim to offer advice that would 'train those bound by what the neighbours say to break free from stereotypes. It will urge those who are lacking in confidence to go the extra mile in order to gain that much needed self-belief'. However, they also reassure at the same time that it 'will enable girls to make dressing decision on their own, without the help of competitive peers'—save for the dictates of the expert duo, though.

The other example comes from an article, published in the *New York Times*, which reported an account of a guessing game by a group of experts trying to place New Yorkers socially, personally and geographically by their appearance. The expert panel was quite senior and included Jane Rinzler Buckingham, president of Youth Intelligence, a trend-spotting firm; Ginny Hilfiger, a senior vice president of Tommy Hilfiger; Kal Ruttenstein, a senior vice president of Bloomingdale's; Valerie Steele, chief curator at the Fashion Institute of Technology; Cathy Horyn, a fashion reporter for the *New York Times*; and the designer Bill Blass. Their task consisted of reading biographical clues from one photo of various characters. Their guesses were then compared with the actual biographical details and found badly wanting: an interesting picture of stereotypes with more misses than hits, and with a few rather safe bets, such as reading upmarket location from the possession of a branded or pricey item (Ellin and Pener 1999).

How can meaning be perceived as so fixed and yet be so fluid?

The unexamined assumption underlying research on the meaning of clothes holds that they constitute a transparent language. Whether they are likened to a dictionary where the sign unproblematically signifies a specific meaning of a particular object, or whether they are likened to a grammar of combining certain units which gain meaning by contrast with other arrangements or whether they are thought to signify in a more gestalt fashion—clothes are assumed to convey meaning which is shared by local or global communities. We can look at the work of Kress and Van Leeuwen (2006) for a comparison with another visual field: they elaborate a method of visual grammar which refers to contemporary Western visual design and provide an account of the elements and rules underlying this form of visual communication. They do acknowledge, however, that the grammar of visual language is culturally specific and not transparent or universally understood, and they also mention the possibility of social or regional variations deriving from a long history of cultural connection and interchange as well as from the global power of cultural industries and the media.

Barry Brummett (2008), in *A Rhetoric of Style*, illustrates how style is increasingly a global system of communication as people around the world understand what it means to dress a certain way, to dance a certain way, to decorate a certain way, to speak a certain way.

How the encounter with global culture impacts local meanings is not so straightforward, though, and doesn't mean that consumers share the same tastes or values. The globalization and standardization of modern consumer culture around the world have stimulated localization and heterogeneity of demand. On the global scale, globalization has created common symbols (styles, brands) that offer entry points for shared conversation as well as contestation and resistance to global companies and

Table 7.1: Assumptions about Meaning

A. *Assumptions on the nature of meaning:*

1. That clothes themselves carry meaning (popular culture discourse)

2. That interaction and context frame clothing meaning (academic discourse)

B. *Assumptions on the nature of the clothing system of meaning:*

1. That it functions like a language (de Saussure's 'langue' or Chomsky's 'competence') where each object corresponds to a specific meaning, or set of meanings, or that it functions like speech (de Saussure's 'parole' or Chomsky's 'performance'), where combining elements in practice in relation to other utterances generates meaning

2. That it functions in a more holistic manner, not through 'feature analysis' but in a gestalt, intuitive way (e.g. semiotics)

---

brands (Featherstone 1991). Consumer lifestyle tribes are increasingly seen as the globalized replacement of traditional communities (Cova and Cova 2002).

Before addressing the potential impact of global cultural context on communicating meaning through clothing, we need to examine the assumptions about meaning that are embedded in the research and practice of clothing (see Table 7.1).

But can clothing communication be conceived of as 'language' in the way verbal input communicates or 'signification' in the way visual signs communicate? Lurie (1981) advocated a popular thesis on the 'language of clothes'; Enninger (1985) had his doubts. According to him, such metaphors provide only preliminary insights. They are useful insofar as they suggest that there are some similarities between clothing and language, but they obscure the differences between the two systems, while not specifying which features they share.

Meaning in the sense of A1B1 exists only in highly homogenous and distinctive communities with well-defined dressing rules, such as the Amish, who provided Enninger (1985) with his template for the grammar of clothing. Some researchers (e.g. Hebdige in *Subculture: The Meaning of Style* [1979]) regarded youth culture in that way. Thirty years on, is the notion of a dictionary of style still valid? We think we can recognize typical members of youth culture dressing groups of our time (for example: Goths, Preps, Emo, Punks, Chavs, Rahs or Nerds). But what about the less typical members? Would we even identify them? The spread of youth culture's ideology about resistance expressed through style has become a global template for identity politics. It has not created homogeneity of outlook, just a shared basis for conversation and reflexivity (Kjeldgaard 2009). In fact, it is hard to find consensus on meaning even in more coherent communities, as the examples in Figure 7.1 suggest.

(a)

(b)

(c)

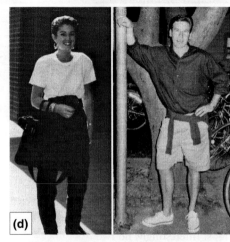
(d)

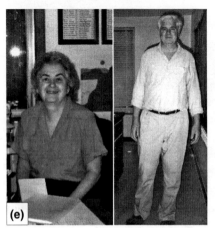
(e)

(f)

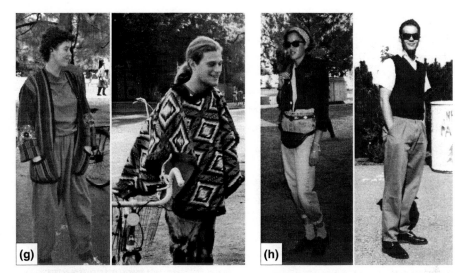

Figure 7.1: A selection of images from style tribes identified by some students on UC Davis campus in 1991. The categories chosen varied from student to student; even labels differed, indicating different semantic fields: (a) Greek; (b) Casual; (c) Plain; (d) New Wave (left) and Preppy (right); (e) Professor; (f) Fashion oriented (left) and Fashionable (right); (g) Earthy (left) and Hippie (right); (h) Trendy.

A few years ago, I asked my students on a California campus to divide the student body at the university into categories of people with similar looks and outlooks and take pictures to show their divisions (for some examples, see Figure 7.1). The task was easy for them: each student produced a series of images of typical members of those groups. Interestingly, no two students came up with the same classifications. In 1982, Peter Marsh (see Frosdick and Marsh 2005) studied the attire of fans at a local football club. The outfits were evaluated on a series of scales and yielded a system of signs with clear and accurate messages along 'hardness' and 'loyalty' dimensions. In contrast, in 2010 Luke Tallant did a study of football hooligans. He showed football fans photos of fans from the same club and asked them to select those whom they thought were hooligans. He found a mixed degree of recognition of the 'real hooligans', even though each of the photos contained some elements of dressing that are identified with this category.

Who Defines the Meaning of Clothes?

A key question in the study of the meaning of objects is the source of authority of the meaning. In essence, the study of clothing communication is at once a study of human behaviour and human artefact. Since clothes are worn on the body, it is tempting to see them as conveying a visual representation of psychological processes. Because they are a part of a system of objects whose use is subject to fashions and social norms, it is tempting to see them as representing material culture and social trends.

Hence, at the outset we must separate these two domains. Are we going to look at the *meaning of clothes*, or are we going to look at the *meanings we give to the clothes we wear*? A corollary of this question is: Do clothes have a meaning independent of our intentions? And if they do, who is to tell us about this meaning? The wearer? The researcher? A lay observer? A rulebook?

But in order to understand the process of creating meaning, it is not sufficient to view the piece of clothing outside its communicative context. We couldn't, for example, study the meaning of isolated outfits, nor could we study pictures of headless figures. For the same reason, it is not enough to look at somebody's wardrobe and interpret the meaning of the signals he or she is sending off with various outfits. We need to include his or her version of reality as well, and evaluate both wearers' and observers' accounts.

Why should there be a difference between wearers and viewers? Do we not all play either part at different times?

If I make a judgement on the communicative intention of someone wearing a certain outfit, would it correspond to what I would want to communicate if I were wearing the same outfit? Not necessarily. The reasons are both contextual and psychological. It is rarely the outfit itself that conveys the messages, but usually the sum total of ingredients that make a look, as well as the fit and manner in which it is worn. The same outfit can look sublime on one person and ridiculous on another.

Further, psychologists tell us in attribution theory that when accounting for behaviour of self and others, people use different kinds of explanations. For example, they tend to view other people's behaviour as more personally caused and their own as environmentally influenced. This indicates differences in agency and accountability in that they are less responsible for their actions and more controlled by their circumstances.

Ethnographers would say that our informants, perceptive as they may be about their own and their culture's practices, lack the critical distance enjoyed by the participant observer, the ethnographer, who lives among them. Discourse analysts, however, would tell us that a community of speakers uses the available linguistic repertoires as the basis for their reasons. The discourse approach relies on accounts of the wearers. It acknowledges the dynamic, changing, contingent and negotiated nature of meanings in any given context. It brings to light what might be invisible to the speakers themselves as evidence of linguistic strategies, rather than unconscious processes.

This means that even accounts that appear personal and individual do not, in fact, originate in the person, but rather are created by the language used to describe them and are, therefore, shared meanings, part of a public and collective reality.

We are, in fact, talking about different levels of analysis. One level is that of how people interpret the meanings of other people's dress, which is closer to the cultural stereotype semiotic approach. Another level is that of how people explain their own clothing choices and preferences.

Is Intention Required for Communication through Clothes?

We have established the widely shared agreement in the research literature by clothing researchers that clothes and personal appearance are means of non-verbal communication used to exchange personal and social information.

Personal indexing (characteristics, states of mind, mood, taste, creativity, conformity) and *social indexing* (lifestyle, political ideology, ethnic and religious group, gender, sexual orientation, fashion, group identity) are the two functions of *identity and identification* (Gregory Stone [1965] referred to them as 'identification with' and 'identification of'). Visual language, even more than verbal language, always sends a message regardless of intention to communicate.

The main difference between verbal and visual sign systems is that with words one cannot signify without communicating (although one can signify with silence), while with clothing (and pictures), one can.

Explicit communication is the *main message*, the intended meaning: what we say, what we try to say, what we think we say and what we don't want to say (Barthes's [1983/1977] notion of 'denotative' meaning and Goffman's notion of information given). Implicit communication is the *meta-message*, the unintended meaning: what can be read off, inferred, attributed or reconstructed in the presences, but also in the absences (Barthes's notion of 'connotative' meaning and Goffman's notion of information given off).

A few researchers identified intent as a relevant factor in communication (referring to information given or given off). Buck (1988) incorporated both types of communication into one theory by distinguishing two simultaneous communication streams: (1) spontaneous—which is biologically based, intuitive, direct and non-propositional; and (2) symbolic—which is learned, rational, intentional and propositional. The study of clothes provides one such illustration to this dual conception since some clothing messages require recognition of intention in order to be comprehended, and some do not, as is shown by Fouquier (1981) in his four ways of interpreting dress: (1) spontaneous—involuntary

Table 7.2: Role of Intent in Communication

Message	*Meta-message*	*Success of Communication*
Spontaneous	With no conscious intent to signify	Recognition of intentions
Fake spontaneous	With concealed intent to signify	Recognition of information, not of intentions
Symbolic	With intent to signify	Recognition of intentions and information

gestures or utterances; (2) fake spontaneous—made to look like spontaneous; (3) intentional—whose interpretation is dependent on recognition of the intention (e.g. status symbols); and (4) informational—whose interpretation is independent on recognition of information (e.g. costly jewellery).

Drawing on the work of Gregory Bateson (1972), Deborah Tannen (1990) views a communication act as made up of message—the obvious meaning—and the meta-message, which frames the conversation and provides information about the relations among the participants and their attitude towards their communication partners. In other words, if the message of wearing a fur coat is 'I like it and I can afford it', the meta-message might be 'I am above caring for ethical or environmental issues', which is a meta-message of ideological and social affiliation. But there may be conflicting or ambiguous messages. And so the meta-message might really be 'I am a romantic, and I think a woman looks best in furs.'

Adapting from the joint conceptions of Buck, Fouquier, and Tannen, the notion of intent in communication can be summarized in Table 7.2.

What Does Successful Communication Mean?

This question brings us back to the main examination of the nature of the clothing code between uniformity and diversity.

Referring to Table 7.2, it is obvious that while the success of spontaneous communication is in the decoding of information, symbolic communication, however, needs also be judged by decoding intentions.

In order to assess the success of a communicative act, we need to distinguish between two definitions of communication: *transmission of information* or *transmission of intentions* (Sperber and Wilson 1995) through the exchange of symbols. The first definition is represented by the code model, which portrays communication as the process of encoding and decoding signals. It focuses on the structural properties of the signals in isolation from the context and deals with denotative meaning and propositional content. Austin (1962) calls it the locutionary force of the utterance. The second definition is represented by the inferential model, which views communication as the transmission and recognition of intentions (Grice 1957). It refers to the communicative use of sentences in the performing of social actions—what Austin (1962) calls the illocutionary force of an utterance: its intentional meaning.

The concept of successful communication presupposes some sort of expectation that is being met or a standard that is being matched. The criteria for successful communication depend on the definition of communication adopted: if communication is regarded as the transmission of information, then decoding the message is a successful communication. If communication is regarded as the transmission of intention, then recognition of the sender's intent is a successful communication. To demonstrate that the two are not identical, we can think, for example, of someone habitually wearing, for sentimental reasons, a piece of diamond jewellery passed down in the family for generations. Here, decoding the meaning of the item (i.e. recognizing its worth) conveys the information that the wearer is in possession of expensive jewellery. In other words, this information is independent of the intention. In this case, failure to recognize the meaning of the item is not miscommunication since there was no conscious intention to communicate in the first place. If, however, the person was wearing the jewellery in order to flaunt his or her status or wealth, recognizing the meaning of the item indicates a successful communication, while failure to do so indicates miscommunication.

CRITIQUE OF COMMUNICATION RESEARCH PARADIGM

The idea that clothes communicate is one of the most assumed and least critically examined notions in clothing research. The field of communication through clothing abounds with folk wisdom but lacks in empirical backing of its theoretical and common-sense views. Communication research on fashion in the 1970s and 1980s was characterized by the *stereotype approach* and focused on *occasion wear*. The stereotype approach views meanings as fixed, pre-given, classified in categories and, for the most part, inferred or attributed by the viewer rather than solicited from the wearer.

It worked on the assumption that the meaning of clothes is inherent in the objects themselves, independent of communicative context (see Table 7.1 A1). The focus on occasion dressing reified stereotypes based on style (mostly formal casual, though there were some exceptions for studying specific uniforms, business attire or a few style stereotypes [e.g. Sweat and Zentner 1985]). Methodologically, it was based on inference from pictures or drawings of a person wearing a particular outfit. Inference on the basis of drawings resembles the study of a concept more than the study of a concrete person or group. Photos, on the other hand, refer to clothes of particular individuals, but they constitute just one-off instances out of a possible range of clothes worn by that person, as well as of a potential range of body postures, gestures, and facial expressions. This research tradition, which derives from cognitive social psychological theories of person perception, has come under attack both in social psychology and in fashion studies. In psychology, it has been criticized for its lack of ecological validity (see for example Martin and Macrae 2007) and its tendency to reproduce stereotypes (e.g. Macrae and Bodenhausen 2001) by eliciting people's schematic preconceptions and categorical thinking.

Very little research has looked empirically and systematically at the success of communication through clothing, but instead had continued to reinforce folk wisdom and stereotyping theory.

Two studies conducted in the 1980s provided a useful handle on the analogy of clothing to language. Peter Marsh (1982) studied costumes of fans of a local football club. Stimulus elicitation was based on the actual clothes worn in this subculture reproduced in a series of watercolour paintings. The outfits were evaluated on a series of scales selected on the basis of their occurrence in the fans' accounts. Analysis produced a system of signs with clear and accurate messages along 'hardness' and 'loyalty' dimensions. This pattern resembles the symbolism of certain tribal costumes and demonstrates how the utility of a system of clothing symbols is greatest for homogeneous and well-defined groups. What would happen outside such well-defined groups?

McCracken and Roth (1989) looked at a few looks (punk, preppie, new romantic, suburban leisure, heavy metal) representing a diversity of clothing practice in modern North America. They generated typical examples of each look and systematically replaced a detail in the look (colour, fabric, pattern or accessory) with alternative variations. The test of the existence of a code was measured by the ability to identify the correct group and to distinguish the 'proper variations'. The researchers found pockets of shared code, by some people more than others, and for some items more than others.

These two interesting studies join a long tradition of studies that empirically manipulated one aspect of clothing (e.g. style: formal/casual, occasion dressing, uniform, workwear) and asked people to make context-free judgements (usually pen and paper) of attired people or headless figures wearing one example of a general category.

This type of experiment is no longer the only method of studying clothing communication. Over the years, there has been some development in the study of communication in clothing. In fashion theory it has been superseded by a range of contextual approaches from a holistic semiotic perspective (e.g. Calefato 2004; Rubinstein 2001), symbolic interactionists who regard meaning as created in an interpersonal context (e.g. Kaiser 1990, 2002; Tseëlon 1992), discourse theorists who analyse meaning as a function of discursive formations and practices (e.g. Thompson and Haytko 1990) or anthropologists using ethnographic methods (e.g. Woodward 2007).

Methodologically, this research tradition evidences the following limitations:

1. It focused on the viewer's perspective, not the wearer's perspective. More recently, studies which reverse this tradition have emerged, but not studies that combine both.

2. It focused on the visual (e.g. style) or structural (e.g. social group, occupation, residence) aspects of clothing messages to the exception of experiential ones. Inference from visual or location (social, geographical) to character, biographical, motivational or mental relies on the age-old assumption about unity between external appearance and internal essence (Finkelstein 1991), and the corollary that a change of appearance affects a change of essence underlies public policies to introduce dress codes for teachers or school uniforms for children to solve problems of professional respect or discipline or to change the corporate image of the police in an attempt to combat civil disorder.

3. It cherry-picked easily identifiable or marked social occasions, thus privileging occasion wear, designer work and glamorous people over unmarked everyday clothes of everyday people. Thus, it tended to focus on extremely crude stereotypical cliché examples and to reify styles and treat them as unquestioned shorthand for a visual code. The most common was formal/casual, and a proverbial example, in the context of role theory, for instance, used to be that to wear a bathing suit to a formal occasion would be out of place. Such use of extreme examples while intending to be heuristic and deliberately exaggerated reflected nonetheless what was lacking from dress research which tended to cherry-pick absurd or caricature examples to make a point. It reflected the tendency to paint in broad brush, so crude that it only skimmed the surface and did not begin to reflect the richness and intricacies of sartorial behaviour. Such an approach is reproduced today with the study of designer couture clothes to the exclusion of ordinary clothes of ordinary people.

Between them, the three limitations result in a reification of social categories and social stereotypes and the creation of a research artefact that appears to suggest more homogeneity in outlook than actually exists. In fact, it exaggerates the claims of the efficiency of the clothing code.

A Proposal of an Alternative Paradigm

To address the shortcomings of the current paradigm, I proposed an alternative paradigm, one that embraced what the current paradigm left out. This paradigm is based on a series of studies I conducted over several years. Some parts of it are based on self-report methods and involve drawings but incorporate the aforementioned critique in the following manner:

1. Conducting a series of pilot studies to ensure that all the parameters that figure in the research are 'user generated' and not 'experimenter's bias'
2. Extending the scope of clothing messages to include informational (visual) but also intentional messages
3. Supplementing single-outfit drawings with a series of drawings representing the wearer in more than one context
4. Combining pen-and-paper studies with interpersonal contexts involving real-life people in real-life settings
5. Contrasting viewers' versus wearers' interpretation of their own outfits

However, the fundamental paradigm I have introduced in my research has departed from the *special occasion approach* or *stereotype approach* and has laid the groundwork for *wardrobe research* with a series of studies that explored the 'lived experience' of wearing clothes and participating in the fashion system. The full scale of the research is beyond the scope of this article (for full details see Tseëlon 1989).

I would like to single out one study which compared women's dressing intentions with others' interpretations.

The Study

Two of the groups that participated in my study consisted of nine and ten women respectively. The participants were previously unacquainted women of a variety of ages and clothing styles who responded to requests for volunteers published in women's and fashion magazines. About half worked full-time, and the other half were part-timers, housewives and students; half had children; most came from the South of England and the Midlands.

The women were invited to attend a bring-and-share party, on a Sunday afternoon, at a garden party in Oxford. They were asked to dress 'in a way which you feel best represents you' and it was emphasized, 'please note, I'm not saying necessarily "dress up," but dress in a way which will capture you best.' The purpose of the event was explained as 'an interesting "guessing game" that will be both (I hope) fun, and give you some insight into my research. An opportunity to see how close we can get to getting ourselves across to a bunch of complete strangers.' Shortly after arrival, the women were asked to describe the messages they intended to convey through their clothes and their own impressions of the messages the other women intended to convey through their clothes. In addition, they were asked to judge both themselves and all the others on a series of scales. On the basis of previous extensive research, I have identified user-generated dimensions that kept coming up as relevant intentional dimensions of clothing communication. Many hours of focus groups, individual interviews, self-report studies and statistical analyses yielded seven recurring dimensions that were nothing like what one would assume when studying the communicability of clothes.

The dimensions were the following: *effort* (taking effort with one's appearance, which may or may not be visible in terms of results); *style* (how visible and unique one wants to look, as opposed to fitting in); *anxiety* (how much one needs the clothes to provide confidence); *visibility* (how 'visible and observed' they perceive the situation for which they dress to be); *fashionability* (how important it is to be fashionably dressed); *sexiness* (how much they want to look sexy); and *affluence* (whether they want the clothes to tell about their ability to afford expensive or labelled clothes). For each dimension, a four-point scale was constructed. The response categories ranged from 'definitely' through 'slightly' (or 'subtly' and 'not particularly') to 'definitely not'. *The wording of the scales was taken out of the language used by the respondents.*

For example, the scale for style was as follows:

1. I *definitely* dressed to be noticed and unique.
2. I dressed to be *subtly* noticed and unique.
3. I dressed to *subtly* fit in.
4. I *definitely* dressed to fit in.

The only scale which had a discrete and not dimensional structure was effort. It consisted of the following:

1. Looking my best
2. Much more effort than my usual standard
3. My usual standard of effort
4. Less than my usual standard of effort

Each participant was given one set of scales to describe herself and nine additional sets for each participant.

In order to determine whether clothing stimuli were easily decodable, I had to establish that decoding would be better than chance. Since every scale had four answer categories, the chance probability of choosing any of them should be 25 per cent. Examination of the distribution of responses both on the self and others scales showed that there was not a 25 per cent chance of choosing any one response category because some categories were chosen more often than others, and some response categories were more preferred for self and not for others, and vice versa. Hence, the probability of choosing a response category was worked out for each scale separately, taking into account frequency of response to both self and others scales.

The following tables summarize the observed and expected frequencies of correct guesses (when the answer of the woman matched that of another woman judging her) and the associated values of chi square for each scale (see Tables 7.3, 7.4, 7.5 and 7.6).

In summary: for both groups, whether the accurate or the approximate method of decoding was considered, each time a different dimension came out as better decoded than others above chance level. The results did not suggest any systematic pattern but rather an accidental one. Hence, it can be concluded that decodability of all dimensions was not greater than chance.

Hypothesis 2 was that decodability was a property of the clothes, rather than the individuals. Tables 7.7 and 7.8 show the distribution of correct decoding, broken down by individuals and dimensions. An ANOVA with individuals as one factor and dimensions as another revealed a significant main effect for dimensions in Group 2 ($F = 5.46$; $df = 6$; $p < 0.01$), but not in Group 1 (see Tables 7.8 and 7.9).

Since point-to-point correspondence draws rather arbitrary distinctions between degree of accurateness (when 'very' is judged as incorrect in comparison with

Table 7.3: Observed and Expected Frequencies of Accurate[†] Guesses and the Values of χ^2: Group 1 ($N = 9$)

Scale	Observed	Expected	χ^2
Effort	32	30.1	0.2
Style	31	19	6.46*
Anxiety	17	14.7	0.45
Visibility	29	25.6	0.69
Fashionability	29	24.2	1.43
Sexiness	30	22.9	3.22
Affluence	20	20.9	0.05

* $p < 0.05$.
[†] Response that matched perfectly.
With $df = 1$, only the style scale was significant with a probability of less than 0.05. In other words, only the style dimension was decoded with a better-than-chance probability. The same procedure was repeated for the approximate* guesses.

Table 7.4: Observed and Expected Frequencies of Approximate[†] Guesses and the Values of χ^2: Group 1 ($N = 9$)

Scale	Observed	Expected	χ^2
Effort**			
Style	39	30.75	0.8
Anxiety	38	34.66	0.61
Visibility	51	50.76	0
Fashionability	45	37.1	3.46
Sexiness	51	41.66	4.96*
Affluence	34	40.44	2.33

* $p < 0.05$.
** The effort scale had no approximate version since each category was discrete. With $df = 1$, only the sexiness dimension was decoded with a better-than-chance probability.
† When collapsed categories (definitely + subtly) were counted together as correct.

Table 7.5: Observed and Expected Frequencies of Accurate[†] Guesses and the Values of χ^2: Group 2 ($N = 10$)

Scale	Observed	Expected	χ^2
Effort	45	44.6	0.01
Style	26	21.8	1.05
Anxiety	20	23.8	0.81
Visibility	36	27	4.28*
Fashionability	23	26.3	0.58
Sexiness	27	29.8	0.39
Affluence	43	34.2	3.64

* $p < 0.05$.
† Response that matched perfectly.
With $df = 1$, only the visibility scale was decoded with a better-than-chance probability.

'slightly'), this analysis was repeated with respect to the approximate scoring (where 'very' is judged as correct in comparison with 'slightly'). Here, as was anticipated, the level of correct decodability was higher than in the accurate group and was about 45 per cent.

Table 7.6: Observed and Expected Frequencies of Approximate[†] Guesses and the Values of χ^2: Group 2 ($N = 10$)

Scale	Observed	Expected	χ^2
Effort**			
Style	50	44.2	0.8
Anxiety	45	50.2	1.2
Visibility	55	55	0
Fashionability	33	45.4	7.69*
Sexiness	68	67.4	0.01
Affluence	62	62	0

* $p < 0.05$.
** The effort scale had no approximate version since each category was discrete. With $df = 1$, only the fashionability dimension was decoded with a better-than-chance probability.
[†] When collapsed categories (definitely + subtly) were counted together as correct.

Table 7.7: Distribution of Correct Decoding (Group 1): Accurate Scoring ($N = 9$)

Subject:	A	H	E	JO	JA	L	R	WE	WI	Total
Scale:										
Effort	4	2	4	5	4	3	2	4	4	32
Style	4	5	5	1	5	4	5	1	1	31
Anxiety	2	2	1	3	2	1	1	2	3	17
Visibility	1	3	6	2	2	4	5	2	4	29
Fashionability	2	4	4	3	4	3	3	3	3	29
Sexiness	2	4	4	5	5	3	3	1	3	30
Affluence	0	2	2	4	3	1	4	3	1	20
Total	15	22	26	23	25	19	23	16	19	188
%	23.8	34.9	41.2	36.5	39.6	30.1	36.5	25.3	30.1	100

On visual inspection, it can be seen that the general level of correct decoding (the general total against the possible total) was about a third.
Group 1: 188 out of 9 (9 × 7) = 33.1%
Group 2: 220 out of 10 (10 × 7) = 31.4%
An ANOVA with individuals as one factor and dimensions as another revealed a significant main effect for dimensions in Group 2 ($F = 5.46$; $df = 6$; $p < 0.01$), but not in Group 1 (see Tables 7.9 and 7.10).

Table 7.8: Distribution of Correct Decoding (Group 2): Accurate Scoring ($N = 10$)

Subject:	E	F	H	J	K	L	M	P	S	W	Total
Scale:											
Effort	3	5	5	5	5	3	3	6	4	6	45
Style	3	2	2	5	1	3	2	3	3	2	26
Anxiety	3	2	2	2	3	0	0	3	3	2	20
Visibility	3	2	5	1	1	7	3	4	6	4	36
Fashionability	1	4	2	0	3	2	3	2	3	3	23
Sexiness	4	3	2	2	3	2	3	2	2	4	27
Affluence	3	6	2	5	4	4	6	3	5	5	43
Total	20	24	20	20	20	21	20	23	26	26	220
%	28.5	34.2	28.5	28.5	28.5	30.0	28.5	32.8	37.1	37.1	100

Table 7.9: Analysis of Variance (ANOVA) of Correct Decoding (Group 1): Accurate Scoring ($N = 9$)

Source	df	S of Squares	Mean Square	F
Individuals	8	16.98	2.12	1.28
Dimensions	6	22.98	3.83	2.32

Table 7.10: Analysis of Variance (ANOVA) of Correct Decoding (Group 2): Accurate Scoring ($N = 10$)

Source	df	S of Squares	Mean Square	F
Individuals	9	8.29	0.92	0.51
Dimensions	6	58.97	9.83	5.46*

*$p < 0.01$.

Group 1: 258 out of 9 (9×6) = 53.08%
Group 2: 313 out of 10 (10×6) = 52.16%

As with accurate decoding, an analysis of variance with individuals as one factor and dimensions as another found a significant main effect for dimensions in Group 2 ($F = 6.03$; $df = 5$; $p < 0.01$). Since a significant main effect was found only with regard to one group, it is possible that in this particular group some individuals were more easily encodable.

As with previous hypotheses, it seems that some individuals were particularly easy to read off and some were relatively good at detecting messages. It should be noted that this finding refers to the groups under study and is hard to generalize; it is also not clear whether the ability is constant across situations—that is to say, whether someone who is a good decoder, for example, is always a good decoder or only with some types of people or clothes, as the one-off significant correlation suggests. On the whole, the results seem to question the assumption regarding the uniform meaning of clothes and point to the potential of individual interpretations and misunderstanding in the area of communicating with clothes.

The results of these particular groups suggest that no consistent dimension was decoded with a better-than-chance probability. In other words: all the messages that were supposed to transfer from encoders to decoders were only poorly decoded—below chance level. This suggests that there is a scope of individual and local differences. Perhaps in each group some dimensions were more easily recognizable than others? Perhaps there was an element of skill involved, and some observers are simply better decoders than others? Perhaps. But from the point of view of what I set out to find—that is, how justified we are in talking about a 'socially shared clothing code'—it certainly suggests that such a code, if it exists, is rather elusive. This is even more obvious when one examines the micro level—the accuracy of decoding specific individuals. I would like to illustrate this point through a close-up focus on two individuals (from Group 2) representing the two archetypes that have been typically used in clothing research: smart and casual.

The Smart-Looking Woman

A is the most enigmatic of the subjects (see Figure 7.2). She is 22, lives in a provincial town in the Midlands and is working full-time. She has an original style and puts attention and thought into her appearance, as she wants it to leave an unambiguous impression of her self. Her stylish appearance was generally commented on by observers, although not necessarily her individual style. It is obvious that some of the messages that were attributed to her clothes derive from a generalized stereotype of an elegant-looking lady. For some observers, a stylish appearance is synonymous with fashionable appearance (i.e. like everybody else), while for others stylish is conceived in terms of a personal look (i.e. unlike everybody else). Other characteristics (more effort than usual, sexiness, affluence) that were attributed to her apparently form part of the elegant stereotype and in this particular case seem to reflect the observers more than the wearer.

How did A describe her clothing message? She admitted to being 'individual in style (I'd like to pride myself that my clothes, not necessarily expensive, are at least individualistic, reflecting personal style) well controlled yet easy-going. Chic but not totally aloof; independent, being at ease with self & therefore others.'

The ways she was described by others are as follows:

1. 'Affluent, a bit overdone'
2. 'Extrovert'
3. 'Stylish & flamboyant, wanting to be noticed, very feminine'
4. 'Has own style, adores the good life, city girl, very fashionable, confident, serious'
5. 'Fashion-conscious. hair style, make up, jewellery & dress all conform to magazine fashion'
6. 'Fashionable, smart, tasteful, feminine'

Figure 7.2: The smart-looking woman.

7. 'Smart, elegant style'
8. 'Stylish, fashion conscious, elegant'
9. 'Unusual style and up-to-the-minute mix of colours, shoes, hair: doesn't want to look dated'

Thus, contrary to her intentions to look stylish but not fashionable, and chic yet easy-going, she was perceived as fashion-conscious, elegant, and making a strong statement.

This is highlighted even more in the difference between her self rating and others' ratings on the same scales. In response to the question about the level of effort characterizing her appearance, A indicated that it was her usual standard of effort, while seven out of the ten participants thought she was putting her best effort. According to her answers, A dressed to be slightly noticed and unique. She definitely did not need her clothes to give her confidence; she expected to be only subtly visible and observed, not particularly fashionable, not particularly expensive looking and definitely not sexy. The ratings of the other participants differed from her own in two ways, although some differed only in degree. For example, most participants thought A dressed to be definitely noticed and unique, as well as visible and observed. Other responses differed in direction. Thus, most participants thought that A slightly needed her clothes to give her confidence, definitely dressed to look fashionable, subtly dressed to look sexy and dressed to be expensive looking (four thought definitely, and four thought subtly).

The comparison between self and others' ratings revealed that A was misinterpreted on almost every dimension. Many of the misattributions derive from an application of a stereotype.

An opposite example is presented in the case of B.

The Casual-Looking Woman

B is 25 and a student at a university in the North (see Figure 7.3). She is the most transparent among the participants. She dresses in a simple, practical, casual style, not to be confused with not caring about her appearance. B likes to convey her individuality but does so in a very subtle way. Dressed in the almost classic 'studenty' uniform, she was evaluated according to the 'jeans and T-shirt' stereotype and was attributed much more confidence and 'no nonsense' attitude than she actually claimed. Some observers did notice the little details that conveyed the individual message.

According to her own testimony, B is 'fairly undaring & unadventurous though not particularly conventional either. Individual is fairly accurate for my usual mode of dress. I hate looking like other people! But I don't believe in swinging to the opposite extreme just for the hell of it. I like casual comfort (!).'

Figure 7.3: The casual-looking woman.

The ways she was described by others are as follows:

1. 'Young, serious, free, limited budget'
2. 'Self sufficient'
3. 'Down-to-earth but attentive to detail and comfort'
4. 'Self assured, serious minded but full of life, hard-working but casual in appearance, accepts life as it comes, friendly'
5. 'College/prep appearance. casual. adventurous. sporty'
6. 'Studenty. not the normal "high-street" fashion but arty; not too way-out as a student but scarf & sailor top give game away, as well as jeans + earrings. wants to say "I'm going to be casual & different"'

7. 'Casual, comfortable, "studenty", not trying to impress, tight clothes which accentuate bulges but also a bit sexy'
8. 'Casual, comfortable clothes, splash of colour with scarf'
9. 'Active, no nonsense dressing—looks as though it takes her 5 minutes to get out in the morning'

Thus, even though B was on the whole perceived more accurately than A, she was over-interpreted and attributed many messages she did not claim (e.g. attention to detail, arty, sporty, sexy) by almost every respondent. On the other hand, her claim to individuality and 'not looking like others' was noticed by only three of the observers. The others placed her in a broad category where everybody looks very studenty and very casual.

The ratings also revealed a great deal of consensus. There was complete agreement between B and most participants that she put in her usual level of effort and that she did not particularly wish to appear sexy, fashionable and definitely not expensive looking. On two dimensions there was a discrepancy: while B admitted she expected to feel slightly visible and observed—most participants thought she didn't—and while she said she did not particularly need her clothes to give her confidence, half thought she definitely did not. Finally, while B indicated that she dressed to subtly fit in, only half the participants agreed to that. The other half thought she wanted to be noticed and unique. Thus, to the extent that B possessed the characteristics that are associated with the 'hip' look, she was accurately decoded. But when she exhibited a characteristic which did not form part of the stereotype (e.g. being self-conscious), she was likely to be misread.

As the illustration of A and B shows, 'group membership' is not a guarantee for correct decoding. While belonging to highly stereotyped categories, both were trying in their own way to communicate a message of their individuality. Yet the smart woman was inaccurately decoded, while the casual one came across rather unambiguously. To the extent that their individual messages corresponded to the stereotype of their look, they were correctly identified, while messages which did not fit the stereotype were misinterpreted.

Together, the two women represent both ends of the limits of the stereotype approach to the decoding of specific individuals. Errors of interpretation can range from a complete misunderstanding (as in the case of A) to a basic understanding with some (crucial or trivial) distortions (as in the case of B). But groups—apart from certain very definite subcultures—do not have a clear and precise dress code. Rather, the reality of clothing meaning is far more divergent, diffuse and idiosyncratic (see also Davis 1985).

What distinguishes this study from the more intuitive 'guessing game' that I mentioned earlier (Ellin and Penner 1999) is the fact that it was based on real interaction, not a picture; that intentions were compared with interpretations; and that the measuring instrument was a combination of quantitative and qualitative methods which were derived from categories that are relevant for the wearers themselves, rather than imposed by the researcher. In being a paradigmatic study, it establishes a principled, rather than an anecdotal point.

CONCLUSION

In summary, the results show that there is more to the communication of personal information through clothes than just applying stereotypes. At the interpersonal level, communicating personal information through clothes is a more complex process than just an attribution of categorical properties. Some dimensions are better decoded than others, but it is not a clear, unambiguous process free of miscommunications. In a context of ongoing interaction, meanings get transformed as familiarization increases, or as more contextual details are added. Some information—sometimes trivial, sometimes crucial—gets distorted. But even at a social encounter of the most superficial kind (as this study was), communication is more than 'costume display' alone.

References and Further Reading

Austin, J. (1962), *How to Do Things with Words*, Cambridge, MA: Harvard University Press.

Barthes, R. (1983/1977), *The Fashion System*, trans. M. Ward and R. Howard, New York: Hill & Wang.

Bateson, G. (1972), *Steps to an Ecology of Mind*, Chicago: University of Chicago Press.

Brummett, Barry (2008), *A Rhetoric of Style*, Carbondale: Southern Illinois University Press.

Buck, R. (1988), 'Nonverbal Communication: Spontaneous and Symbolic Aspects', *American Behavioral Scientist*, 31: 341–54.

Calefato, P. (2004), *The Clothed Body*, London: Berg.

Clark, J., and Phillips, A. (2010), *The Concise Dictionary of Dress*, London: Violette Editions.

Constantine, Susannah, and Woodall, Trinny (2003), *What Not to Wear for Every Occasion: Pt. 2*, New York: Riverhead Trade.

Cova, B., and Cova, V. (2002), 'Tribal Marketing: The Tribalisation of Society and Its Impact on the Conduct of Marketing', *European Journal of Marketing*, 36/5–6: 595–620.

Davis, Fred (1985), 'Clothing and Fashion as Communication', in Michael R. Solomon (ed.), *The Psychology of Clothing*, Lexington, MA: Lexington Books.

Ellin, A., and Penner, D. (1999), 'Who Am I?' [Electronic version]. *New York Times* (14 Nov.), http://www.nytimes.com/1999/11/14/magazine/who-am-i.html?scp=17&sq=Valerie%20Steele&st=cse.

Enninger, W. (1984), *Structural and Pragmatic Properties of Grooming and Garment Grammars*, Berlin: De Gruyter Mouton.

Enninger, W. (1985), *The Design Features of Clothing Codes: The Functions of Clothing Displays in Interaction*, Tübingen, Germany: Gunter Narr Verlag.

Featherstone, M. (1991), *Consumer Culture and Postmodernism,* Thousand Oaks, CA: Sage Publications.

Finkelstein, J. (1991), *The Fashioned Self,* Cambridge: Polity.

Fouquier, E. (1981), 'On the Interpretation of Other People's Dress', *Diogenes*, 29/113: 177–94.

Frosdick, S., and Marsh, P. (2005), *Football Hooliganism*, Abingdon, UK: Willan.

Grice, H. (1957), 'Meaning', *Philosophical Review*, 66: 377–88.

Hebdige, Dick (1979), *Subculture: The Meaning of Style,* London: Methuen.

Hedström, S., and Ingesson, C. (2008), 'The End of Trend. Stockholm', *Bon* (Spring): 62–66.

Kaiser, S. (1990), 'The Semiotics of Clothing: Linking Structural Analysis with Social Process', in T. Sebeok and J. Umiker-Sebeok (eds), *The Semiotic Web,* Berlin: De Gruyter Mouton.

Kaiser, S. (2002), *Social Psychology of Clothing: Symbolic Appearances in Context*, 2nd ed., New York: Fairchild Books.

Kjeldgaard, D. (2009), 'The Meaning of Style? Style Reflexivity among Danish High School Youths', *Journal of Consumer Behaviour,* 8: 71–83.

Kress, G., and Van Leeuwen, T. (2006), *Reading Images: The Grammar of Visual Design*, 2nd ed., London: Routledge.

Lurie, A. (1981), *The Language of Clothes,* New York: Random House.

Macrae, C., and Bodenhausen, G. (2001), 'Social Cognition: Categorical Person Perception', *British Journal of Psychology*, 92: 239–55.

Marsh, P. (1982), *Rule Governed Expressions of Aggression among Football Fans and Youths,* PhD thesis, Oxford University.

Martin, D., and Macrae, C. (2007), 'A Face with a Cue: Exploring the Inevitability of Person Categorization', *European Journal of Social Psychology,* 37: 806–16.

McCracken, G., and Roth, V. (1989), 'Does Clothing Have a Code? Empirical Findings and Theoretical Implications in the Study of Clothing as a Means of Communication', *International Journal of Research in Marketing*, 6: 13–33.

Rubinstein, R. (2001), *Dress Codes: Meanings and Messages in American Culture,* Boulder, CO: Westview Press.

Simon-Miller, F. (1985), 'Signs and Cycles in the Fashion System', in M. Solomon (ed.), *The Psychology of Clothing*, Lexington, MA: Lexington Books.

Sperber, D., and Wilson, D. (1995), *Relevance: Communication and Cognition,* Oxford: Blackwell.

Stone, G. (1965), 'Appearance and the Self', in M. Roach and J. Eicher (eds), *In Dress, Adornment, and the Social Order,* New York: Wiley.

Sweat, S., and Zentner, M. (1985), 'Attributions toward Female Appearance Styles', in M. Solomon (ed.), *The Psychology of Fashion*, Lexington, MA: Lexington Books.

Tallant, L. (2010), *How Far the Dress Code of Football Hooligans Forms Part of its Identification as a Group by Insiders and Outsiders,* PhD thesis, University of Leeds.

Tannen, D. (1990), *You Just Don't Understand: Women and Men in Conversation,* London: Virago.

Thompson, C., and Haytko, D. (1997), 'Speaking of Fashion', *Journal of Consumer Research,* 24/1: 15–42.

Tseëlon, E. (1989), *Communicating via Clothing,* PhD thesis, Oxford University.

Tseëlon, E. (1992), 'Self-Presentation through Appearance: A Manipulative vs. a Dramaturgical Approach', *Symbolic Interaction,* 15: 501–14.

Woodward, S. (2007), *Why Women Wear What They Wear,* Oxford: Berg.

8 ADOLESCENCE: IDENTITY, FASHION AND NARCISSISM

MARÍA ELENA LARRAÍN

The human being expresses itself, its intimacy and its identity through body language and action. A person is at the same time a body and its owner. The body is a means of communication with the world and with those who surround us. The body and its appearance are the way in which we present ourselves; it could be stated that it is our basic means of establishing contact with others. Due to the importance of the human body, interest in fashion has been permanent and immutable, although fashion is ephemeral and ever changing (Figueras 2000).

Nowadays, it seems that the body has finally gained value. It could be affirmed that it is actually cared for; it is liberated and has achieved its plenitude thanks to the development and progress of nutrition, the abandonment of moral restrictions and the evolution of fashion in clothing. Many actions are undertaken to keep the body in shape and to preserve its healthy and youthful appearance, to the extent of denying generational differences. Frequently, fathers and mothers imitate their children in their style of dress. Fashion, up to now, was almost the exclusive territory of adult women, but today, the market has discovered the potential profits of capturing the worlds of adolescents and men. Models are very commonly chosen from the ranks of adolescents of increasingly younger ages; however, models in the recent past were usually women who had achieved the plenitude of feminine forms of the body. This fact could be easily dismissed, but it actually has profound psychological repercussions because it offers a certain ideal of beauty in which adult femininity and masculinity are annulled, thus affecting the development and formation of adult identity.

The focus of this chapter is to analyse, from a psychological perspective, the relationship between adolescent identity, its development and its links to fashion. We will revisit some ideas regarding the crucial period of adolescence and the process of identity formation. The influence of dynamics within the family, models, advertising images and the values of society will be addressed as important variables.

As Lipovetsky (1990) has stated, there is no style in fashion that can immediately be imposed on the public today. Styles and appearances are pluralistic and democratic. People, and specifically adults, are aware of what is in vogue, but they adapt and accommodate fashion to their own taste or just ignore it. Fashion is therefore a complex phenomenon that cannot be explained by a single theory. Narcissistic individualism affirms Lipovetsky and leads to a diminished or relaxed interest in fashion. This affirmation, we could add, applies to some narcissistic personalities who develop their grandiose self through language and intellectual exhibitionism. Nevertheless, other personalities of this type deal with their disproportionate love for themselves by worshipping their body, figure and appearance. These persons are usually endowed with beauty and have been valued mainly for it. Narcissism as a psychological dimension related to fashion, self-concept and self-esteem will also be addressed.

Are adolescents affected by fashion in the same way as adults? If narcissism is a risk during adolescence, how is this associated with self-image, the importance of personal style and identity? The idea that our clothes say something about us has become commonplace, but what sort of communication is it, and what sorts of things do our clothes say about us (Barnard 1996)? Our interest in this chapter is to establish a relationship between adolescent identities, which are very frequently unstable and still in the process of formation, and the risk of narcissism during this developmental period. The influence of peer-group pressure and the models these groups offer will also be taken into account as another strong variable related to identity formation during adolescence. Fashion comes in as part of this process of acquiring a personal identity and as a means of social differentiation that can express the ambivalence of our personalities, our main character traits—in short, our identity. Fashion will be seen as a kind of language with symbols of images that adolescents use to express themselves.

I will begin by highlighting some general ideas on the concept of identity and relating them to the developmental period of adolescence. Then a relationship between narcissism and fashion during adolescence will be established. I will comment on the reasons why some adolescents are intensely vulnerable to styles and the models offered by the market. I will conclude by commenting upon the implications these factors can have for identity formation.

SOME IDEAS ON IDENTITY AND ADOLESCENCE

Although Erikson (1968) noted that identity formation is a continuous task through life and recognized its roots in the earliest self-recognition, he emphasized the period of adolescence as the one in which identity consolidates itself. Following Akhtar and Samuel, Erikson defined the attempt to integrate what one knows of oneself and one's world into a stable continuum of past knowledge, present experiences and future goals, in order to establish a cohesive sense of personal feelings as a major goal in adolescence. Failure in this task leads to a chaotic sense of personhood in both its subjective and social senses (Akhtar and Samuel 1996).

Identity formation develops from the outside to the inside. This is the main reason why appearance, looks, personal style and all related phenomena are so crucial during early adolescence. Adolescents must undergo several changes in different spheres of their lives and selves, and there are diverse ways of living this period. Offer (1991) differentiates between those adolescents who live this period simply as the continuity of previous phases, others who live it as an emergent phase and still others who live it tumultuously. These last two groups experience feelings of anguish, insecurity, shame about self and confusion or a grandiose sense of self-esteem and exhibitionism. The literature indicates that physical appearance, self-image, body image and the feelings associated with it significantly affect one's sense of self (Offer et al. 1981 and Benson et al. 1987 in Pletsch et al. 1991).

Social acceptance and relatedness are therefore very important variables that influence personal growth and the formation of identity during the years of young adulthood. Normal adolescents belong to groups of friends who have enormous influence over them. It is well known that during this period of development, parents become less important models than the peer group. What the group establishes as a valued fashion comes from the outside and will be determining during identity formation. Adolescents, being unstable and without defined identities, are then in a continuous process of comparing themselves to the group and have a strong desire to belong. Why adolescents choose one group over another to belong to is a matter that we will not analyse in this paper, but we can say that there are different reasons and motives. Some are conscious, some are not, and adolescents often are not clear about the decisions they make regarding appearance, fashion and style.[1]

For the aforementioned reasons, identity is very vulnerable at this age, unstable and in a process of construction. Identity is formed based on the adolescent's primary love figures from childhood and current relationships with family members, intimate friends, teachers and so forth who become the mirrors of the adolescent. He sees himself in them. The opinions and criticisms of these different loved figures and being accepted by them are of crucial importance. This acceptance or lack of it tells the adolescent who he is and what people think and feel about him. All this information becomes the material he uses to build his personal identity.

Authors such as Erikson (1968) and Marcia (1993) have discussed different concepts of identity. We will mention both definitions, which have similarities as well as some differences that are interesting but which will highlight the risk of not developing a healthy identity. When Erikson focuses in the psychosocial development of identity, he is not only recognizing its psychological dimension but its social and personal dimensions. Thus, for Erikson, psychosocial identity includes three dimensions: A) the subjective or personal dimension; B) a behavioural repertoire and character which differentiates individuals; and C) the social dimension or the recognition of roles in a community (Côté 1996). These components must integrate, otherwise identity crises are inevitable. Identity consolidation is key to normal adolescent development: 'The process of identity formation, according to Erikson, is one in which the adolescent synthesizes and sheds previous identifications and introjections so that an integrated personal identity results. The recognition and acceptance of that person by her community is an important part of the process. However, according to Erikson, acute identity confusion can result when an adolescent faces the demands for his simultaneous commitment to physical intimacy, to decisive occupational choice, to energetic competition, and to psychosocial definition' (Kernberg, Weiner and Bardenstein 2000: 22). When adolescents are under these simultaneous pressures, identity confusion may develop, and the ability to acquire a solid identity is at stake. Psychosocial development as Erikson understands it has to integrate early identifications (with parental figures) and new ones that have their roots in peer groups and in the community to which the adolescent belongs.

Marcia (Moshman 1999) approaches the concept of identity from the viewpoint of personal commitments. Mature identity is a matter of having strong, self-conscious and self-chosen commitments in matters such as vocation, sexuality, religion and political ideology. This author differentiates the identity-diffused individual (who has no strong commitments and is not seeking any) from the identity-foreclosed individual (who does not have clear commitments and whose commitments are not self-chosen). An individual who is either identity-foreclosed or identity-diffused can move into an identity crisis which I refer to as a state of moratorium, a state where one has no current identity commitments but is seeking to make such commitments. Identity diffusion and identity foreclosure may continue indefinitely, but a moratorium is a relatively unstable state, and the individual is likely to resolve his or her identity crisis in one of two ways.

Taylor (1989) has added the concept of strong evaluations. He says that the answer to the question of 'who am I?' cannot only be answered by giving one's name and genealogy. He says that the profound understanding of what is of crucial importance to us is how to answer this question in the right way. 'To know who I am is a species of knowing where I stand. My identity is defined by the commitments and identifications which provide the frame or horizon within which I try to determine from case to case what is good, or valuable, or what ought to be done, or what

I endorse or oppose' (Taylor 1989). The decisions one makes in regard to a personal life project, which includes definitions on values and religious beliefs, vocation, style and fashion, reveal aspects of the commitments and identifications one has made. These are strong evaluations that an individual with an achieved identity has made. While adolescents go through this period of life, they strive to find these answers and personal definitions.

Erikson, Akhtar (2003), Marcia and Taylor all emphasize the importance of acquiring a solid and mature identity. If this task is not achieved normally, psychopathologies or psychological conflicts may appear. Adolescents are in the process of identity formation and will complete this period of development when they possess a solid identity. While in the process of acquiring it, they are very fragile and vulnerable subjects, both to internal influences and to external ones which come through different pathways, such as peer-group pressure or the mass media, and the models it presents and the evaluations from the adult world to which they relate. Adolescents are unstable individuals who can succumb to external cultural influences. Forming a solid identity is thus the major task during adolescence. The adult world should nurture this objective in order to help adolescents become healthy adults with strong evaluations of themselves and commitments they ascribe to and follow.

Since adolescence is in itself a period of ambivalence and ambiguity, the risk of not developing a solid identity and of staying trapped in love for oneself is high. Identity has not yet consolidated so falling in love with one's own image can be a part of this period. The myth of Narcissus, according to Doltó (1990), represents an extreme: the pathology in which the individual denies the election of sexuality. 'Adolescents want to be both sexual identities. They do not want to change and have the need of a complementary half' (Doltó 1990). An adolescent who stays in this type of relationship with himself will not be able to love anyone, and his identity will be at risk.

Therefore, as a mutation period or as a crisis period in which major changes take place, adolescence is especially vulnerable to what is innate to man. Van den Aardweg has stated that 'the force of narcissism or self love has an easy grip, for man is innately egocentric and a "lover" of himself' (Van den Aardweg 1986). We could add that during this period of life this force is especially present and active.

Narcissism or healthy self-esteem, a realistic or unrealistic body image and feelings of authenticity are all related to the state of identity during adolescence. How does an adolescent acquire a healthy identity? What are the characteristics of this identity? What are the actual effects of narcissism over personal identity and character? Does identity have anything to do with style and one's looks? Is style just a copy or imitation of what one sees? Identity, we think, is the knowledge, plans, ideals and values that the individual has about himself. Are adolescents only imitating what they see? Are all adolescents so vulnerable to fashion, new ways of communicating, new words and language? Is there a moment in which exploration and experimentation end and an integrated and rather stable self-identity appears? When does this happen? Are all adolescents equally influenced by peer-group pressure? Understanding how identity is formed and the differences between a consolidated identity and identity diffusion can help us find answers to these questions.

A SOLID IDENTITY

A solid and cohesive identity consists of the following characteristics: '(1) a sustained feeling of self-sameness displaying roughly similar character traits to varied others, (2) temporal continuity in the self experience, (3) genuineness and authenticity, (4) a realistic body image, (5) a sense of inner solidity and the associated capacity for peaceful solitude, (6) subjective clarity regarding one's gender, and (7) an inner solidarity with an ethnic group's ideals and a well-internalized conscience. Disturbances in these areas of functioning comprise the syndrome of identity diffusion' (Akhtar 1992).

Consolidated identity provides an individual with the intra-psychic experience of subjective self-sameness (Akhtar and Samuel 1996; Akhtar 1992). This self-sameness is expressed in similar character traits manifested before different people and in different circumstances. The individual experiences himself as essentially one and the same personality, maintains similar preferences and has a sense of temporal continuity. 'Although interacting with different age groups or with individuals with whom they have various levels of intimacy, they can modulate their behaviors without losing a core sense of inner sameness' (Akhtar and Samuel 1996).

Consistent attitudes and behaviours are other characteristics of consolidated identity. Because these individuals display a stable investment in personal values and ideologies, they develop 'the ability to recognize, focus on and articulate what is meaningful. Such persons also possess a repertoire of behaviors with congruous and predictable parameters' (Akhtar and Samuel 1996: 258). They display character traits which are not contradictory or incompatible. At the same time, 'their political ideologies, aesthetic interests and tastes in food or music remain unaltered regardless of context. Wishes to act in ways that deviate too much from the prevailing sense of self are repressed or consciously inhibited and discouraged, thus maintaining a sense of internal consistency' (Akhtar and Samuel 1996: 258), without implying rigid or monolithic homogeneity. Flexibility may be highly adaptive and useful in many contexts. 'A cohesive identity is different from a poorly integrated one because of the former's overall synthesis, comfortable transition among various self-representations and optimal mixture of reality principle and ego-ideal dictated direction in manifesting or not manifesting various facets of oneself' (Akhtar and Samuel 1996).

Genuineness and authenticity are other characteristics of a well-integrated identity (Akhtar 1992). To possess an identity, it is necessary to recognize it in an 'identification' that one and others carry out. A myriad of definitions of authenticity can be found in the field of psychological research. Akhtar and Samuel (1996) follow the one given by *Webster's Ninth New Collegiate Dictionary*. Authenticity should be that which is 'worthy of acceptance or belief, conforming to fact or reality, not imaginary or false'. In addition, *Webster's* affirms that authenticity involves being actually and exactly what is claimed: without counterfeit; being fully genuine, sincere and trustworthy (Akhtar and Samuel 1996).

From this perspective, individuals with a solid identity are authentic. They are knowledgeable about and committed to an intra-psychic and interpersonal ideology that has as its credo being true to oneself and others, as well as having a capacity for originality. Such persons are able to recognize and accept the 'facts' about themselves as they see them. Dietary preferences; selection of clothing; likes and dislikes in art, literature or music; taste in home decoration; and selection of leisure activities emanate from a deep and mostly unconscious synthesis of early identifications with one's own life experience. There is little effort to imitate others in these matters (Akhtar and Samuel 1996). Styles and fashion represent, in these cases, the personal synthesis of the individual and of its own harmonious originality. Subjective clarity regarding gender and a realistic body image are also traits of a consolidated identity (Akhtar 1992). Gender identity 'consists of three aspects that are essential for an integrated self identity: core gender identity, or the awareness and acceptance of having one type of genitals or another, and therefore of being male or female; gender role, or one's overt behavior in relationship to other people with respect to one's gender; and sexual partner orientation, or one's preferred sex of the love object … Such solid gender identity emerges from the interplay of constitutional givens and cultural factors, with deep acceptance of the distinction between the sexes, predominance of identifications with the same-sex parent, and a recognition of the complementarity of the opposite sex' (Akhtar and Samuel 1996). Adolescents with clarity in this respect will prefer to dress and have a congruent style with the sex they belong to.

A realistic body image involves an objective and stable perception of the body, a normal concern for its dimensions and sizing, with a prevalent feeling of satisfaction. For adolescents, and especially girls, one of the most visibly striking changes happens to their bodies, and for that reason they can be severely concerned with it. Bodies change in size, shape and hormonal structures. Fashion is a symbol of self-identity and part of the language of the body, therefore closely related to this aspect of identity. Different authors (Durkin and Paxton 2002; Schutz, Paxton and Wertheim 2002; Kostanski and Sallechia 2003) have addressed and studied issues such as stable body satisfaction or dissatisfaction, the physical-appearance comparison tendency, the internalization of thin ideal, self-esteem, depression, identity confusion and body mass. These studies reveal a relationship between idealized female images with a significant decrease in body satisfaction and a significant increase in the state of depression attributable to viewing these images. Appearance and nonappearance social comparisons increase with age, and in some of these studies, girls were reported to compare their bodies most frequently with peers and fashion models. The body-comparison tendency was significantly predicted by the importance of thinness, the internalization of sociocultural ideals, a friend's concern with weight, body-image instability, competitiveness, public self-consciousness, perfectionism and the family's concern with weight. Many authors have discussed the importance of the effect of the media on body satisfaction in adolescents, especially girls (Champion and Furnham 1999; Hamilton and Turner 1997; Shaw 1995), and have concluded that fashion magazines and idealized female images, such as the Barbie doll, do have an influence on body image and self-perception. Adolescent girls tend to respond to fashion images by showing greater body dissatisfaction than adults, and both groups respond more to pictures of adults than to those of adolescents. Greater adolescent dissatisfaction has been related to increased age within this developmental period, weight and bulimic tendencies. It is important for adolescents to value their own experience of body beauty. There are beautiful bodies and faces which only express coldness and weakness. This is the case of the Barbie doll, with her exclusively external beauty. Many of today's adolescents played with this doll in their childhood. They dressed and undressed her, and these experiences left a mark on their minds: some of them unconsciously became like her in adulthood. Even more, in some of these young women, the body transformations associated with maternity are felt as a threat to the ideal feminine body. In these cases, early identifications and idealized models during infancy actually have an effect on the type of body and appearance a young adolescent girl wishes to have. Models that resemble Barbie dolls and friends who also want to look or be like her will surely put pressure on the young girl without a consolidated identity.

Inner solidarity with the ideals and values of groups and an inner moral conscience are traits of consolidated identity (Akhtar 1992). This dimension 'refers to the culture of a people and includes values, child-rearing practices, sense of history, modes of expression, and patterns of interpersonal behavior' (Akhtar and Samuel 1996). Relatedness and feeling part of a group is of crucial importance at this age. Until this relatedness is achieved, adolescent girls do not feel that their desire for status and acceptance is consolidated. This is an important subject of adolescent girls' culture and group values that can most accurately be described as 'social dependency' (Hurtes 2002). Adolescents are hence very vulnerable to group pressure in defining their style and appearance: they depend on the group. Some adolescents with a fragile identity can become members of groups with a very definite style and ideology.

By being part of the group, their subjective identity is strongly influenced by the ideas, language, appearance, taste and music the group defines. Groups at this age can help individuals achieve their identity, but, for the aforementioned reason, they also constitute pressure to acquire not only an external style but also an ideology and the dominant stereotype. Simmel's ideas on fashion (Barnard 1996) are of help here to understand these dynamics: people appear to need to be social and individual at the same time, and fashion and clothing are ways in which this complex set of desires and demands may be negotiated. The problem with adolescents is in fact that they appear to have both desires but are very vulnerable and in need of belonging to a same-sex group that can influence them greatly and not help them define themselves. Some adolescents lose their personal identity while belonging to a group with strong values and ideas. Being similar and belonging versus possessing a different identity are desires that can come into conflict at this age. Adolescents judge friends and other groups by their physical appearance, but there are aspects they do not see with which they can also either identify or differentiate from. Subcultures are hence very important. What these subcultures communicate is very interesting and might not be the result of a conscious desire. For instance, ugliness can communicate an oppositional image but can very frequently reflect a feeling of inner vacuum. Adolescents with fragile personalities or split personalities can represent a certain type of person during the day and another night without feeling guilty. Clothing and fashion here express different meanings and can represent contradictory ways of being oneself.

ABOUT NARCISSISM IN ADOLESCENCE AS A CONTEMPORARY VALUE

Perhaps like no other phase of life, the passage through adolescence bears the hallmarks of narcissistic vulnerability, apparent in a proneness to embarrassment and shame, acute self-consciousness and shyness and painful questions about self-esteem and self-worth.

Narcissistic vulnerability is a central feature of both normal and pathological adolescence. Normal adolescents achieve a partial disengagement from their internalized parents without finding themselves bereft of limit-setting and direction-giving capacities or unable to maintain basically good relationships with both their real and their intra-psychic parents. Normal adolescents can construct an ideal that guides their transition into adulthood. In pathological narcissism, by contrast, youngsters crystallize their reliance on an omnipotent sense of self, refuse to acknowledge their shortcomings and vulnerabilities, project onto others disowned self-experiences and demand public affirmation of their illusory power.

Following Akhtar (2003), it can be said that Freud introduced the term *narcissistic* into the psychiatric literature in 1905 and later described the narcissistic character type. Jones in 1913 described the 'god complex' as the portrayal of this personality. Some of its characteristics are narcissistic grandiosity, an exaggerated need for praise, a search for glory and a love of language. Interestingly enough, he also stated that some of these traits were sometimes masked by their opposite: undue humility, social reserve and a pretended lack of interest in status, wealth and material goods in real life.

Akhtar (2003) and Kohut (1971) have noted a second type of narcissistic personality: the so-called shy narcissist who presents narcissistic deficiency, including low self-esteem, lack of initiative, marked propensity towards shame, intense discomfort about his/her need to display him/herself and often suffering from a severe case of stage fright. Cooper (in Akhtar 2003) added that 'the surface manifestations of narcissistic personality might be charm, ambition and accomplishment, or these might include depression, invitations to humiliation and feelings of failure. Cooper emphasized that narcissistic and masochistic tendencies frequently co-exist' (Akhtar 2003).

The *Diagnostic and Statistical Manual of Mental Disorders* (1994) provides a profile of the narcissistic personality disorder: a pervasive pattern of grandiosity (in fantasy or behaviour), a need for admiration and a lack of empathy beginning in early adulthood and present in a variety of contexts. Also, some of the following characteristics must be present: a grandiose sense of self-importance (exaggeration of achievements and talents, expectation of being recognized as superior without commensurate achievements); a preoccupation with fantasies of unlimited success, power, brilliance, beauty or ideal love; a belief that he or she is 'special' and unique and can only be understood by or should associate with other special or high-status people (or institutions); a need for excessive admiration; a sense of entitlement; interpersonal exploitation; a lack of empathy; envy of others or the belief that others are envious of him or her; and arrogant, haughty behaviours or attitudes. Akhtar (2003) affirms that many of these characteristics are also applicable to the shy type of narcissistic personality.

The overt narcissist appears as the typical personality who is excessively interested in his/her appearance for praise and admiration, with an almost obsessive worry for the body, health and beauty and an intense anguish associated with aging and finally dying.

Lipovetsky (1990) writes about contemporary individualism for both sexes and mentions mental and bodily narcissism. He says that with the coming of neonarcissism there is a general interest of both sexes in their private autonomy and attention towards themselves, an obsession with the body, health and relationship problems. He differentiates masculine and feminine narcissism by saying that men usually have a global image of themselves, one that they have to maintain healthy and in shape with little interest for details and with rare preoccupations for certain partial regions of their bodies, with exception of the critical points: wrinkles on the face, abdomen size and baldness. On the contrary, and in Lipovetsky's opinion, women rarely have a global image of their bodies, instead having a fragmented and analytical view. Lipovetsky emphasizes an analytical narcissism in either mature or young women through which they maintain a self-concept and appreciation of certain parts of their bodies as more valuable than others. This analytical narcissism is closely related to the code of feminine beauty. Beauty, here, is understood to be a phobia of fatness and a passion shared by women. Men are becoming increasingly worried about their appearance, body, looks and style. This confirms Lipovetsky's hypothesis of masculine neonarcissism.

According to Herrero (2002), contemporary identity is marked by the aesthetics of thinness, sports and ecology and is defined merely by its exterior components. In the 'appearance era', the new moral goal is one's looks. The radical definition of looks has its basis in the body, which becomes an object. If appearance and exteriority are the main values, there is no way of differentiating the human body from other objects. Baudrillard (in Herrero 2002), one of the principal postmodern gurus, states that in consumer society every object, even the body, has a functional operation. Artificial changes to the body have become a new religion.

The development of a healthy conceptualization of the self is key to adequate functioning later in life. Self-image and self-esteem are concepts that help clinicians and researchers evaluate adolescent narcissism, as well as normal and adequate self-perception. Many adolescent girls are excessively worried about their bodies, as stated earlier, and have acute body and self-image dissatisfaction. Casper and Offer (1990) mention that the fairly common fear of being overweight and thoughts of dieting experienced by contemporary female adolescents, in part, seem to reflect the greater aesthetic value that contemporary society places on the thinness of women. Therefore, it can be affirmed that society, group values and models presented by society through fashion and the media have a significant influence on adolescents, who are in a developmental period characterized by physical, psychological, cognitive and social transitions (Pletsch et al. 1991). From this standpoint, fashion can be dangerous because it is full of this desire to be original, creative and admired by others, especially in this hedonistic age in which the primary cultural values are pleasure, freedom and independence. The values and style of the group to which the adolescent belongs become a great influence over the self-concept the young person is developing.

Adolescents who are defining their identity and immature adults with narcissistic problems can become constantly worried about their appearance and allergic to imposed standards and homogeneous rules. In Lipovetsky's (1990) words, Narcissus seeks psychological intimacy and authenticity but, on the other hand, tends to engage in playful exhibitionism and the feast of appearances. With fashion one can feel and look younger, different, similar to the ideal image of oneself; it is just a matter of playing with one's own created image and renewing it at will. Since the external signs of death are disappearing from the public space, the fantasy of omnipotence, or the 'god complex' described by Jones, appears to be stimulated. It is the pleasure and sense of power associated with metamorphosis and mutation described by Doltó (1990) as an intrinsic characteristic of adolescence.

Adolescents who have not yet been able to achieve a solid identity and whose characters have a predominantly narcissistic and hysterical type, or who suffer from eating disorders, will probably be extremely worried about and in conflict with their body, self-image and appearance. They will also be extremely worried by feelings of belonging to a group and therefore will be very vulnerable to that pressure. Important areas of their self-esteem and self-concept depend on the evaluations of the group, and the process of differentiation will be a conflictive one. The same is true for narcissistic adults who continue to be immature and who have severe difficulty establishing love relationships based on commitment and dependence.

But normal adolescents going through the mutation period and feeling fragile will also have a conflictive relationship with their body image and appearance. Adolescents very commonly do not know what to wear or frequently feel discomfort with their style because they actually do not yet have a personal style. They still have not achieved a sustained feeling of self-sameness and of temporal continuity in self-experience. This can make them feel different with different people or in different circumstances. They might adapt to these situations and appear to have several styles.

Since genuineness and authenticity are in the process of being acquired, adolescents will probably have doubts about who they are and whether they are being true or projecting a false image of themselves to others. Adolescents have not yet achieved a realistic body image or a sense of inner solidity. They are developing a subjective clarity regarding their gender, so the perception of their body can be expressed in the way they dress and appear. Adolescents may search in clothes and cosmetics for a way to compensate or feel closer to their ideal image of themselves. According to their body weight and their feelings about it, they can wear heavy clothes or very tight ones, either to show their body or to hide it.

Self-concept and self-esteem can also be expressed through clothes and style. An adolescent who feels depressed and empty inside might try to defend himself from these bad feelings by trying to obtain praise and admiration. Adolescents can become extremely original in their style just to be looked at and feel cared for. Through clothes, adolescents communicate many things, such as the need for psychological and physical protection, the way they are relating to the opposite sex and the means they use to show they are different from others or absorbed by their peer group. They also express the ideology of the group they belong to, their feelings of approval or rejection towards society and family and their need to be the centre of attention or go unnoticed. Many adolescents dress in eccentric ways which may express their inner dissociations. To give an example, we can recall youngsters who wore a cross-shaped earring in one ear and snake in the other, or others who would dress in a sporty way but with heavy-duty boots. Some adolescents cover themselves to hide self-aggressions done to their body. Many times it is the wearing of certain clothes that makes someone a member of a group. While items of fashion or clothing may be neutral or innocent, the uses to which they are put and the functions they have are not (Barnard 1996). And even though this is true, we should add that there are meanings of clothes, regardless of the type of individual wearing them. This is the case of a ballgown or a suit. Therefore, fashion can widely express meanings, but there is also a limit set by the object itself, which has an intrinsic one.

Clothes, style and personal appearance tell us something about that person, but, in the case of adolescents, what is expressed can be exactly the opposite of how they feel. Appearances are not always true, but they should not be underestimated (Zegers 1993). Clinicians who work with adolescents develop an acute sensibility to decoding the messages that they are trying to express through their appearance and use this to enter into their inner worlds.

As Marías (2002) points out, appearance is what we deal with constantly every day, and it is what regulates the experience of others and their behaviours. He emphasizes the importance of self-appearance in interpersonal relations as a means of communication. Fashion can conceal and mask physical defects, insecurities and complexes, but it is also a sign of actual function and status. It plays a role in the human condition: 'This is how I see you; this is how I treat you.' Anyone who does not show his personal dignity can be taken for something he is not.

Doltó (1990) states that present models have substituted the great heroes of the past. The era of idols has begun. Adolescents compare themselves to the models promoted by fashion and very frequently desire to look like them. Such fashion images motivate adolescents to present a body image that gains approval and acceptance. Beauty and a perfect body have become gods to be worshipped. Adolescents and adults influenced by these ideals undergo incredible sacrifice in order to achieve the goals society proposes. Hedonistic society stimulates an excessive, unhealthy emphasis on body image. People are following these trends in an obsessive way by divinizing beauty, eternal youth and thinness. Plastic surgery as a means of obtaining this objective has put itself under the power of these divinities. The idols are movie stars and members of music groups, and they may appear on television or the news talking about their private lives, including all the body transformations they have gone through. Nowadays, diets and exercise and fashion and cosmetics are not enough; today you can rebuild and remodel your body and image (Peña Vial 2004a,b).

SUMMARY

Image and appearances reveal our inner psychology and personality. Some even say that our appearance is our greeting card. Fashion and taking care of oneself are very important, but their preponderance has been exaggerated. Consumerism and compulsive shopping (especially for clothes) have become strategies to alleviate depression and anxiety (Figueras 2000). These compulsive buyers are very different from the expert buyer who buys in a reflexive way with common sense and good information. The fashion victim responds to the progressive individualism which dictates the interest of choice and election as synonyms of freedom (Figueras 2000).

Since adolescence appears to be a crucial period in the development of identity definition and body concept, beauty standards, correct proportions and weight become influenced by fashion. Adolescents are defining who they are and are affected by many variables: their inner world and objects of primary love, their actual relationships with adults (parents, educators, etc.) and friends. Groups and subcultures are very relevant at this age, as are mass-media models, values and ideals of beauty and charm.

Today's culture places great value on the way people look, especially women, but also men. When societies focus on 'body image', the body is no longer seen as subjectively experienced, but rather as an object (Rosenbaum 1993, in Oliver 1999), and fashion and self-appearance become overwhelmingly influential. Adolescents can learn through fashion whether their bodies are 'right' or 'wrong', 'normal' or 'not normal'. Fashion can represent one of the cultural codes or rules that set the backdrop for the lives of young girls as they begin to develop into young women (Oliver 1999). However, it has to be said that, through trial and error and experimentation, normal adolescents learn about themselves and end up defining their personal style. Almost through playing, they achieve their unique and original modes. Fashion at this age and also later in life can introduce the aspect of ease and play into human life, which is sometimes too serious. It can also be the means of communicating the conflicts, dissociations and pathological aspects of the self.

Fashion is a language through which adolescents and adults express many meanings, but, as Simmel has specifically pointed out, 'fashion is what makes it possible for humans to recognize themselves as members of a group, a society, a professional corporation, without their identity becoming diluted in the group. Fashion is at the same time something that renders possible generalization and differentiation' (in Figueras 2000: 179). If vanities, narcissism, self-centredness and the need for attention are the values that society is proclaiming, there is no doubt that fashion can fall into exhibitionism. The human body is then considered as an object of seduction that fashion must exhibit, undress and uncover. Courréges and other fashion professionals who react against nudism have stated that 'the work of a dressmaker or modiste is to dress people, not strip them' (in Figueras 2000: 188). However, nudism is slowly invading society. This ugly and graceless tendency to undress is part of the self-erotic psychology that overvalues exhibitionism. To show everything, just as to say everything, with the excuse of being authentic and spontaneous, is actually a lack of interiority of the person (Anatrella 1990). Interestingly enough, this is a task that a child of six or eight years of age achieves and expresses by opposing his parents when they want to clean him. The child has learned to hide and protect his nakedness. Modesty is part of normal development. It seems that many adolescents and adults nowadays have not assumed this task.

Figueras (2000) says that when fashion does not present a definite style—that is, when it is less authoritarian, more diverse and democratic—consumers become tyrannized by aesthetics and shape. This is what is happening today. Thin bodies and eternal youthfulness are two of the goals people seek when building their appearance through clothes and style (and other invasive strategies such as plastic surgery). Since the 1990s, advertising has disseminated images of young women with ravaged appearances as the ideal of beauty. Adolescents are exposed to this influence and are at risk of acquiring different eating problems and related psychopathologies (anorexia, bulimia, etc.). The prevalence of these illnesses is increasing at present. But even more serious cases are adolescents who have built their identity based on these values. They are at risk of conforming to deceitful pseudo-identities, identities that are ever changing following fashion's lead. This may also be expressed in their permanent interest in changing home decorations and in experiencing new forms of nutrition, new religions and spiritual interests and so forth.

On the other hand, mature and healthy adolescents and adults already have a self-definition and self-esteem that are not as vulnerable. Their relationship to models and the influence of the mass media on their identity are evidently less. Normal adults without narcissistic problems know who they are, have a defined life project and follow it and feel comfortable and at ease with their body, appearance and style. Since they have a solid identity, they possess a personal and original style that is to a certain extent independent of fashion trends. Mature and normal adults relate to fashion models and to the values that society proposes in a different and more independent way. Beauty should be founded on solid principles that consider the inner attitude and attitude towards others, and not only relate to questions of looks and external appearances. Today you do not have to be born beautiful because personal beauty is built and is a result of a combination of spiritual, mental and physical characteristics that can be enhanced by age (Figueras 1997).

The myth of Narcissus, of looking at oneself in a haughty way, full of self-pride, sets the basis for an unfortunate and unhappy enterprise which puts humans under the despotism of fashion and its related values. Adolescents make decisions about themselves, their appearance and their style influenced or conditioned by many factors. As mentioned earlier, parental figures are important models during infancy and are introjected during childhood. Peer groups and belonging to a community that presents models, values and appearances that are accepted or rejected will also condition adolescent decision-making. Voluntary, conscious or unconscious choices about fashion are thus very complex and cannot be attributed to one factor alone. It is the combination of personal biography (physical and psychological), influences to which the person is exposed during adolescence and the strength to oppose or reject whatever is not part of the personal life project that will finally guide the adolescent in one direction or another. All this happens while the young person is going through the task of building an identity, which, as we have described, is a process that can end with a normal consolidated identity or with a diffused or abnormal one.

Adolescents should be helped by adults to achieve a solid and normal identity with a healthy self-concept. They should also be helped to differentiate from their group. They should develop a strong capacity to accept similarities but at the same time to oppose and be assertive to whatever goes against their values and life project. This is the only way in which they will be able to relate in a normal way to fashion and appearance and be authentic and honest to themselves. Otherwise, they might emphasize their appearance as objects of desire for the opposite sex, thus diminishing their human dignity. Or they might use fashion in an extreme way as a means of acquiring self-esteem.

Helping adolescents develop virtues such as modesty, authenticity and strength of the self is of central importance. In consequence, fashion, style and looks will be ways of communicating healthy character and normal consolidated identity traits. When adolescence has been left behind, the young person is less vulnerable to the power of fashion because the consolidated identity becomes an intra-psychic narrative of the self that every person carries with him- or herself. With maturity the person gains a certain independence from fashion, knows who he/she is and understands the appearance that is in accordance with his/her identity. Identity formation and identification processes are completed by adulthood, and the relationship to fashion has changed to a more stable one.

References and Further Reading

Akhtar, S. (2003), *New Clinical Realms. Pushing the Envelope of Theory and Technique*, Lanham, MD: Jason Aronson.

Akthar, S., and Samuel, S. (1996), 'The Concept of Identity: Developmental Origins, Phenomenology, Clinical Relevance, and Measurement', *Harvard Review of Psychiatry*, 3/5: 254–67.

Anatrella, T. (1990), *El sexo olvidado*, Santander: Editorial Sal Térrea.

Barnard, M. (1996), *Fashion as Communication*, New York: Routledge.

Casper, R., and Offer, D. (1990), 'Weight and Dieting Concerns in Adolescents: Fashion or Symptom?' *Pediatrics*, 86/3 (Sept.): 384.

Champion, H., and Furnham, A. (1999), 'The Effect of the Media on Body Satisfaction in Adolescent Girls', *European Eating Disorders Review*, 7/3 (June): 213.

Côté, J. (1996), 'Identity: A Multidimensional Analysis', in G. Adams, R. Montemayor and T. Gullota (eds), *Psychosocial Development during Adolescence: Progress in Developmental Contextualism*, London: Sage Publications.

Diagnostic and Statistical Manual of Mental Disorders: DSM-IV (1994), Washington, D.C.: American Psychiatric Association.

Doltó, F. (1990), *La causa de los adolescentes: el verdadero lenguaje para dialogar con los adolescents*, Barcelona: Ed. Seix Barral.

Durkin, S., and Paxton, S. (2002), 'Predictor of Vulnerability to Reduced Body Image Satisfaction and Psychological Well-being in Response to Exposure to Idealized Female Media Images in Adolescent Girls', *Journal of Psychosomatic Research*, 53/5 (Nov.): 995.

Erikson, E. (1968), *Identity: Youth and Crisis*, New York: W. W. Norton.

Figueras, J. (1997), *La moda, sus secretos y su poder*, Madrid: Albacore S.L.

Figueras, J. (2000), *El feminismo ha muerto ¡Viva la mujer!* Madrid: Ediciones Internacionales Universitarias, S.A.

Hamilton, H., and Turner, S. (1997), 'The Influence of Fashion Magazines on the Body Image Satisfaction of College Women: An Exploratory Analysis', *Adolescence*, 32/127 (Fall): 603–15.

Herrero, M. (2002), 'La moda en la postmodernidad', *Humanitas*, 27: 392–403.

Hurtes, K. P. (2002), 'Social Dependency: The Impact of Adolescent Female Culture', *Leisure Sciences*, 24/1 (Jan.): 109.

Kernberg, P., Weiner, A., and Bardenstein, K. (2000), *Personality Disorders in Children and Adolescents*, New York: Basic Books.

Kohut, H. (1971), *The Restoration of the Self*, New York: International Universities Press.

Kostanski, M., and Sallechia, S. (2003), 'An Examination of One's Perception of the Importance of Fashion and the Experience of Shopping on Body Image Satisfaction', *Australian Journal of Psychology*, 55: 190.

Lipovetsky, G. (1986), *La Era del Vacío*, Barcelona: Editorial Anagrama.

Lipovetsky, G. (1990), *El Imperio de lo Efímero*, Barcelona: Editorial Anagrama.

Marcia, J. (1993), *Ego Identity: A Handbook for Psychosocial Research*, London: Springer-Verlag.

Marías, J. (2002), 'Las Apariencias' [electronic version], *ABC*, September 9, 2004.

Moshman, D. (1999), *Adolescent Psychological Development: Rationality, Morality and Identity*, London: Lawrence Erlbaum Associates.

Offer, D. (1991), 'Adolescent Development: A Normative Perspective', in S. Greenspan and G. Pollock (eds), *The Course of Life*, iv, *Adolescence*, 181–99, Madison, Connecticut: International Universities Press.

Oliver, K. (1999), 'Adolescent Girls' Body Narratives: Learning to Desire and Create a "Fashionable" Image', *Teachers College Record*, 101/2 (Winter): 220–46.

Peña Vial, J. (2004a), 'La idolatría de la juventud', *El Mercurio*, apuntes, Artes y Letras, March 14.

Peña Vial, J. (2004b), 'La religión del cuerpo', *El Mercurio*, apuntes, Artes y Letras, Jan. 11.

Pletsch, P., Jonson, M., Tosi, C., Thurston, C., and Riesch, S. (1991), 'Self-image among Early Adolescents: Revisited', *Journal of Community Health Nursing*, 8/4: 215.

Schutz, H., Paxton, S., and Wertheim, E. (2002), 'Investigation of Body Comparison among Adolescent Girls', *Journal of Applied Social Psychology*, 32/9 (Sept.): 1906.

Shaw, J. (1995), 'Effects of Fashion Magazines on Body Dissatisfaction and Eating Psychopathology in Adolescent and Adult Females', *European Eating Disorders Review*, 3/1: 15–23.

Taylor, C. (1989), *Sources of the Self: The Making of the Modern Identity*, Cambridge: Cambridge University Press.

Van den Aardweg, G. (1986), *On the Origins and Treatment of Homosexuality: A Psychoanalytic Reinterpretation*, New York: Praeger Publishers.

Zegers, B. (1993), 'Las apariencias engañan', *Encuentros en Familia*, 4 (Sept.), Santiago Provida.

PART III FASHION, IMAG
AND HEALTH

9 FASHION, LIFESTYLE AND PSYCHIATRY

RAPHAEL M. BONELLI

This chapter deals with the psychiatric implications of fashion, image and identity in contemporary culture. I will therefore focus on the individual level, though I will often cross over to other specialties such as sociology, philosophy and psychology because of their wider view of this topic and in the hopes that an interdisciplinary approach will help us gain a better grasp of the whole phenomenon.

The first concern arising is if there is any link between fashion, image and identity on the one hand and human disease on the other. Can fashion increase or decrease illness? Can fashion help psychiatrically ill persons? In fact, we find increasing interest in fashion in our depressed patients at the moment when depression wanes and people start to participate in society again. Similarly, schizophrenic patients gravely neglect their attire to a radical extent, and improvement in their symptomatology can be noticed by improvement in personal appearance. In fact, art and aesthetics play a major role in the healing process of some psychiatrically ill persons. On the other hand, we find that some contemporary psychiatric diseases—such as anorexia nervosa, body dysmorphic disorder, body-image dissatisfaction and unneeded plastic surgery—in an increasing number of patients today are probably stimulated by abnormally perfect models presented by society. Moreover, sexual activity might, especially in adolescents, be artificially forced by fashionable media and/or peer pressure, thus possibly leading to impaired relationships years later. Though not discussed in this chapter, gender-identity disorder and transvestitism (Yunger, Carver and Perry 2004; Zucker 2004) are also of growing importance in modern psychiatry.

One of the pitfalls of my topic could be a merely negative view of fashion, as psychiatry necessarily deals with disease (which is a negative phenomenon). As an example of this aspect, shopping, the main characteristic of our affluent society, can become pathological in a medical sense. Peer pressure can force one to buy whatever

is 'in', and people can lose control of this conduct (McCarthy 2004). This loss of control is called compulsive shopping disorder (Aboujaoude, Gamel and Koran 2003). With a negative approach, we could therefore conclude that shopping itself is highly problematic as a pure symptom of consumerism. However, by doing so, we would not solve the problem. Shopping is reasonable behaviour which can simply be exaggerated by wrong attitudes and insufficient personal control. I shall approach the topic of fashion as it relates to mental health in a similar way: by highlighting its risks and also pointing out its useful and healthy elements and doses.

FASHION AND LIFESTYLE

This chapter deals with the interdependence of fashion and the human psyche. On the one hand, fashion is obviously created by humans, thereby necessarily expressing somehow parts of the human psyche. Fashion is actually a merely human phenomenon, as no other species shows a similar 'needless' pattern of behaviour. Fashion is able to influence human life significantly by initiating social trends, thus making people change lifestyles, attitudes and relationships and thereby affecting the human psyche as well. These changes often improve subjective quality of life but sometimes may also decrease it or even lead to psychiatric disturbances. It is this social influence on the human psyche that makes fashion overbear ephemerality and develop into a notable social factor.

In a comprehensive review of the sociology of fashion, Thomas Schnierer suggested three cardinal attributes to define the sociologic phenomenon of fashion: its temporal, social and material aspects (Schnierer 1995).

1. The temporal aspect indicates that fashion has to be ephemeral. According to some authors, the term *fashion* should only be employed when something new appears rapidly and disappears swiftly as well. For Günter Wiswede, fashion is a fluctuating change of marginal forms of conduct, driven by arbitrary settings of paradigms without significant influence on social structure and including larger parts of a population (Wiswede 1976). Georg Simmel, born in 1858 in Berlin, is said to be the godfather of sociologic research on fashion. He stated, 'The question of fashion is not "to be or not to be", but fashion is and is not at the same moment, standing at the borderline of the past and the future, giving us a strong feeling of being in the present' (Simmel 1923). In other words, fashion tries to reach something it will never achieve (Müller 2003); otherwise, it would lack further drive. Johannes B. Torello stated that fashion itself is never new; in his view, this phenomenon is actually an abysmal human disposition (Torello 1967). However, without getting too involved in this

sociological discussion, ephemerality seems to be a limiting factor for psychiatric research on fashion. For this reason, I try to focus on the personal attitude towards fashion, which is usually quite constant in a person. Moreover, some short-dated waves of fashion may leave more stable human habits behind.

2. The second attribute is the social aspect. Fashion obviously has to show a certain amount of collectivity—that is, must include several individuals. For Georg Simmel, the limited character (i.e. not a social entirety performs fashion) is an essential part of the phenomenon. He declared that 'the nature of fashion consists in the fact that only a part of a group actually performs it, whereas the rest of the group is on the way to adopt it' (Simmel 1923). Translating sociologic mechanisms into the psychodynamic individual level, a person desires to be what he/she adores and therefore identifies with idols or pure images of some given standard (Torello 1968a). Advertisements are based on this human phenomenon.

However, for psychiatry, Malcolm Barnard's personal focus on the social aspect is more interesting: 'Everyday experience, in which clothes are selected according to what one will be doing that day, what mood one is in, who one expects to meet and so on, appears to confirm the view that fashions and clothing are used to send messages about oneself to others' (Barnard 1996). In fact, people tell us a lot about themselves by the way they dress. The outfit is actually of imminent importance for psychiatric assessment of patients in daily clinical practice, and changes in clothing often reflect mood changes. In psychiatry, observation of the outfit is part of the diagnostic method. Fashion is actually a method of self-revelation and therefore communication. According to Valerie Mendes (2001), it is possible through style of dress to express who somebody is, or who somebody wants to be. Fashion is representation, expression, identity and status. 'Call it fashion, costume, or dress, what we wear and how we decorate ourselves tells the world who we are, even in less-than-fashionable circumstances' (Mendes 2001). The interaction between humans based on their outfits is an elementary form of communication that can be interrupted by neglecting this aspect.

3. The third sociologic characteristic is the material dimension. Fashion needs a concrete material to reify. It includes a large spectrum of styles, colours, manners and behaviour, although mostly applied to clothing. The term *fashion* includes hairstyle, colours, accessories, decoration, jewellery, customs, architecture and so forth. The more the peripheral equipment of some objects can be refined and altered, the more prone to fashionable styling they are. Therefore, clothing and hairstyles are susceptible to fashion, while nails and bricks definitely are not (Wiswede 1976). In this chapter, I refer to the term *fashion* as (1) material decorating of the human body (e.g. clothing, hairstyle, etc.),

thus interfering somehow with human communication, or (2) human behaviour, also including social trends such as 'You have to have a boyfriend by the time you are fourteen.' Therefore, this chapter does not consider fashion not directly related to human relationships, such as architecture or decoration.

The next step introduces the differentiation between fashion and lifestyle. Whereas the former might be more interesting for sociology, psychology and possibly philosophy (whereas it is mainly ignored by medicine), the latter is actually an evolving research topic in medicine (Rimm and Stampfer 2004). Lifestyle is usually defined as a set of behaviours which are considered to influence health and are generally considered to involve a good amount of free choice (Contoyannis and Jones 2004). Fashion and social trends are interdependent, and both significantly influence lifestyle. A new discipline of lifestyle medicine was created recently (Gilbert, Walley and New 2000) due to the fact that some lifestyles constitute clear-cut risk behaviours for somatic and psychiatric problems. For this reason, fashion is definitely connected to psychiatry via its influence on lifestyle. The topic of lifestyle actually lies at the heart of modern preventive medicine. The threat of injury or infection has been replaced in the Western imagination by the dangers of everyday activity: smoking, slothfulness, sunbathing, promiscuity and other sexual risk behaviour and drug and alcohol consumption, to name but a few (Hirota et al. 1992; Miauton, Narring and Michaud 2003; Pope, Ionescu-Pioggia and Pope 2001; Ruidavets, Bataille and Dallongeville 2004; Yarnell et al. 2004).

The word *lifestyle* was first used in the early 1930s by followers of the Austrian psychiatrist Alfred Adler. Adler himself saw lifestyle as a defence mechanism: a pattern of behaviour adopted at an early age to disguise physical weaknesses or inferiorities (Adler 1912). In 1934, Walter Langdon-Brown claimed that 'styles of life' were the clinical fantasies of patients, with different illnesses being used to disguise particular personal failures. It was not until the early 1960s that advertising and marketing took over the term *lifestyle* as shorthand for aspirational identities and their attendant consumption patterns. This usage received popular support; youth movements celebrated *lifestyle* as a form of individual and cultural expression (Hayward 2004). It was this usage that was taken up in epidemiology; the clustering of modes of behaviour and consumption allowed the easy elision of statistical and moral significance. Finally, in its seventy-year career, *lifestyle* has moved from being a symptom of illness to a cause of disease (Hayward 2004).

THE HUMAN NEED FOR FASHION

Fashion is in fact a merely human phenomenon that animals never develop. Johannes B. Torello (1967) observed that 'those frowning serious people condemn fashion as caprice, insanity, vanity, immorality, extravagance or simple waste: as if fashion was invented by the devil.' In fact, there is an ivory-tower, quixotic, body-hostile contempt of human phenomena like fashion in some parts of our society today (the 'intellectuals') as a backlash against the growing importance of fashion in some other parts (the majority, in fact). The ability to enjoy life, superficiality, feelings and fun are important parts of human existence. The lack of this ability is called anhedonia in psychiatry. This anhedonic attitude condemns fashion as mere superficiality without significance. Aristotle wrote that 'men who are deficient with regard to pleasures and enjoy them less than they should scarcely exist, for such insensibility is not human; for even the other animals distinguish kinds of food, enjoying some but not others, so if there be someone who finds nothing pleasurable and no difference between one kind of food and another kind, he would be far from being a man' (Book C, 14; see Apostle 1984).

In a certain way, 'fashion is play. Every fineness, every fashion, every play is delicate. It is threatened from all directions. But man may not abandon fashion, because rigor in material or mental aspects might asphyxiate him' (Torello 1967). In his famous book, Johan Huizinga (1939) compared *Homo ludens* with *Homo sapiens* and *Homo faber*. Huizinga saw the instinct for play as the central element in human culture—that is to say, all human activities involve play: 'Now in myth and ritual the great instinctive forces of civilized life have their origin: law and order, commerce and profit, craft and art, poetry, wisdom and science. All are rooted in the primeval soil of play' (Huizinga 1939). Moreover, he stated that 'in play there is something "at play" which transcends the immediate needs of life and imparts meaning to the action. All play means something. If we call the active principle that makes up the essence of play "instinct", we explain nothing; if we call it "mind" or "will" we say too much. However we may regard it, the very fact that play has a meaning implies a non-materialistic quality in the nature of the thing itself' (Huizinga 1939).

Torello emphasizes that fashion is necessary play, and as such it should be integrated into personal life. He cites Plato by saying that the very best of man is to play, and Thomas Aquinas found playing as important for internal life as resting (Torello 1967). Old Greek ethics referred to the ideal person as Eutrapelos (i.e. the serious-cheerful), who holds balance between the Bomolochos (clown) and the Agroikos (the rigid grumbler). According to Torello, the playful Eutrapelos knows his existence is meaningful but unnecessary, and therefore he escapes from the danger of carelessness on the one hand and from the danger of tragedy on the other. An abundance of play was the characteristic of most contemplative persons, like the troubadour of Assisi, the comical Thomas More, a cheerful Teresa of Avila and the mystical clown Philipp Neri; all were endowed with eternal wisdom by not taking themselves too seriously (Torello 1967). From this point of view, fashion changes its character when it is taken too seriously, when it lacks the characteristics of play, when it pretends to be more than it is.

From a puritan, utilitarian point of view, the playfulness of fashion is superfluous and useless. But most ethicists agree that fashion is not intrinsically good or bad, and therefore may be used the right or wrong way. No human being can totally avoid its influence, as we are all social beings. We actually have to dress somehow, and what we wear is either fashionable, classic or old-fashioned.

Pure clothing meets the needs of protection against cold and curiosity. Fashion provides the rest. The refreshing changes in personal outfit are due to a healthy yearning for variety. We find a major difference between the generations in terms of interest in clothing (older people being less concerned about their outfit; they have found their style) and between the sexes. With increasing age, people might focus more on their interior life and responsibilities so that their interest in their own attire wanes. With the years, we know what to wear to form part of the group and define our identity. Most recent psychological research on fashion has been carried out on adolescent girls. We know today that the so-called 'fashion alienation' is positively related to age (i.e. the older the person, the less interest in fashion) and negatively related to frequency of use of the media for fashion (Kaiser and Chandler 1984). Three significant factors were recently found in 358 girls in senior secondary school completing the measures assessing the importance of clothing: self-enhancement, experimentation and conformity (Fung and Yuen 2002).

FASHION CANNOT SUBSTITUTE VALUES

The modern media makes it possible for new trends to reach every single person in a period of days (whereas in ancient times it took decades). Therefore, we now find increasing peer pressure in the phenomenon of fashionable clothing, fashionable attitudes, fashionable ideas and fashionable behaviour (Devos and Banaji 2003; Van Vugt and Hart 2004). Fashionable 'modern' opinions often develop in society after being declared by the mass media and obediently accepted by the apparent majority. The term 'political correctness' was coined to describe the phenomenon of a new unified dictatorial morality. According to some philosophers, 'the crisis in modernity involves a degradation, indeed a pulverization, of the fundamental uniqueness of each human person' (Weigel 1999).

As mentioned earlier, fashion is an important element of play for human life, but when it is taken too seriously, it may take on a role it cannot fulfil. Fashion seems to be increasingly important in large parts of our society today due to a lack of higher values (Covey 1989). People lacking higher values are actually highly susceptible to peer pressure.

This social phenomenon seems to be connected with a certain loss of interiority, of values, of religion, of transcendence and therefore a loss of identity. When there is no interiority left, the exterior must replace it. Parts of today's society are increasingly focused on the image, rather than the content. 'The new imagery, with photography at its forefront, did not merely function as a supplement to language, but to replace it as our dominant means for constructing, understanding and testing reality. The new focus on the image undermined traditional definitions of information, news and, to a large extent, reality itself . . . For countless Americans, seeing, not reading became the basis of believing' (Postmann 1985).

The decreasing importance of transcendence (Frankl 1969) implies a growing importance of fashion, which might reflect increasing egocentrism, including an emphasis on body culture. However, this is not the problem of fashion itself, but rather of the lack of a necessarily serious purpose in life. As early as in primary school, it is of high importance for parents to have their children wear a trendy T-shirt, thereby satisfying their lust for succeeding in competition with others. Thus, their offspring assimilate this attitude of competing with their peers in superficialities. We find a similar phenomenon in adults with regard to the automobile industry. Without this lust to keep up with the Joneses, a whole branch of industry would be in terrible trouble. Incidentally, an important factor in this development is the fact that single-child families have a lot of money to spend on their only child.

FASHION IS STIMULATED BY THE POLARITY OF SEXES

A large part of the human phenomenon of fashion is driven by the polarity between maleness and femaleness. In fact, fashion is able to highlight the differences between the sexes to make them more attractive to each other. The dynamic of fashion requires this complementary difference of the sexes—in other words, the sexual attraction between male and female. However, due to the differences between the sexes in this aspect, females send many more courtship messages through clothing with males as the receivers. Interestingly, males send their courtship messages more on the behavioural level and not to the same extent through clothing. This is why females in general are much more prone to fashion (especially if we reduce fashion to clothing). Indeed, practically all fashion magazines are dedicated to women, and most models are female as well. Interestingly, Sigmund Freud commented that 'all women are clothes fetishists' and explained that a woman uses clothes to show that 'one can find in her everything that one can expect from women' (Richards 1996).

Public exhibition harms the psychic integrity of both the 'sender' and the 're-ceiver' through the depersonalization of the body and turning it into pure eroticism

(Torello 1969). The so-called sex wave, emphasizing the exposure of the human body, erroneously pretends that we live in a time of body culture (Torello 1969). Its revelation causes a loss of intimacy and therefore a loss of (often female) identity. Moreover, high susceptibility to such exhibitions in the male recipient analogously cause damage to his image of the female's role in his own life, thus damaging his inter-gender relationship.

Desired sexual attractiveness and activity can play important roles in female dressing; it is up to each woman to define the intensity of her exposure. Karl Grammer and co-workers analysed the relationship between a female's clothing choice, sexual motivation and hormone levels in 351 females attending Austrian discotheques (Grammer, Renninger and Fischer 2004). The group digitally analysed clothing choice to determine the amount of skin display, sheerness and clothing tightness. Participants self-reported sexual motivation, and the team assessed hormone levels through saliva sampling. The results show that females are aware of the social signal function of their clothing and that in some cases they alter their clothing style to match their courtship motivation. In particular, sheer clothing positively correlated with the motivation for sex. Moreover, hormone levels correlated positively with physique display (Grammer et al. 2004).

The DSM-IV (American Psychiatric Association 1994) defined voyeurism, a psychiatric disturbance, as 'recurrent, intense sexually arousing fantasies, sexual urges or behaviors involving the act of observing an unsuspecting person who is naked, in the process of disrobing, or engaging in sexual activity'. Without a doubt, we are developing towards a voyeuristic society, as we simply have more possibilities to view this kind of content than in the past (television, the Internet, journals, cinema, advertisements, etc.).

THE HISTRIONIC ATTITUDE TOWARDS FASHION

The psychiatric study of personality disorders has identified two unhealthy attitudes towards society in general and fashion in particular. One gives fashion too much attention, and the other condemns it. Histrionic personalities, on the one hand, are prone to superficiality. They are dependent on the opinion of others and therefore put an exaggerated amount of effort into their personal fashionable outlook. They are characterized by an exaggerated and often inappropriate display of emotional reactions that approaches theatricality in everyday behaviour. This attitude towards fashion is increasingly common in our society. In contrast, schizoid personalities (predominately males) do not care about the opinions of others. They have a very limited range of emotion, both in the expression and experiencing of feelings, and are especially indifferent to social relationships. While the schizoid way of thinking consists of an underestimation of the body, the histrionic approach undervalues intellectual integrity and values.

It might be useful to replicate the exact definition of this pattern of conduct. According to the World Health Organization (WHO)'s ICD-10 (World Health Organization 1994), the histrionic personality disorder (with the diagnostic number F60.4) is characterized by

> at least three of the following six items: (a) self-dramatization, theatricality, exaggerated expression of emotions; (b) suggestibility, easily influenced by others or by circumstances; (c) shallow and labile affectivity; (d) continual seeking for excitement, appreciation by others and activities in which the person is the center of attention; (e) inappropriate seductiveness in appearance or behavior; and (f) over-concern with physical attractiveness.

The second important psychiatric classification, the DSM-IV, provides some new aspects. It defines the histrionic personality disorder by

> a pervasive pattern of excessive emotionality and attention seeking, beginning by early adulthood and present in a variety of contexts, as indicated by five (or more) of the following eight items: (1) is uncomfortable in situations in which he or she is not the center of attention, (2) interaction with others is often characterized by inappropriate sexually seductive or provocative behavior, (3) displays rapidly shifting and shallow expression of emotions, (4) consistently uses physical appearance to draw attention to self, (5) has a style of speech that is excessively impressionistic and lacking in detail, (6) shows self-dramatization, theatricality, and exaggerated expression of emotion, (7) is suggestible, i.e., easily influenced by others or circumstances, and (8) considers relationships to be more intimate than they actually are.

Stephen R. Covey gives an interesting analysis of the contemporaneous histrionic society on the topic of feeling and love in his remarkable bestseller *The Seven Habits of Highly Effective People*. In his view, love is a verb, thus implying action. In contrast, histrionic ('reactive') people make it a feeling. 'They're driven by feelings. Hollywood has generally scribed us to believe that we are not responsible, that we are a product of our feelings. But the Hollywood script does not describe the reality. If our feelings control our actions, it is because we have abdicated our responsibility and empowered them to do so' (Covey 1989).

The Austrian psychiatrist Victor E. Frankl (1969) emphasized that in contrast to the animal, man is open to the world. It is a characteristic constituent of human existence to break through the barriers of the environment of the species *Homo sapiens*.

According to him, the lack of self-transcendence and higher values makes a life empty and meaningless. Fashion has an irresistible attraction for histrionic persons if there is nothing else important in their lives that transcends their own small world. Therefore, trifles like fashion might unsatisfactorily fill this hole without being able to substitute it sufficiently, as fashion never can substitute for higher values.

THE SCHIZOID ATTITUDE TOWARDS FASHION

On the other extreme, we find a patient group in psychiatry that is not at all interested in fashion, social trends or modern lifestyle. These people avoid relationships and do not show much emotion; their psychiatric disturbance is called schizoid personality disorder. They genuinely prefer to be alone and do not secretly wish for popularity. They tend to seek jobs that require little social contact. Their social skills are often weak, and they do not show a need for attention or acceptance. They are perceived as humourless and distant and are often termed 'loners'. Trying to be fashionable would be extremely exhausting, strange and annoying for them, and they would never produce a believable performance.

According to the WHO's ICD-10,

> the schizoid personality disorder is characterized by at least three of the following nine items: (a) few, if any activities, provide pleasure; (b) emotional coldness, detachment or flattened affectivity; (c) limited capacity to express either warm, tender feelings or anger towards others; (d) apparent indifference to either praise or criticism; (e) little interest in having sexual experiences with another person; (f) almost invariable preference for solitary activities; (g) excessive preoccupation with fantasy and introspection; (h) lack of close friends or confiding relationships and of desire for such relationships; and (i) marked insensitivity to prevailing social norms and conventions.

According to Fritz Riemann, the schizoid personality exaggerates *Selbstbewahrung* (self-protection) and *Ich-Abgrenzung* (I-separation) due to an excessive fear of commitment (Riemann 1961). Individuals with schizoid personality utilize intellectualization to detach and form an emotional barrier (Magnavita 1997). These individuals tend to be abstract and matter-of-fact about their emotional and social lives (Millon and Davis 1996). Their lack of reactivity results in little need for complex intrapsychic defences (Kavaler-Adler 2004). Moreover, a property that defines schizoids is withdrawal into fantasy, mathematics or 'philosophy' (McWilliams 1994). The external world feels so full of consuming threats against safety and individuality that schizoid individuals manifest a tendency to withdraw and seek satisfaction in their own world. Their most adaptive capacity is creativity. Self-esteem is often maintained by creative activity as they seek confirmation of their originality and uniqueness (McWilliams 1994).

Rigid Victorian principles can lead to a sort of schizoid attitude towards fashion, the body and sexuality. In fact, hostility against one's own body and hostility against fashion go hand in hand. Disrespect for the body, rigidity, frigidity, pseudo-morality and cold charisma are all part of the same story. People need the desire to be beautiful; it is a sign of psychic health.

BODY DISSATISFACTION

There is evidence today that images of fashion models influence the self-image of the average (healthy) woman (Paquette and Raine 2004), as women usually compare their body size with the women around them (McLaren and Gauvin 2003). Males appear much more satisfied than females with their body and more diverse in choice of a larger or smaller ideal body type (Yates, Edman and Aruguete 2004). The only exceptions are homosexual men, who resemble the female attitude in this aspect (Conner, Johnson and Grogan 2004; Yelland and Tiggemann 2003). For girls, sociocultural influences and feedback from their best female friend and mother are important predictors for body-change strategies (McCabe and Ricciardelli 2003). The more problems girls have with their self-image, the greater the number of depressive symptoms (Erkolahti et al. 2003). Accordingly, happiness in 144 women significantly and positively correlated with the three components of body esteem: sexual attractiveness, weight concern and physical condition (Stokes and Frederick-Recascino 2003).

We find an alarming impact of fashion magazines on female body satisfaction. Turner and colleagues examined the impact of exposure to fashion magazines on healthy women's body-image satisfaction. Participants were undergraduate women, randomly assigned to two experimental conditions: half looked at fashion magazines prior to completing a body-image satisfaction survey, and the remaining half, news magazines. The women who looked at fashion magazines wanted to weigh less, were less satisfied with their bodies, were more frustrated about their weight, were more preoccupied with the desire to be thin and were more afraid of getting fat than their peers who looked at news magazines (Turner et al. 1997). Analogously, Tiggemann and Slater (2004) investigated the impact of thin, idealized images of women as presented in music television, a popular form of entertainment for young people. A sample of 84 women viewed a videotape containing either appearance music videos (which emphasized appearance and featured thin, attractive women) or non-appearance music videos. Viewing the appearance music videos featuring thin women led to significantly increased social comparison and body dissatisfaction.

When interpreting these findings, we could definitely define this 'normal female re-action' as a certain vulnerability to two major pathological decompensations of body dissatisfaction: weight and appearance (Grant and Phillips 2004). The first leads to eating disorders, the second to plastic surgery.

EATING DISORDERS

Weight is the predominant reason for distress in the majority of women today. Society's way of thinking about body image seems to influence an individual's subjective well-being. Teasing and internalization (peer pressure) mediate the effect of body-mass index on body dissatisfaction (Rotenberg, Taylor and Davis 2004; Shroff and Thompson 2004). In one study, 8 per cent of the 11-year-olds, 10 per cent of the 13-year-olds and 14 per cent of the 15-year-olds said they were on a diet (Borresen and Rosenvinge 2003). The fairly common fear of being overweight and thoughts about dieting experienced by contemporary female adolescents seem to reflect the greater aesthetic value that contemporary society places on thinness for women (Casper and Offer 1990). However, the line between (normal) body dissatisfaction and abnormal eating behaviour is very thin. In a recent survey of 502 schoolgirls, Thomsen and colleagues (Thomsen, Weber and Brown 2002) found positive associa-tions between reading women's beauty and fashion magazines and the use of patho-genic dieting methods (appetite suppressants/diet pills, skipping two meals a day, intentional vomiting and restricting calories to 1,200 or less each day). A determin-ing factor in developing an eating disorder is psychic instability due to a lack of more relevant interests ('values'). Casper and Offer (1990) investigated the relationship between psychological adjustment and attitudes towards body weight and dieting in 497 randomly selected normal adolescents. Two-thirds of female adolescents were preoccupied with weight and dieting, compared with only a small number (approxi-mately 15 per cent) of male adolescents. Increased weight and dieting concerns were associated with greater body and self-image dissatisfaction, with a depressed mood and greater overall symptomatic distress.

Apparently, the media holds an awesome ability to influence young women, bombarding them with images of abnormally thin models who seem to represent the ideal. In fact, 26 per cent of female beauty-pageant contestants themselves have an eating disorder (Thompson and Hammond 2003). Although sociocultural fac-tors, as a group, were significantly associated with the internalization of the thin ideal in a recent study, perceived media pressure was the only sociocultural influence uniquely related to the internalization of the thin ideal (Blowers et al. 2003). When the majority of adolescents inevitably fail to achieve the extremely thin image they crave, body dissatisfaction results, and disordered eating can begin (Andrist 2003).

Anorexia nervosa is the psychiatric disorder evolving out of this phenomenon. It is characterized by deliberate weight loss, induced and/or sustained by the patient, and has a poor prognosis (33 per cent chronicity, 33 per cent deaths and only 33 per cent recovery to a healthy life). According to the DSM-IV, it is defined by (1) refusal to maintain normal body weight; (2) intense fear of gaining weight or becoming fat, even though underweight; (3) disturbance in the way in which one's body weight or shape is experienced, undue influence of body weight or shape on self-evaluation, or denial of the seriousness of the current low body weight; and (4) amenorrhea. Emerging research in the paediatric and adolescent literature demonstrates that girls as young as five are already anxious about their bodies and want to be thinner (Ambrosi-Randic and Tokuda 2004; Andrist 2003). This obsessive interest in body weight is only fuelled by a dramatic increase in the number of Internet Web sites devoted to disordered eating. Unfortunately, many of the Web sites today are 'pro-ana' (pro anorexia nervosa) and 'pro-mia' (pro bulimia nervosa) and encourage young people at risk to begin starving themselves (Andrist 2003).

PLASTIC SURGERY

The aforementioned ideal body image might drive some people, especially histrionic personalities, to another form of (fairly untreatable) psychiatric condition: the so-called body dysmorphic disorder (Jefferys and Castle 2003; Jordan and Mawn 2003). This disorder is defined as a preoccupation with an imagined defect in one's appearance. Alternatively, where there is a slight physical anomaly, the person's concern is markedly excessive (Herren, Armentrout and Higgins 2003). The preoccupation is associated with many time-consuming rituals such as mirror gazing, constant comparing and showing unhealthy perfectionism (Eisen et al. 2004; Frare et al. 2004). Body dysmorphic disorder patients have a distorted body image. Such patients have a poor quality of life and are socially isolated, depressed and at high risk of committing suicide. They often have needless dermatological treatment and cosmetic surgery (McLearie, Orr and O'Dwyer 2004; Veale 2004). In fact, the disorder is highly over-represented among people who seek cosmetic plastic surgery (Grossbart and Sarwer 2003; Sarwer, Crerand and Didie 2003a), which has experienced a tremendous boom in the last decade. The plasticity of the body is hardly a modern discovery, as such traditional (and multicultural) practices as foot binding, corseting, the use of arsenic powders to whiten skin and plates placed in the lips to extend them may attest. In Europe in the sixteenth century, physicians began making early surgical attempts to alter physical appearance, largely to mask evidence of syphilis, which produced major disfigurement in its victims, especially in the nose (Rosen 2004). What began as an effort to mask genuine disfigurement eventually became a way to conceal more modern woes, such as aging; the treatment of a medical emergency turned into a paid service of the client's image of beauty and perfectibility. The five most frequent reasons for cosmetic (non-medically explained) surgery today are mammoplasty, abdominoplasty, rhinoplasty, liposuction and blepharoplasty— breast, belly, nose, fat and eyelid manipulation, respectively (Kisely et al. 2002).

Women interested in breast augmentation consequently report greater investment in their appearance, greater distress about their appearance in a variety of situations and more frequent teasing about their appearance than age-matched controls (Sarwer et al. 2003b). In an interesting study on new referrals to a plastic-surgery clinic for cosmetic, non-medically explained reasons, patients presenting for cosmetic reasons were thirteen times more likely to be female and nine times more likely to have high dysmorphic concerns compared to an age- and sex-matched control group seeking surgery for some medically explained reason (Kisely et al. 2002). However, plastic surgery does not solve this problem. Evidence suggests that these people do not benefit from cosmetic treatments and frequently experience a worsening of their body dysmorphic disorder symptoms (Honigman, Phillips and Castle 2004; Sarwer et al. 2003a). In fact, epidemiologic studies have found that risk of death from suicide is two to three times higher among women with cosmetic silicone gel-filled breast implants than among women of comparable age in the general population (Klesmer 2003; McLaughlin, Lipworth and Tarone 2003; McLaughlin, Wise and Lipworth 2004).

ADOLESCENT SEXUAL LIFESTYLE

The personal lifestyle chosen by somebody for his/her private life is always to some extent influenced by society via certain 'fashions' conveyed by the media (DSM-IV) and the person's peer group (Rosenthal 1997; Zimmer-Gembeck, Siebenbruner and Collins 2004), which itself is often guided by the media as well. Mainly in adolescence, these two factors have a strong impact, though they lose some importance with age. However, no other suggested 'fashionable behaviour' has such a powerful impact on long-term personal lifestyle as the positive or negative influence of the media on adolescent sexual lifestyle. The key period of sexual development occurs during adolescence, a stage that is highly vulnerable to pathogenic external stimuli. During this period, individuals begin to define their inter-gender relationship and consider which sexual behaviours are enjoyable, appropriate and moral for themselves (Collins, Elliott and Berry 2004).

Therefore, the main target to focus on seems to be to show interesting alternatives to premature sexual activity. The most important issue is to offer youth some higher values to help them achieve interiority, inner strength and moral stability to survive the wave of sensuality in their surroundings. The external influence can hardly be abolished, so inner values must be cultivated. The result of depriving adolescents of all mundane contact produces anaemic marionettes who are ill-equipped for life. In fact, as a more powerful influence, religiosity reduces the likelihood of coital debut for both males and females in all surveys on adolescent sexual behaviour (Forste and Haas 2002; Lammers et al. 2000; Lefkowitz et al. 2004; Nicholas 2004; Rostosky, Regnerus and Wright 2003). So perhaps 'fashion' in dealing with sexuality in adolescence is once again warranted.

CONCLUSIONS

Fashion contributes greatly to a successful life by introducing the aspect of easiness and play into this sometimes too serious human life. Plato insisted that the very best of man is to play, and Thomas Aquinas found play as important for internal life as resting. It is highly appropriate to participate in the social play of fashion. Rigid puritan utilitarianism criticizes this very human phenomenon as useless, ephemeral and superficial in a schizoid concentration on interiority with ignorance (and even hostility) towards the human body and the social dimension. Fashion should not be despised because 'material or mental rigor asphyxiates the person' (Torello 1967). Admittedly, fashion sometimes is overestimated by contemporaneous histrionic society. This is due to a lack of self-transcendence and higher values, which therefore abuses fashion for self-enhancement and the search for identity. But this overestimated fashion is the victim of histrionic meaning-deprived society, rather than the culprit. The exaggerated importance of fashion might lead to negative changes in lifestyle and may therefore influence somatic and psychic health. An especially vulnerable aspect is adolescent sexuality. Adolescents should be helped to form part of the world by actively deciding how to dress and behave; they should not be driven by social trends. 'Reactive people are driven by feelings, by circumstances, by conditions, by their environment. Proactive people are driven by values—carefully thought about, selected and internalized values' (Covey 1989).

References and Further Reading

Aboujaoude, E., Gamel, N., and Koran, L. M. (2003), 'A One-year Naturalistic Follow-up of Patients with Compulsive Shopping Disorder', *Journal of Clinical Psychiatry*, 64: 946–50.

Adler, A. (1912), *Über den nervösen Charakter. Grundzüge einer vergleichenden Individualpsychologie und Psychotherapie*, Vienna, Austria.

Ambrosi-Randic, N., and Tokuda, K. (2004), 'Perceptions of Body Image among Japanese and Croatian Children of Preschool Age', *Perceptual and Motor Skills*, 98: 473–8.

American Psychiatric Association (1994), *Diagnostic and Statistical Manual of Mental Disorders (DSM-IV)*, 4th ed., Washington, DC: American Psychiatric Association.

Andrist, L. C. (2003), 'Media Images, Body Dissatisfaction, and Disordered Eating in Adolescent Women', *MCN American Journal of Maternal Child Nursing*, 28: 119–23.

Apostle, A. G. (1984), *Aristotle's Nicomachean Ethics*, Grinnell, Iowa: Peripatetic Press.

Barnard, M. (1996), *Fashion as Communication*, London, New York: Routledge.

Blowers, L. C., Loxton, N. J., Grady-Flesser, M., Occhipinti, S., and Dawe, S. (2003), 'The Relationship between Sociocultural Pressure to be Thin and Body Dissatisfaction in Preadolescent Girls', *Eating Behaviors*, 4: 229–44.

Borresen, R., and Rosenvinge, J. H. (2003), 'Body Dissatisfaction and Dieting in 4,952 Norwegian Children Aged 11–15 Years: Less Evidence for Gender and Age Differences', *Eating and Weight Disorders*, 8: 238–41.

Casper, R. C., and Offer, D. (1990), 'Weight and Dieting Concerns in Adolescents: Fashion or Symptom?' *Pediatrics*, 86: 384–90.

Collins, R. L., Elliott, M. N., and Berry, S. H. (2004), 'Watching Sex on Television Predicts Adolescent Initiation of Sexual Behavior', *Pediatrics*, 114: e280–9.

Conner, M., Johnson, C., and Grogan, S. (2004), 'Gender, Sexuality, Body Image and Eating Behaviors', *Journal of Health Psychology*, 9: 505–15.

Contoyannis, P., and Jones, A. M. (2004), 'Socio-economic Status, Health and Lifestyle', *Journal of Health Economics*, 23: 965–95.

Covey, S. R. (1989), *The Seven Habits of Highly Effective People*, New York: Simon & Schuster.

Devos, T., and Banaji, M. R. (2003), 'Implicit Self and Identity', *Annals of the New York Academy of Sciences*, 1001: 177–211.

Eisen, J. L., Phillips, K. A., Coles, M. E., and Rasmussen, S. A. (2004), 'Insight in Obsessive Compulsive Disorder and Body Dysmorphic Disorder', *Comprehensive Psychiatry*, 45: 10–15.

Erkolahti, R., Ilonen, T., Saarijarvi, S., and Terho, P. (2003), 'Self-image and Depressive Symptoms among Adolescents in a Non-clinical Sample', *Nordic Journal of Psychiatry*, 57: 447–51.

Forste, R., and Haas, D. W. (2002), 'The Transition of Adolescent Males to First Sexual Intercourse: Anticipated or Delayed?' *Perspectives on Sexual and Reproductive Health*, 34: 184–90.

Frankl, V. E. (1969), *The Will to Meaning*, New York: A Meridian Book, New American Library.

Frare, F., Perugi, G., Ruffolo, G., and Toni, C. (2004), 'Obsessive-compulsive Disorder and Body Dysmorphic Disorder: A Comparison of Clinical Features', *European Psychiatry: The Journal of the Association of European Psychiatrists*, 19: 292–8.

Fung, M. S., and Yuen, M. (2002), 'Clothing Interest among Chinese Adolescent Girls in Hong Kong in Relation to Socioeconomic Status', *Psychological Reports*, 90: 387–90.

Gilbert, D., Walley, T., and New, B. (2000), 'Lifestyle Medicines', *British Medical Journal*, 321: 1341–4.

Grammer, K., Renninger, L., and Fischer, B. (2004), 'Disco Clothing, Female Sexual Motivation, and Relationship Status: Is She Dressed to Impress?' *Journal of Sex Research*, 41: 66–74.

Grant, J. E., and Phillips, K.A. (2004), 'Is Anorexia Nervosa a Subtype of Body Dysmorphic Disorder? Probably Not, but Read On', *Harvard Review of Psychiatry*, 12: 123–6.

Grossbart, T.A., and Sarwer, D.B. (2003), 'Psychosocial Issues and Their Relevance to the Cosmetic Surgery Patient', *Seminars in Cutaneous Medicine and Surgery*, 22: 136–47.

Hayward, R. (2004), 'Historical Keywords: Lifestyle', *Lancet*, 364: 495.

Herren, C., Armentrout, T., and Higgins, M. (2003), 'Body Dysmorphic Disorder: Diagnosis and Treatment', *General Dentistry*, 51: 164–6.

Hirota, T., Nara, M., Ohguri, M., Manago, E., and Hirota, K. (1992), 'Effect of Diet and Lifestyle on Bone Mass in Asian Young Women', *American Journal of Clinical Nutrition*, 55: 1168–73.

Honigman, R. J., Phillips, K A., and Castle, D.J. (2004), 'A Review of Psychosocial Outcomes for Patients Seeking Cosmetic Surgery', *Plastic and Reconstructive Surgery*, 113: 1229–37.

Huizinga, J. (1939), *Homo Ludens. Vom Ursprung der Kultur im Spiel*, Stuttgart: Rowohlt Taschenbuch Verlag.

Jefferys, D. E., and Castle, D.J. (2003), 'Body Dysmorphic Disorder—A Fear of Imagined Ugliness', *Australian Family Physician*, 32: 722–5.

Jordan, D. R., and Mawn, L.A. (2003), 'Dysmorphophobia', *Canadian Journal of Ophthalmology. Journal Canadien d'ophtalmologie*, 38: 223–4.

Kaiser, S. B., and Chandler, J. L. (1984), 'Fashion Alienation: Older Adults and the Mass Media', *International Journal of Aging & Human Development*, 19: 203–21.

Kavaler-Adler, S. (2004), 'Anatomy of Regret: A Developmental View of the Depressive Position and a Critical Turn towards Love and Creativity in the Transforming Schizoid Personality', *American Journal of Psychoanalysis*, 64: 39–76.

Kisely, S., Morkell, D., Allbrook, B., Briggs, P., and Jovanovic, J. (2002), 'Factors Associated with Dysmorphic Concern and Psychiatric Morbidity in Plastic Surgery Outpatients', *Australian and New Zealand Journal of Psychiatry*, 36: 121–6.

Klesmer, J. (2003), 'Mortality in Swedish Women with Cosmetic Breast Implants: Body Dysmorphic Disorder Should Be Considered', *British Medical Journal*, 326: 1266–7.

Lammers, C., Ireland, M., Resnick, M., and Blum, R. (2000), 'Influences on Adolescents' Decision to Postpone Onset of Sexual Intercourse: A Survival Analysis of Virginity among Youths Aged 13 to 18 Years', *Journal of Adolescent Health*, 26: 42–8.

Lefkowitz, E. S., Gillen, M. M., Shearer, C. L., and Boone, T. L. (2004), 'Religiosity, Sexual Behaviors, and Sexual Attitudes during Emerging Adulthood', *Journal of Sex Research*, 41: 150–9.

Magnavita, J. J. (1997), *Restructuring Personality Disorders: A Short-term Dynamic Approach*, New York: Guilford Press.

McCabe, M. P., and Ricciardelli, L.A. (2003), 'Sociocultural Influences on Body Image and Body Changes among Adolescent Boys and Girls', *Journal of Social Psychology*, 143: 5–26.

McCarthy, M. (2004), 'Shopping 'til We Drop. Can Psychology Save Us from Our Lust for Possessions?' *Lancet*, 363: 296–7.

McLaren, L., and Gauvin, L. (2003), 'Does the "Average Size" of Women in the Neighbourhood Influence a Woman's Likelihood of Body Dissatisfaction?' *Health Place*, 9: 327–35.

McLaughlin, J. K., Lipworth, L., and Tarone, R. E. (2003), 'Suicide among Women with Cosmetic Breast Implants: A Review of the Epidemiologic Evidence', *Journal of Long-term Effects of Medical Implants*, 13: 445–50.

McLaughlin, J. K., Wise, T. N., and Lipworth, L. (2004), 'Increased Risk of Suicide among Patients with Breast Implants: Do the Epidemiologic Data Support Psychiatric Consultation?' *Psychosomatics*, 45: 277–80.

McLearie, S., Orr, D. J., and O'Dwyer, A. M. (2004), 'Psychiatric Morbidity in a Regional Plastic Surgery Centre—One-year Review with a Proposed Categorisation', *British Journal of Plastic Surgery*, 57: 440–5.

McWilliams, N. (1994), *Psychoanalytic Diagnosis: Understanding Personality Structure in the Clinical Process,* New York: The Guilford Press.

Mendes, V. (2001), 'Introduction: The Fashion of Fashion', in C. Newman (ed.), *Fashion,* 28–35, Washington, DC: National Geographic Society.

Miauton, L., Narring, F., and Michaud, P. A. (2003), 'Chronic Illness, Lifestyle and Emotional Health in Adolescence: Results of a Cross-sectional Survey on the Health of 15–20-year-olds in Switzerland', *European Journal of Pediatrics*, 162: 682–9.

Millon, T., and Davis, R. (1996), *Disorders of Personality: DSM-IV and Beyond,* 2nd ed., Hoboken, New Jersey: Wiley.

Müller, E. (2003), *Georg Simmels Modetheorie,* Zürich: Soziologisches Institut der Universität Zürich.

Nicholas, L. J. (2004), 'The Association between Religiosity, Sexual Fantasy, Participation in Sexual Acts, Sexual Enjoyment, Exposure, and Reaction to Sexual Materials among Black South Africans', *Journal of Sex & Marital Therapy*, 30: 37–42.

Paquette, M. C., and Raine, K. (2004), 'Sociocultural Context of Women's Body Image', *Social Science & Medicine*, 59: 1047–58.

Parkes, L. M., Rashid, W., Chard, D. T., and Tofts, P. S. (2004), 'Normal Cerebral Perfusion Measurements Using Arterial Spin Labeling: Reproducibility, Stability, and Age and Gender Effects', *Magnetic Resonance in Medicine: Official Journal of the Society of Magnetic Resonance in Medicine / Society of Magnetic Resonance in Medicine*, 51: 736–43.

Pope, H. G., Jr, Ionescu-Pioggia, M., and Pope, K. W. (2001), 'Drug Use and Lifestyle among College Undergraduates: A 30-year Longitudinal Study', *American Journal of Psychiatry*, 158: 1519–21.

Postmann, N. (1985), *Amusing Ourselves to Death,* New York: Penguin Books.

Richards, A. K. (1996), 'Ladies of Fashion: Pleasure, Perversion or Paraphilia', *International Journal of Psychoanalysis*, 77 (Pt 2): 337–51.

Riemann, F. (1961), *Grundformen der Angst: eine tiefenpsycholigische Studie,* München and Basel: Ernst Reinhardt Verlag.

Rimm, E. B., and Stampfer, M. J. (2004), 'Diet, Lifestyle, and Longevity—The Next Steps?' *JAMA*, 292: 1490–2.

Roberts, D.F., Foehr, U.G., Rideout, V.J., and Brodie, M. (1999), *Kids & Media @ the New Millennium: A Kaiser Family Foundation Report: A Comprehensive National Analysis of Children's Media Use: Executive Summary*, Menlo Park, California: Henry J. Kaiser Family Foundation.

Rosen, C. (2004), 'The Democratization of Beauty', *New Atlantis*, 5: 19–35.

Rosenthal, D.A. (1997), 'Understanding Sexual Coercion among Young Adolescents: Communicative Clarity, Pressure, and Acceptance', *Archives of Sexual Behavior*, 26: 481–93.

Rostosky, S.S., Regnerus, M.D., and Wright, M.L. (2003), 'Coital Debut: The Role of Religiosity and Sex Attitudes in the Add Health Survey', *Journal of Sex Research*, 40: 358–67.

Rotenberg, K.J., Taylor, D., and Davis, R. (2004), 'Selective Mood-induced Body Image Disparagement and Enhancement Effects: Are They Due to Cognitive Priming or Subjective Mood?' *International Journal of Eating Disorders*, 35: 317–32.

Ruidavets, J.B., Bataille, V., and Dallongeville, J. (2004), 'Alcohol Intake and Diet in France, the Prominent Role of Lifestyle', *European Heart Journal*, 25: 1153–62.

Sarwer, D.B., Crerand, C.E., and Didie, E.R. (2003a), 'Body Dysmorphic Disorder in Cosmetic Surgery Patients', *Facial Plastic Surgery*, 19: 7–18.

Sarwer, D.B., LaRossa, D., Bartlett, S.P., Low, D.W., Bucky, L.P., and Whitaker, L.A. (2003b), 'Body Image Concerns of Breast Augmentation Patients', *Plastic and Reconstructive Surgery*, 112: 83–90.

Schnierer, T. (1995), *Modewandel und Gesellschaft. Die Dynamik von 'in' und 'out'*, Opladen: Leske und Budrich.

Shroff, H., and Thompson, J.K. (2004), 'Body Image and Eating Disturbance in India: Media and Interpersonal Influences', *International Journal of Eating Disorders*, 35: 198–203.

Simmel, G. (1923), *Philosophische Kultur. Über das Abenteuer, die Geschlechter und die Krise der Moderne*, Potsdam: Gustav Kiepenheuer Verlag.

Stokes, R., and Frederick-Recascino, C. (2003), 'Women's Perceived Body Image: Relations with Personal Happiness', *Journal of Women & Aging*, 15:17–29.

Thompson, S.H., and Hammond, K. (2003), 'Beauty Is as Beauty Does: Body Image and Self-esteem of Pageant Contestants', *Eating and Weight Disorders*, 8: 231–7.

Thomsen, S.R., Weber, M.M., and Brown, L.B. (2002), 'The Relationship between Reading Beauty and Fashion Magazines and the Use of Pathogenic Dieting Methods among Adolescent Females', *Adolescence*, 37: 1–18.

Tiggemann, M., and Slater, A. (2004), 'Thin Ideals in Music Television: A Source of Social Comparison and Body Dissatisfaction', *International Journal of Eating Disorders*, 35: 48–58.

Torello, J.B. (1967), 'Mode', *Analyse*, 3: 14–15.

Torello, J.B. (1968a), 'Modelle', *Analyse*, 4: 16–17.

Torello, J.B. (1968b), 'Tanz', *Analyse*, 4: 16–17.

Torello, J.B. (1969), 'Weiblichkeit', *Analyse*, 5: 16–17.

Turner, S.L., Hamilton, H., Jacobs, M., Angood, L.M., and Dwyer, D.H. (1997), 'The Influence of Fashion Magazines on the Body Image Satisfaction of College Women: An Exploratory Analysis', *Adolescence*, 32: 603–14.

Van Vugt, M., and Hart, C. M. (2004), 'Social Identity as Social Glue: The Origins of Group Loyalty', *Journal of Personality and Social Psychology*, 86: 585–98.

Veale, D. (2004), 'Body Dysmorphic Disorder', *Postgraduate Medical Journal*, 80: 67–71.

Weigel, G. (1999), *Witness to Hope*, New York: HarperCollins Publishers.

Wiswede, G. (1976), 'Theorien der Mode aus soziologischer Sicht', in K. G. Specht and G. Wiswede (eds), *Marketing-Soziologie. Soziale Interaktionen als Determinanten des Marktverhaltens*, 393–409, Berlin: Duncker und Humblot.

World Health Organization (1994), *Pocket Guide to the ICD-10 Classification of Mental and Behavioral Disorders*, Washington, DC: American Psychiatric Press.

Yarnell, J., Yu, S., McCrum, E., et al. (2004), 'Education, Socioeconomic and Lifestyle Factors, and Risk of Coronary Heart Disease: The PRIME Study', *International Journal of Epidemiology*, 34/2: 268–75.

Yates, A., Edman, J., and Aruguete, M. (2004), 'Ethnic Differences in BMI and Body/self-Dissatisfaction among Whites, Asian Subgroups, Pacific Islanders, and African-Americans', *Journal of Adolescent Health: Official Publication of the Society for Adolescent Medicine*, 34: 300–7.

Yelland, C., and Tiggemann, M. (2003), 'Muscularity and the Gay Ideal: Body Dissatisfaction and Disordered Eating in Homosexual Men', *Eating Behaviors*, 4: 107–16.

Yunger, J. L., Carver, P. R., and Perry, D. G. (2004), 'Does Gender Identity Influence Children's Psychological Well-being?' *Developmental Psychology*, 40: 572–82.

Zimmer-Gembeck, M. J., Siebenbruner, J., and Collins, W. A. (2004), 'A Prospective Study of Intraindividual and Peer Influences on Adolescents' Heterosexual Romantic and Sexual Behavior', *Archives of Sexual Behavior*, 33: 381–94.

Zucker, K. J. (2004), 'Gender Identity Development and Issues', *Child and Adolescent Psychiatric Clinics of North America*, 13: vii, 551–68.

10 THE IMPACT OF THE TERM 'FASHION' ON MEDICAL AND PSYCHIATRIC LITERATURE

FRANCESCO CECERE

In our personal experience, many patients affected by eating disorders (EDs: e.g. anorexia nervosa, bulimia nervosa, binge eating disorder, etc.) often talk during therapeutic sessions about the influence of fashion, top models, media, advertising, television programs and so forth on their evaluations of their own bodies. In a similar way, these topics are attributed a relevant role (to a greater or lesser degree, according to patients' opinions) in the etiopathogenesis of their illnesses. It is easy to believe these connections because we know that EDs are diseases with multi-causative origins. We must consider a number of different etiopathogenetic causes involved: genetic, social, familial and individual factors contribute in different ways to provoke the onset of these illnesses. It is very difficult to actually prevent such diseases due to the complexity of the causative process. We have very little data on the genetics of EDs; we can say that there is probably a genetic predisposition to become ill, but not much more than this. We have not identified a typical family of ED patients. Many years ago, some family therapists tried to describe the classical structure of the anorectic family: the father was often absent or had an external role in conducting the family; the mother was very intrusive. Subsequent studies have delegitimized these impressions. Nor does our experience indicate a typical family structure: our patients can occur in broken or whole, warm or cold families. We do find in many families a key role in terms of the management of emotions. Patients represent a wide social range, from upper-class to lower-class girls. These patients have a discrete number of similar characteristics. However, when we look for the pathognomonic characteristics of premorbid personalities, we find a strict number of very specific common traits. When we look at the possible social risk factors for EDs, we can find a terribly long list of heterogeneous social factors characterized by their non-specificity: victims are female, Western, watch television and so on. If we try to plan preventive campaigns based on these general risk factors, we generally fail.

Faced with the task of planning a large preventive campaign in public and private schools in Rome (Italy), we have cautiously chosen the topics of our meeting with students, parents and teachers and, in a special way, those related to the media world. Right from the start, we were aware of the difficulties of planning such a campaign: the first problem was time. Each meeting lasted only one to two hours; we planned two or three meetings for each group. It was therefore very difficult to evaluate, in such a short time, the massive attack of media advertisements on young people. We needed to have an impact on their imagination and feed their minds with critical thinking. It is very difficult to find the right way to improve this maturation process because there is the serious risk of producing imitative behaviors. For instance, speaking about vomiting and the different ways to be more and more slender (laxative and diuretics abuse, excessive physical activity and so on) can generate in adolescent minds the wish to experiment with some of these methods, just for curiosity, transgressiveness, attraction to risk or for all these reasons combined. Finding the best language to speak with young people seems to be the most relevant challenge for health personnel involved in preventive campaigns against EDs. We have found that traditional ways of communication, such as booklets and traditional sessions, are totally ineffective.

Adolescents are bombarded with thousands of commercials every day. In addition, some research on the role of television in generating EDs has shown that young girls spend many hours a day watching pseudo-health programs entitled, for instance, *Thinner: Healthier* or *Thinner: More Beautiful* (Levine and Smolak 1996). In these programs, it is possible to find physicians or dietitians who speak about the incredible results of special diets set up by themselves. They promise that anyone can lose many pounds in a week or less. This is the goal of many people: to obtain spectacular results in a very short time. To achieve thinness, they are willing to use illicit drugs actually prescribed by physicians. For all these reasons, we often find adolescents who repeat in their minds that 'thin is beautiful' and 'whoever is beautiful is also successful'.

The media plays a role in generating pathological habits in sensitive people, but it plays a more relevant role in perpetuating these unhealthy behaviors. Every day, we can watch television shows with young, very thin actresses; in many interviews, they claim that they eat pasta, pizza and similar foods, and also that they don't exercise. Spectators are astonished by their perfect bodies and become depressed. It is impossible to eat a lot of food and be that thin. In fact, the rate of bulimia in top models is higher than in the general population (Santonastaso, Mondini and Favaro 2002). During the course of our studies, we have sometimes found people in the fashion world who instigate models to pathological behaviors that can lead to EDs. To obtain such perfect bodies, many models are on a diet all the time, exercise many times a week or every day or must use plastic surgery. It seems that this matter does not concern the world of media and fashion, for, despite the claims of fashion operators at Milan Fashion Week that they refuse very slender models, one clearly sees the images of anorexic models in their fashion magazines! Economic concerns appear to be more relevant than people's health in the fashion world.

EDs have a high incidence and prevalence rates in the general population, especially among young people (Walsh and Klein 2003). If Hilde Bruch (1978) could say in the mid-twentieth century that anorexia appeared to be a strange disease affecting upper-class, well-educated young girls, now we can find ED patients in all social classes. In recent years, the epidemiological data related to these diseases have shown a worrying global increase. This phenomenon is more frequently detected in Western countries. In developing countries, the upper classes are as affected as Western populations. But when the use of television has spread in these countries, the epidemiological rates of EDs have risen, as in the case of the Fiji Islands (Becker et al. 2002). Obviously, many other factors influence the etiopathogenesis of EDs: changes in family structure, different sex roles in modern society, management of emotions at the individual and group levels, changes in eating habits and so on. For example, the introduction of fast-food habits, which are very appealing to younger generations, and the consequent change observed in eating in Europe, can be considered an important risk factor for the spread of EDs. Adolescents are driven to eat fat and unhealthy food, and at the same time the fashion and media world propose very thin bodies as a unique style option. The only possible way to reconcile these opposite goals is bulimia.

But now, if we consider all the variables probably involved in the etiopathogenesis of EDs, we find that emotional management is very important. In a few words, we can say that people use food intake to control emotional changes. Bulimic patients feel somatic sensations (restlessness, stomach pain, hunger) and begin to binge. In this way, they control emotional arousal: the level of distress decreases, and they feel good for a moment. After this acme, they begin to feel guilty, depressed and angry and start to vomit. The problem is that they do not recognize their emotions; they do not say, 'I am sad, or happy, or angry, or anxious' and so on. Instead, these patients say, 'I want to eat, I am restless, I have bowel pain' and so forth. Often, we find a similar pattern of emotional misrecognition in patients' families. Children learn to use bodily sensations to recognize and manage emotions just as they learn a mother tongue.

Some have spoken of an 'ED epidemic' in reference to this increase in the spread of EDs. The importance of this group of diseases, from a public health point of view, is universally confirmed: EDs (especially anorexia nervosa) show the largest mortality rate among mental disorders in young people overall. Patients die from the effects of starvation or from suicide. These chronic diseases also have an important direct and indirect economic impact on public health services: aside from medical expenses, there is an economic loss related to the organic and psychological disabilities/troubles of the patients and/or their families. In addition, some authors are describing new forms of EDs: for instance, they have found that a large group of young male athletes are very concerned about their muscles and food intake (bigorexia or reverse anorexia; see Pope, Katz and Hudson 1993). This is only one of a very large new group of EDs, especially in the United States and other Western countries.

Despite these facts, the medical literature does not seem to be very interested in the relationship between fashion and EDs, or in the media world and EDs. We conducted a search using MedLine, the most popular online text-based search-and-retrieval system in the medical literature. The results confirmed our impression: we only found seven scientific papers using the keywords 'fashion and EDs'; in another search we used the keywords 'fashion and body dissatisfaction' and found only five papers. It is noteworthy that there is a strong relationship between body dissatisfaction and EDs. All patients suffering from EDs are dissatisfied with their bodies and are very concerned with food intake because they believe they are too fat.

Only when we used the terms 'media and EDs' did we find 112 references. We found a larger amount of research on the relationship between hours spent watching television and rates of EDs. Now, we intend to focus our attention on two recent papers published by the *International Journal of Eating Disorders*. The first is a meta-analytic review conducted by Groesz, Levine and Murnen (2002) of the effect of the experimental presentation of thin media images on body satisfaction. Meta-analysis is essentially a summary of the available literature on a topic. This method is very useful in outcome studies to improve the results of single studies using small samples of patients. This statistical methodology is often used in evidence-based medicine, the new branch of research designed to identify and improve truly effective treatments.

In their paper, Groesz and colleagues underline some very interesting findings: 'The glorification of slenderness omnipresent in magazines targeting young adolescent girls will have its most deleterious effect during or immediately after the early adolescent transition and on girls who are entering that transition already possessing a strong investment in thinness and beauty. It is more frequent that girls ages 13–14 are more likely to compare themselves to slender models than girls ages 9–10, and that females ages 10–25 who have low self-esteem and poor body image are particularly likely to seek out and "enjoy" advertisements with slender, attractive models' (Groesz et al. 2002: 12). The authors then pointed out two important implications for future research: 'Theory and research need to elucidate why girls and women are motivated to read fashion magazines, sometimes against their better judgment; second, how images of slender beauty affect females in general and some females in particular. It is evident that an important construct has received too little attention, by medical researchers: Social comparison. Theorists on this matter typically distinguish three types of motives for social comparison: self-evaluation, self-improvement and self- (or ego) enhancement' (13). But there is another relevant implication of these studies: the role of media literacy in ED prevention. 'We refer to media literacy like to a cycle of critique that includes awareness of media use, analysis of content and intentions, and caution in the form of activism towards the media or advocacy using the media' (13).

Tiggemann and Slater investigated the impact of thin, idealized images of women as presented in music television, a popular form of entertainment for adolescents. They found the following:

> Brief exposure to music videos containing thin and attractive images of women led to an increase in body dissatisfaction. Previous research demonstrated that music videos, as a popular form of mass media entertainment, may be sending multiple messages and may be influential in a multitude of ways. The results of the video comparisons were more clear-cut than the results of most of the previously reviewed research, because music videos provide a more naturalistic medium. Viewers may be more aware and resistant to the efforts of advertisers to influence them (as in television commercials or fashion magazine shots) than they are of actual television content. Content analyses of music videos have revealed a preponderance of video clips that emphasize appearance and feature thin and attractive idealized images of women. (Tiggemann and Slater 2003: 55)

There are many explanations for this lack of interest in scientific research about the relationship between fashion and EDs. Medical and psychiatric researchers probably consider fashion to be a very trifling topic. On the contrary, it may be that there are some methodological difficulties involved in studying this topic with traditional descriptive approaches. The classical epidemiological methodology, essentially a quantitative one, is a not a good fit for these topics, as there are many variables and confounders to control. Multiple regression analysis is probably not the best approach to this problem, either. Probably the best method is to use a qualitative approach to study these causative relationships. A sociological approach may be more useful than a traditional causative epidemiological one. This is true not only for the causative mechanisms of EDs, but probably for all mental illnesses or, in general, for those diseases with multiple-cause pathogenesis.

In any case, as a main goal for the public health services, we advocate starting prevention strategies for these disorders using existing scientific information and other wisdom. Health personnel should involve all caregivers (parents, grandparents, teachers, etc.), as well as media operators and fashion professionals. It is important for the language used in these preventive campaigns, especially those aimed at young people, to be similar to media language. As mentioned earlier, it is very difficult or even impossible to attract adolescents' attention using traditional communication strategies.

A very interesting example of a preventive/critical activity is the Web site About-Face.org (http://www.about-face.org). This Web site is conceived and managed by a nonprofit organization in San Francisco. It is made up of a group of professionals (psychologists, journalists, advertisers, etc.) and some lay young people. It shows advertising campaigns, fashion photos and so forth classified as a top-ten list of offenders and a top-ten list of non-offenders. All this visual material is correlated with critical comments from different sources: psychological manuals and papers, sociological and philosophical issues, and so on. This is a very good example of an appealing way to interest young people in these critical topics.

In conclusion, I would stress that far from a lack of connection between fashion and serious health problems, the relationship between them is very telling. It tells of the importance of self-image and its connection with the idealized image fashion presents. It also is descriptive of what kinds of tactics are effective in reaching the consciousness of young people. If preventive programs for these types of illnesses could be as compelling to the attention of young people as the media that foments the problems to begin with, then we might be able to fight on a level playing field. By studying and adopting the methodologies and dissemination tactics of the fashion industry, the medical community could turn the tables and reach the increasing number of patients at risk of EDs.

References and Further Reading

Becker, A. E., Burwell, R. A., Gilman, S. E., Herzog, D. B., and Hamburg, P. (2002), 'Eating Behaviors and Attitudes Following Prolonged Exposure to Television among Ethnic Fijian Adolescent Girls', *British Journal of Psychiatry*, 180 (June): 509–14.

Bruch, H. (1978), *The Golden Cage,* Cambridge: Harvard University Press.

Cosin, J. M., Frederickx, Y., Yousif, A., Hamoir, M., and Van den Eeckhaut, J. (1986), 'Mannequin Syndrome', *Acta Otorhinolaryngol Belgica*, 40 (April): 678–81.

Field, A. E., Cheung, L., Wolf, A. M., Herzog, D. B., Gortmaker, S. L., and Colditz, C. (1999), 'Exposure to the Mass Media and Weight Concerns among Girls', *Pediatrics*, 103 (March): E36.

Groesz, L. M., Levine, M. P., and Murnen, S. K. (2002), 'The Effect of Experimental Presentation of Thin Media Images on Body Satisfaction: A Meta-Analytic Review', *International Journal of Eating Disorders*, 31 (January): 1–16.

Hamilton, K., and Walzer, G. (1993), 'Media Influences on Body Size Estimation in Anorexia and Bulimia. An Experimental Study', *British Journal of Psychiatry*, 162 (June): 837–40.

Labay Matias, M. (2000), 'Eating Disorders and Their Etiology. Not Only Fashion and Media', *Ann Esp Pediatr*, 52 (January): 223–6.

Levine, M. P., and Smolak, L. (1996), 'Media as a Context for Development of Disordered Eating', in L. Smolak and M. P. Levine, *The Developmental Psychopathology of Eating Disorders*, Mahwah, New Jersey, Lawrence Erlbaum Associates.

Pinas, L, Toner, B. B., Ali, A., Garfinkel, P. E., and Stuckless, N. (1999), 'The Effects of the Ideal of Female Beauty on Mood and Body Dissatisfaction', *International Journal of Eating Disorders*, 5 (March): 223–6.

Pope, H. G., Jr, Katz, D. L., and Hudson, J. I. (1993), 'Anorexia Nervosa and "Reverse Anorexia" among 108 Male Bodybuilders', *Comprehensive Psychiatry*, 34 (Nov.–Dec.): 406–9.

Santonastaso, P., Mondini, S., and Favaro, A. (2002), 'Are Fashion Models a Group at Risk for Eating Disorders and Substance Abuse?' *Psychother Psychosom*, 71 (May–June): 168–72.

Tiggemann, M., and Slater, A. (2003), 'Thin Ideals in Music Television: A Source of Social Comparison and Body Dissatisfaction', *International Journal of Eating Disorders*, 35 (Jan.): 48–58.

Thomsen, S. R., Weber, M. M., and Brown, L. B. (2002), 'The Relationship between Reading Beauty and Fashion Magazines and the Use of Pathogenic Dieting Methods among Adolescent Females', *Adolescence*, 37 (Spring): 1–18.

Walsh, B. T., and Klein, D. A. (2003), 'Eating Disorders', *International Review of Psychiatry*, 15 (Aug.): 205–16.

11 STRONG FASHION AND WEAK IDENTITY: A NECESSARY ASSOCIATION?

MARIA TERESA RUSSO

In order to discuss the importance and role of fashion in present society, we must first make an important distinction between fashion as a *phenomenon* and fashion as a *system*.

By fashion as a *phenomenon* we mean the evolution of taste that has always characterized social customs, in which we can recognize three factors: the simultaneous need for distinction and belonging; the aesthetic need, which is expressed in the search for elegance (this is also shown as a shared need, a development of social life surrounding the taste of beauty); and the need for play, an irrepressible tendency in the human being (art and fashion participate in this suspension of what is useful, serious and necessary in favour of that which is superfluous, ironic and useless).

When we are speaking about fashion as a *system* we refer to a typical aspect of mass society characterized by generalized consumerism and the predominance of the market.

The present problem is that fashion as a system has almost completely absorbed fashion as a phenomenon. It has thus become necessary to recover the elements of the fashion phenomenon one by one. Perhaps the system would truly succeed if it placed itself at the service of the phenomenon, to find a new balance and rediscover an authentic sense of elegance.

But there is also, at an individual level, a problem of personal identity that contributes to the increasing relevance of fashion. The core of the dilemma is to make clear in what measure this personal identity problem is the cause or the effect of the ruling hegemony of the fashion system. We must also reflect on the characteristics of the new user of fashion to better understand the roots of the changes, together with their possible positive evolutions. There is a weakness in postmodern society, characterized by a fragility of ties, that is both caused and affected by more vulnerable identities. Our present culture of appearance presents all its problematic aspects in the area of body identity.

It is important to regain a greater awareness of the symbolic value of the body as a person's arena for expression. This is possible only if we consider the body in all its integrity and relational nature.

WHAT ARE WE SPEAKING ABOUT WHEN WE SPEAK ABOUT FASHION? THE FASHION PHENOMENON

In order to discuss the importance and role of fashion in today's society, we must first make an important distinction between fashion as a phenomenon and fashion as a system. What follows is a philosophical reflection on certain cultural processes, which are highlighted by sociological research. I offer this interpretation, not in an attempt to find a solution, but rather to understand the playing field.

For fashion as a phenomenon we mean the evolution of taste that has always characterized social customs: such change is certainly linked, as has been rightly pointed out, to a social trend generated by the simultaneous need for distinction and belonging (Simmel 1911: 30–1). The former leads us to look for the characteristics which make us original and therefore different from others, while at the same time the latter induces us to search for the details which make us fashionable—that is, similar to all the others.

Arising from these needs, we might say that an anthropological frame is shown: from the need for distinction emerges the search for identity, and from the need for cohesion comes the search for otherness. We say 'I am myself' from our desire to distinguish ourselves from the others; we say 'to be myself I need you' from our desire for closeness to others.

But to understand fashion as a phenomenon, we have to add two other necessary elements to this double need. The first consists of the drive towards the beautiful, which is expressed in the search for elegance. In this respect, two quotations are enlightening. The first is by Baudelaire and goes back to 1863: 'Every fashion is a new effort, more or less successful, to go closer to the beautiful; it's any closeness to an ideal whose desire stirs without pause in the unsatisfied human spirit' (Baudelaire

1976: 716). The second is by the painter De Pisis, taken from his notebook entitled *Adam or about Elegance*: 'Elegance in dressing is subjected to the general laws of art and beauty' (De Pisis 1983: 11).

By the word *taste* we traditionally mean that part of human nature that makes it possible to enjoy and understand beauty. Aesthetic need is a fundamental element in the evolution of taste; yet, strange to say, Flügel, in his well-known 1930s essay about the psychology of clothes, absolutely ignored it, singling out the aims of clothing as only the three basic needs: for protection, for showing off and for seduction (Flügel 1978: 28–30).

This aesthetic need is also shown to be a shared need, a configuration of social life surrounding the taste for beauty (Maffesoli 1993: 142–3). The historian F. Braudel has included clothing among the *frames of everyday life* by stating that fashion in clothing is something to be taken very seriously because it represents an extremely interesting clue about the orientation of a civilization: 'But is fashion really so vain? Or—as we believe—do these signs profoundly testify on a given society, a given economy, a given civilization, with their enthusiasms, their possibilities, their joy of living?' (Braudel 1982: 291).

We can wonder how it is that sometimes this thrust towards beauty produces diametrically opposed results, such as the recent fashion of *heavy metal,* among others: as a matter of fact, even in these phenomena, in opposition, the same tension can be noticed. In this case, the search for ugliness or for the horrible represents the intentional rejection of something that, exactly in so far as it has been expressly denied, is reaffirmed as natural.

The drive towards beauty that is manifested in fashion is defined not in what we can call *great aesthetics,* represented by the creation and fruition of real artistic work, but by *little aesthetics,* made up of gestures and daily choices inspired in the search, if not for beauty, at least for what is agreeable. In this sense, the semiologist Greimas has spoken of the *seriousness of the grooming,* referring to the importance that is given during the day to the process of getting dressed, where the appreciation of beauty is worked out essentially through an affective and sensitive component that also takes into account the functionality and the convenience of what is chosen (Greimas 1988: 58–65). To Greimas, the phenomenon is also defined as the *pleasure of looking at shop windows*: a cognitive operation in which the evaluation ('I like it'), imagination ('Will it fit me?'), memory ('Haven't I got one like this already?') and comparison ('What can I wear with it?') are all involved.

The function of clothing is so relevant that historically it has often influenced customs and morality. Not by chance, numerous social protests have been in step with unusual clothes and the consequent introduction of new fashions: from the trousers of the sans-culottes to the mini skirt, the phenomenon is recurrent in history. As

Barthes points out, the clothing that is intentionally chosen is not a simple *clue,* but rather a sign or group of signs that constitutes a *code* (Barthes 1970: 73): consequently, it is a vehicle of expression of one's own identity. And more than that, which Barthes does not emphasize, clothing in turn influences one's identity. It is true that someone who dresses up *does* something through his clothes—that is, he expresses himself—but it is also true that the clothing *does* something to the person who wears it—it induces him, let's say, towards specific behaviour. As Balzac wrote in 1830: 'The bearded man's ideas aren't the same as those of the shaved one' (DeBalzac 2000: 46).

The other important element shown in the fashion phenomenon is the taste for play, an irrepressible tendency in the human being. The recreational element of play supposes giving freely, making your own rules and having a sense of fun and playful lightness: art and fashion participate in this suspension of the useful, of the serious and of the necessary, thus giving way to the superfluous, the ironic and the useless. In human existence, the alternation between what is serious and what is recreational is indispensable, just as between work and rest. From this point of view, we cannot exclude that the increasing importance of fashion might be attributed to the so-called *totalitarianism of work* so characteristic of our society, which has the effect of provoking a reaction just as radical: the need for play and escapism. We must also consider another element: the increase of social control typical of present democracies can produce a greater desire for escaping from order and rules. Fashion seems to have the suitable ingredients to carry out this role.

WHAT HAS CHANGED IN FASHION TODAY: THE FASHION SYSTEM

Speaking about fashion as a *system* is a different matter. The word *fashion* refers to a typical aspect of mass society characterized by generalized consumerism and the predominance of the market. It is about the organization of the fashion phenomenon, structured around the basis of production, distribution and proceeds of sales; in short, it is about marketing. On one hand, the fashion system aims at capturing the public's moods in order to interpret it and satisfy it to the utmost; on the other hand, it occasionally tries to impose a *decree or diktat*, with the purpose of maintaining a leading edge in affecting the processes of change. Unlike the phenomenon, the fashion system is ruled by a strict law of *business*, a fact that profoundly alters the features analysed thus far.

The current problem is that fashion as a system has almost completely absorbed fashion as a phenomenon. Some important consequences stem from this:

1. The difficulty on the part of the consumer to practise a *spontaneous aesthetic*, imbued with good taste and balance, because the system tends to influence the public by surprising it with novelty rather than training it to search for elegance.

2. The marketing system gives rise to the following succession: availability at an inferior quality generates more consumption, which generates trends that do not consider quality or good taste.

3. The identification of style with *brand*, so that clothing, instead of reinforcing personal identity, becomes more and more the expression of something impersonal: purchasing power, *status,* and so forth. H. M. Enzensberger, in his *Funeral Oration on Fashion*, has nicely commented that the preponderance of brand labels has turned people into walking advertisements (Enzensberger 1999: 145–6). To wear Armani denotes taste and status, but to do so the brand must be recognizable. Recognition requires a shared code that must be repeatedly advertised in increasingly exaggerated terms. This entails, among other things, two consequences. The first is the transformation of the clothing code. Every code, as a matter of fact, indicates a shared and binding tie that forms a sphere of speech (Davis 1992: 5). However much clothing is a code with particular features,[1] it is also true that, like language, it intends to convey something: with the predominance of the *brand* this communication becomes equivocal and consequently self-referring. Equivocal, because the image I want to transmit with particular objects is often not what others perceive: to be shared, it requires sharing the context that is the knowledge of the *brand*. Therefore, it is self-referring because it creates a new elite, a privileged area where only those who know the Armani *code* (and practice it) can grasp the meaning of the message. The second consequence of mass repetitive advertising is the metamorphosis of luxury, which has ceased to be a search for what is rare or refined and has instead become a pursuit of what is merely and simply expensive in so far as it is the sign (indication) of a status more than of a taste. Style, then, is no longer related to quality of daily life, but rather to signs that denote a certain level of income and a special standard of living.

4. A given clothing style is increasingly a reflection of a correlative style of life. Consumerism is responsible for presenting this tie as necessary. To dress casual, for example, more than an intentional casual way of matching different items of clothing, is an attitude: it is a way of living that strives for freedom from rules, which in its sartorial expression is false because it requires an effort . . . and an expensive one, at that.

5. Fashion has thus become a factor of social change, influencing culture, moulding the attitudes that people adopt and prescribing ways of thinking and

behaving. In the past, fashion did not have the role of creator (maker) of taste, which was entrusted to art instead. The good taste/bad taste distinction was, in fact, mediated above all by the artist, who guided the public's perception of beauty (Gadamer 1995: 33). With the crisis of artistic creation, this guiding role has been taken on by fashion.

Fashion's new role as creator of taste gives it a seriousness that appears extraneous to it, since fashion is the realm of play and the improbable, where the only rule is *I like it* and *it fits me,* quite far from the laws of universal beauty. The fact that fashion feels uneasy in this role is more than evident: it is sufficient to look at the constant fluctuation between the whimsical and the ironic tone in some fashion reportages and at the peremptoriness of some *Diktate*, which impose particular products and only those at distribution and sale points. As a matter of fact, fashion's hegemony is such that when the system, periodically, cunningly launches a statement about the right to spontaneity, implying that *everyone can dress as he likes,* the result is a radical anarchy in which the public, no longer able to discern good taste, wanders lost between vulgarity and kitsch.

Moreover, the fashion system depends on the fashion phenomenon. Business demands that the stylist interpret the unexpressed desires of the public, take them as his/her own and feed them back to the public. But it is this more or less tolerated dependence between market and art which determines the contemporary fashion system crisis. In fact, it is not only fluctuations in taste that are more and more unpredictable, but also the way these fluctuations spread no longer by trickling down, as Simmel wanted, but in a downpour or, in fact, a horizontal rather than vertical effect (Davis 1992: 104).[2] It has become almost impossible to foresee what will modify taste: a film, a political event, a media or sports star and so on.

The boomerang effect of some fashions cannot be stopped; the fashion phenomenon originated by the system ends up having the upper hand. It is enough to think about the fashion of the low waistline, launched as a *Diktate* in the fashion shows of 1999 and until now impossible to uproot, despite all the efforts of stylists. Another example is fashions conceived for teenagers that are adopted by adult women. The miniskirt, for instance, which was launched as a symbol of women's emancipation, has turned into a further factor for the submission of women to a male aesthetic as, somewhere between its creation and its diffusion, it became a symbol of seduction.

It is evident that, nowadays, the fashion phenomenon cannot survive without the system because all fashion has become impossible without market organization. But this brings us to question the role of fashion and specifically to be concerned about whether fashion, structured as it is within the system, can carry out the role of guiding taste.

Many have denounced 'the priority of profit over creativity' in fashion because profit as the priority (which is the defining characteristic of the fashion system versus phenomenon) eliminates the elements necessary for the creative process, such as freshness, fantasy, visionary capability, culture, ability of dissociation and innocence (Molho 2000: 187–8). It thus becomes necessary to recuperate the elements one by one. Perhaps the system should strive to put itself at the service of the phenomenon, to achieve a new balance and rediscover an authentic sense of elegance.

USERS OF THE FASHION SYSTEM: STRONG OR WEAK IDENTITIES?

The problems analysed in this chapter cannot be attributed solely to a deficient ruling system. There is, at an individual level, a problem of personal identity that contributes to the increasing relevance of the fashion system. The core of the problem will become clear if we can elucidate to what extent the problem of personal identity is the cause or the effect of the imbalanced role of fashion in today's society. In other words, we must also reflect on the new characteristics of the new users of fashion to better understand some of the roots of change and its possible positive evolutions.

What are we looking for through fashionable clothing or fashionable attitudes? Moreover, are we looking for something different today than yesterday?

Postmodern individuals have been described as having fragile connections and ties to their environment. This weakness seems to be both the cause and effect of more vulnerable identities in the postmodern society. This *minimum self*, as it has been defined, requires a construction more than a search for identity (Lasch 1984). This new individual relies more on appearing than on being and combats the fear of invisibility through the creation of a reflected image of oneself. The result is almost a confirmation of one's own real existence, framed in the simulacra sent by the media and by fashion. At this point, it becomes difficult to distinguish between reality and appearance, and one might end up pretending to match the former to the latter.

There is a crucial difference between dressing up and disguising oneself. They are two operations that aim for opposite effects: the first at the expression of oneself, the second at the concealing or alteration of oneself. It is not certain if personal identity is strengthened by clothing. The same word *look*, which also means to *appear*, is often used to qualify one form of dress or another and highlights the basic uncertainty: does one aim at *being* more or *looking* more?

This culture of appearance presents problems in the area of body identity, where some worrisome changes have been registered:

1. Shifting from the real body to the fancied body, meant as a simulacra, re-designed over and over again and continually perfectible. This involves the rising of a new shame: that of possessing an imperfect or perishable body and a new wish—a perfect and eternally young body. In this way, the body loses its naturalness, becomes more and more artificial and transforms itself into an object to be pampered and, at the same time, to be monitored—in other words, the kingdom of the sanitary check-up, the healthy regime, hygienic watchfulness and the most exaggerated cosmetics (Perrot 1984: 263). Fashion and fitness blend one into one another and refer to each other, since both refer to the necessity to be fit, a duty that is never sufficiently fulfilled (Bauman 2002: 82).
2. Shifting from the serial nature of clothing to the serial nature of the body. From prêt-a-porter clothing, which has certainly flattened styles and homogenized attitudes, we have gone on to the prêt-a-porter body in a system that imposes as dominant a certain kind of physique, where size becomes a sort of Procrustean bed to which the body must absolutely conform (Calefato 2002: 52).
3. Loss of narrativity of one's own body. We can define as body style the awareness of one's own unique history and the ability to tell it through one's own body. In this lies the meaning of mimicry and gesture, as well as one's very personal way of wearing clothes. Today we have lost this ability because stereotyped styles have prevailed. We think that we are spontaneous, but we really instinctively imitate gestures and styles that bounce from the media and, above all, from television models. It is this very permeability between real life and its simulacra that makes us insensitive to, or even unaware of, the differences of behaviour that exist between public and private spaces, between the familiar and the professional register. Hence, there is a difficulty in practicing the necessary distinctions between proper clothing for the workplace and for the beach, or between formal attitudes and familiar ones.
4. The *liquidity*[3] of the differences between types of bodies: male and female, young and old (Anatrella 1998). The triumph of *unisex* styles in clothing has been associated with the progressive flattening of sexual differences, encouraged by the first feminist movement.[4]
5. The transformation of seduction into pornography. Seduction has always been the constant, if not decisive, element of fashion: it is characterized as the art of attracting attention to one's self, playing with one's own sexuality. Instead, pornography is the exaggeration of sex, exploiting it for a commercial purpose. In seduction there is subjectivity, while pornography is about objectifying. It presents an anonymous body exhibited in its anatomic solidity, nothing more (Henry 1999: 32). A fashion which mixes these two concepts helps the process

of the body's objectification and of the trivialization of sex, thus producing a progressive eroticization of society.

6. The disappearance of modesty, with nakedness losing its significance. If we define modesty as the urge to defend one's privacy regarding the body, in an attempt to be recognized as a person and not only as a body, we can say that there is a close link between modesty and identity. A weak identity is also an identity which cannot possess itself and therefore cannot find a balancing point in its expression of self: it is comparable to a glass house, where the self is nowhere and it is difficult to distinguish between the outside and the inside. Nakedness conveys that we are fully open to relations, something which in the context of modesty only happens in certain intimate relationships. On the contrary, with the disappearance of modesty, nakedness is changed into a neutral sign: it becomes insignificant and instead turns into a barrier which keeps others from grasping the person in his/her totality.

What are some practicable ways of reacting to such transformations in order to strengthen this eroded condition of identity? As a starting point, I propose the recovery of the body's true meaning.

The task is to regain a greater awareness of the symbolic value of the body as a personal expression. On one hand, subjectivity does not identify itself with corporeality; on the other hand, there is no a personal identity which exists and expresses itself outside corporeality. Therefore, identity is what relates subjectivity to corporeality, but only if we consider the body in its integrity and relational nature.

First, the human body expresses a person because, as Augustine states, it has *modus, species, ordo*—that is, measure, beauty, order (*De Civitate Dei*, XI, 22). If it is true that in any living organism the whole is greater than its parts, it is especially true for the human body. A body in its individual parts, dismembered by a fashion incapable of orientating the gaze at the whole person, is lacking in subjectivity and loses humanity. As Merleau-Ponty remarks: 'A living body, seen too close up and without any background from which to distinguish it, is no longer a living body, but a material mass, alien as a lunar landscape' (Merleau-Ponty 1998: 63). The individual parts have no meaning, but the whole and the meaning of the whole are beyond the materiality which makes it visible.

The body also has an identifier value as a body in relation to others: it is not merely a presence, an inert element which stays in a particular space, but rather someone who questions me, even if silently. Gesticulation is filled with meaning and history, as is the personal countenance that signifies 'to be here', which in turn always expresses 'to be here according to one's own sex'. A strong identity can express itself in the same strong way through its body. Faithfulness to oneself and to one's own history is shown also at a visible and empirical level.

Being who I am or wanting to appear as another person is always the eternal dilemma.

References and Further Reading

Anatrella, T. (1998), *La différence interdite. Sexualité, éducation, violence*, Paris: Flammarion.

Barthes, R. (1970), *L'Empire des signes*, Paris: Seuil.

Barthes, R. (1967), *Système de la mode*, Paris: Seuil.

Baudelaire, F. (1976), 'Eloge du maquillage', in *Le peintre de la vie moderne*, Paris: Gallimard.

Bauman, Z. (2002), *Modernità liquida*, Bari: Laterza.

Braudel, F. (1982), *Le strutture del quotidiano*, Torino: Einaudi.

Calefato, P. (2002), *Segni di moda*, Bari: Palomar.

Centro Studi Filosofici di Gallarate, ed. (1977), 'Gusto', in *Dizionario delle idee*, Florence: Sansoni.

Curcio, A., ed. (2000), *La dea delle apparenze. Conversazioni sulla moda*, Milan: Franco Angeli.

Davis, F. (1992), *Fashion, Culture and Identity*, Chicago: University of Chicago Press.

De Balzac, H. (2000), *Traité de la vie élegante*, Paris: Presses Universitaires Blaise Pascal.

De Pisis, F. (1983), *Adamo o dell'eleganza. Per un'estetica del vestire*, Bologna: L'inchiostroblu.

Enzensberger, H.M. (1999), *Zigzag. Saggi sul tempo, il potere e lo stile*, Torino: Einaudi.

Flügel, J.C. (1978), *Psicologia dell'abbigliamento*, Milan: Franco Angeli.

Gadamer, H.G. (1995), *L'attualità del bello*, Genoa: Marietti.

Greimas, A.J. (1988), *Dell'imperfezione*, Palermo: Sellerio.

Henry, M. (1999), *Encarnation. Pour une philosophie de la chair*, Paris: Seuil.

Lasch, C. (1984), *The Minimal Self*, New York: Norton & Company.

Maffesoli, M. (1993), *Nel vuoto delle apparenza. Per un'etica dell'estetica*, Milan: Garzanti.

Merleau-Ponty, M. (1998), *Phénoménologie de la perception*, trad. ital., Milan: Bompiani.

Molho, R. (2000), 'La moda e i suoi tradimenti', in A. Curcio (ed.), *La dea delle apparenze. Conversazioni sulla moda*, 186–9, Milan: Franco Angeli.

Perrot, P. (1984), *Il senso delle apparenze. Le trasformazioni del corpo femminile*, Milan: Longanesi.

Simmel, G. (1911), 'Die mode', in *Philosophische Kultur*, Leipzig: Klinkhart.

NOTES

Chapter 2: The Modern Western Fashion Pattern

1. They actually refer to it as the 'European Fashion Pattern', which, although historically accurate, seems rather anachronistic in the context of both the cultural influence of the United States in the modern world and the ongoing processes of globalization.
2. These included Hutcheson, Hume, Gerard, Burke, Kames, Blair, Reynolds and Alison. See Hooker (1934).
3. Of course, there is also a good case for saying that there is a strong element of socialization present in gustatory taste. However, it is possible to demonstrate that there is an inherited component in such taste preferences, which is something, it would seem, cannot be demonstrated in the case of aesthetic taste.
4. It is worth remembering that no one of these indicators has ever proved to be a very successful index of class or status when used on its own, which is something that would appear to be just as true of dress.
5. The idea that there are few if any restrictions on what clothes people can wear, or on when and where they can wear them, is actually something of a myth. The author's current research suggests that dress regulation is both widespread and significant in contemporary Western societies. See Campbell (2005).
6. Equally, it is important to note that individuals change their style of dress daily as they move from one social context to another (i.e., informal to formal, or work to leisure). However, it is equally implausible to suggest that each of these involves a change of identity rather than merely a shift in the dominant mode of self-expression (see Davis 1992).
7. The most obvious exception to this is when adults undergo religious conversion and may, as a consequence, radically change their appearance, including their dress; those individuals who convert to ISKON (International Society for Krishna Consciousness)—better known as the Hare Krishnas—would be an obvious example.

Chapter 3: Fashion, Image, Identity

1. In this way, Arendt also presents the main lines of recent sociological theory about 'consumer society' (see Arendt 1958: 126).
2. Kant, I. (1784), 'Idea for a Universal History with a Cosmopolitan Intent', Akk, VIII, 20.
3. Kant, I. (1796), 'Anthropology from a Pragmatic Point of View', Akk, VII, 245.

4. 'Mankind is an inventive species; and where an invention is obvious and absolutely nec-essary, it may as properly be said to be natural as any thing that proceeds immediately from original principles, without the intervention of thought or reflexion. Nor is the expression improper to call them Laws of Nature.' David Hume, Treatise, III, 2, 1.

5. Yet something different than humour takes place whenever, instead of playing within conventions, fashion goes systematically against them, by way of reversing them; or every time it becomes cynic instead of simply humoristic. In these cases, fashion is used as a critique of society. While this pattern of behaviour is intrinsic to the dynamic of fashion—we just need to remember Simmel's reflections on anti-fashion—its generaliza-tion in our age has become a mark of postmodern lifestyles.

6. Kant, KrV A 748/B776; Schiller, 26th Letter.

7. 'For himself alone a human being abandoned on a desert island would not adorn either his hut or himself, nor seek out or still less plant flowers in order to decorate himself; rather, only in society does it occur to him to be not merely a human being but also, in his own way, a refined human being (the beginning of civilization): for this is how we judge someone who is inclined to communicate his pleasure to others and is skilled at it, and who is not content with an object if he cannot feel his satisfaction in it in community with others' (Kant 2000: 5/297).

8. Kant even speaks of a correct standard of taste, to be achieved through the communica-tion between the refined upper class and the natural lower class (Kant 2000: 5/356).

9. This is also why, in attention to that standard of taste, even the fertile imagination of genius should be somehow restrained: 'If the question is whether in matters of beautiful art it is more important whether genius or taste is displayed, that is the same as asking whether imagination or the power of judgment counts for more in them . . . Taste, like the power of judgment in general, is the discipline (or corrective) of genius, clipping its wings and making it well behaved or polished . . . Thus if anything must be sacrificed in the conflict of the two properties in one product, it must rather be on the side of genius: and the power of judgment, which in matters of beautiful art makes its pronouncements on the basis of its own principles, will sooner permit damage to the freedom and richness of the imagination than to the understanding' (Kant 2000: 5/319–20).

10. The figure of Schiller is in between: on the one hand, he aspires to a political utopia very similar to Kant's, if only Kant's individuals were more aesthetically developed. However, the primacy he gives to this aesthetic development and his opposition to any form of actual or institutional aesthetic repression makes his political ideal really a utopia, and, at the same time, it brings anarchy to the real historical situation.

11. In the text, Schiller defines the world as 'the formless content of time': this expression assumes Kant's definition of the world as being formalized by the understanding: in the absence of active understanding, our sensibility would receive impressions within a time frame, but those impressions would be without form.

12. Before acquiring its Identity, the 'I' has to go through history. The distance between the 'I' and the Subject—thereby the achieving of identity—is called 'time'. Also, the 'I' can

be called time because, during the process, the 'I' is not a Subject, and therefore it is identical to itself. As a being in time, the 'I' is not Absolute, but merely a possibility of Absolute (see Polo 1999: 49).

13. From this perspective, Žižek's approach to Lacan through Hegel might sound surprising. It is not that surprising, however, if we consider that Žižek proposes a de-centred conception of the Subject, not only in Lacan but also in Hegel (Žižek 1995: 68): not only is a Symbolic Subject in debt with *object a*, but also Hegel's absolute Subject is affected by a contradiction: the fact that, on the one hand, the Subject is the result of a process, while, on the other, it is the object of contemplation (Polo 1999).

14. Likewise, postmodernism has to deny the possibility of a unitary life. Postmodern people are supposed to live in fragmented experiences of time. Continuity in time would risk the emergence of a fixed identity. This is why Baudrillard and Jameson have compared the contemporary subject to the schizophrenic: the experience of the schizophrenic is one of isolated meanings which cannot be united in a coherent sequence: this is why the schizophrenic has no idea of identity (Baudrillard 2002: 177)—the schizophrenic has no project; he has lost the capacity to retain history (Jameson 2002: 185).

15. See also 'Interview with Gene Swenson' (1963), in Harrison and Wood (1992).

16. 'Narcis, he says, is not the triumphant individual; he is rather the fragile and disistabilised individual, because he has to charge with himself, and construct himself on his own, without the former support of collective frames and interiorized social norms' (Lipovetsky 2003b: 28).

Chapter 4: Identity and Intersubjectivity

I am grateful to Robert Sokolowski for many helpful comments on an earlier version of this chapter.

1. 'The principle of adherence to given formulas, of being and of acting like others, is irreconcilably opposed to the striving to advance to ever new and individual forms of life; for this very reason social life represents a battle-ground, of which every inch is stubbornly contested, and social institutions may be looked upon as the peace-treaties, in which the constant antagonism of both principles has been reduced externally to a form of cooperation' (Simmel 1971 [1904]: 295–6).

2. 'Speaking broadly, we may say that the most favorable result for the aggregate value of life will be obtained when all unavoidable dependence is transferred more and more to the periphery, to the externals of life . . . In this respect fashion is also a social form of marvelous expedience, because, like the law, it affects only the externals of life, only those sides of life which are turned to society. It provides us with a formula by means of which we can unequivocally attest our dependence upon what is generally adopted, our obedience to the standards established by our time, our class, and our narrower circle, and enables us to withdraw the freedom given us in life from externals and concentrate it more and more in our innermost nature' (Simmel 1971 [1904]: 314).

3. The narrower meaning of *fashion*, as the style that is current or up to date, characterizes the work of Simmel (1971 [1904]) and Lipovetsky (1994). A broader use of the word to refer to all dress is found in scholars such as Craik (1994) and Crane (2000).

4. Simmel defines style as follows: 'For style refers to a *general* mode of expression, one that is common to many creations, a form ideationally separable from its various contents' (1971 [1908b]: 233).

5. 'Fashion always occupies the dividing-line between the past and the future, and consequently conveys a stronger feeling of the present, at least while it is at its height, than most other phenomena' (Simmel 1971 [1904]: 303).

6. For example, Simmel (1971 [1904]) wrote in the early twentieth century, during a period dominated by a fairly orderly system of fashion generated from predictable, 'authoritative' sources—the fashion houses or couturiers. Lipovetsky (1994), Crane (2000), Davis (1992), Breward (2003) and others, writing decades later, attest to both the more rapid pace of changing fashions and the much wider variety of sources from which fashions originate—from young people and subcultures within society, for example, in addition to the fashion houses of haute couture.

7. Among these types of clothes, Entwistle (2000: 45) refers to traditional clothing as 'fixed', in contrast to the changing nature of fashion.

8. This view runs counter to that of some writers, such as Rubenstein (1995), who see a more explicit language in fashion that can be read in a more straightforward manner.

9. In an article about the designer Giorgio Armani, *Vogue* magazine sums up all four elements when it describes the designer as 'an iconic distillation of himself' (September 2004: 784). He is an image of himself—that is, of an image-maker—taken as such by a representative of another image-making industry.

10. An instance of objectification in clothing fashion may be the development of some haute couture into an art for its own sake rather than an art for the wearer. Haute couture as an art form is a logical development of the refinement of materials and skills in this area and the opportunity it gives for aesthetic expression. However, Lipovetsky discusses the move from a situation in which couturiers worked with a client to reflect the client's personal style in the clothing design to a situation in which couturiers dictated fashion (1994: 64–74). Fashion as art for art's sake would be the next step. Breward provides an example of this with Alexander McQueen's focus on death and violence—ripped clothing stained with blood, tire marks to suggest roadkill (2003: 235)—which would seem to be an artist's personal statement rather than any attempt to establish a real fashion to be worn.

11. Sokolowski discusses the situation in which people seem 'to prefer the preserved image to the imaged event; at ceremonies like important speeches or weddings, for example, which can be perceived only once, some members of the party put all their attention into taking pictures or recording what is said, and do not "see and hear" what is going on . . . Then they have a photograph of the event instead of a memory of it, and look at the picture instead of having seen the thing' (1992b: 12).

Chapter 8: Adolescence

1. In his book *Fashion as Communication* (1996), Barnard refers widely to different adolescent groups, their styles and the symbols they wear to express different ideologies.

Chapter 11: Strong Fashion and Weak Identity

1. For clothes, it is better to speak of *undercoding*, since the significance and the significant undergo a much more rapid variation than in a language and are much more ambiguous (Davis 1992: 5–7).
2. See also the expression *mass fashion* used by P. Calefato to show the extreme and unpredictable spreading of fashion nowadays (cfr. Calefato 2002: 3).
3. The adjective *liquid*, applied to postmodern time, shows the continuous fluctuation of a characteristic to the opposite (cfr. Bauman 2002).
4. The so-called *feminism of difference*, advanced by Luce Irigaray, among others, has most recently emphasized sexual difference.

INDEX